Become a Great Data Storyteller

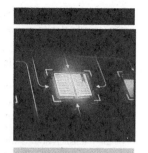

Become a Great Data Storyteller

Learn How You Can Drive Change with Data

Angelica Lo Duca

WILEY

Published by John Wiley & Sons, Inc., Hoboken, New Jersey.
Published simultaneously in Canada and the United Kingdom.

ISBNs: 9781394283316 (Paperback), 9781394283330 (ePDF), 9781394283323 (ePub)

For general information on our other products and services, please contact our Customer Care Department within the United States at (800) 762-2974, outside the United States at (317) 572-3993. For product technical support, you can find answers to frequently asked questions or reach us via live chat at https://support.wiley.com.

If you believe you've found a mistake in this book, please bring it to our attention by emailing our reader support team at wileysupport@wiley.com with the subject line "Possible Book Errata Submission."

Wiley also publishes its books in a variety of electronic formats. Some content that appears in print may not be available in electronic formats. For more information about Wiley products, visit our web site at www.wiley.com.

Library of Congress Control Number: 2024940655

Cover image: © D3Damon/Getty Images
Cover design: Wiley

SKY10094543_122324

To my sister, Rosa, and our childhood spent telling stories.

About the Author

 **Angelica Lo Duca, PhD,** is a researcher at the Institute of Informatics and Telematics of the National Research Council, Italy. She is also an adjunct professor of data journalism at the University of Pisa. Her research interests include data storytelling, data science, data journalism, data engineering, and web applications. She has also worked on network security, semantic web, linked data, and blockchain. She has published more than 60 scientific papers at national and international conferences and journals. She has participated in different national and international projects and events. She is also the author of the book *Comet for Data Science*, published by Packt Publishing Ltd.; coauthor of *Learning and Operating Presto*, published by O'Reilly Media; and author of *Data Storytelling with Altair and AI*, published by Manning Publications.

When she's not busy studying and writing, Angelica loves cooking and spending time with her family.

About the Technical Editor

Victor Yocco, PhD, is a researcher who focuses on communication and psychology. He frequently writes about the application of principles of psychology to digital design, including in his book *Design for the Mind*, from Manning Publications. He graduated with a PhD from Ohio State University, where his research focused on communication and values in informal learning contexts. He has served as a technical editor for books and journals across many fields. Victor lives near Philadelphia with his daughter.

Acknowledgments

This book could never have seen the light of day without the moral support and patience of my husband, Andrea, to whom I am deeply grateful. Thank you, my love, for supporting and putting up with me during the difficult moments of crisis and joy that accompanied the writing of this book. Thanks for listening to my thoughts on the role of the data storyteller and how to build a data-driven story. By the end of this book, you, too, will have become a great data storyteller, and if you are not a great data storyteller, you are certainly a great listener.

This book is also the result of the support of my children, Giulia and Antonio. I realized how much I'd filled your heads with the book's details when I heard you talk about data storytelling and how to organize a story in three acts. Once at the cinema, Giulia told me, "Mom, have you found the first plot point in the story?" And there, I understood how much this book is not only mine but also yours. Thank you, my little ones.

In addition to my family, I would also like to thank the incredible team at Wiley. Profound thanks go to Kenyon Brown, the acquisitions editor of this book. Without your availability, this book would never have seen the light. And then a big thank you to development editor, Jan Lynn Neal, for her impeccable work, even in moments of difficulty. Jan, I want to give you a heartfelt thank you for everything you have done. Without you, this book would not be what it is now. Also, thank you to the rest of the Wiley team, including Satish Gowrishankar, Archana Pragash, and the other members of the Wiley crew.

Special thanks to the technical editor and my friend Victor Yocco. Without your valuable comments and suggestions, Victor, this book wouldn't be half what it is today. Victor, sooner or later, we will write a book together.

A final thank you to you, dear reader, who dreams of becoming a great data storyteller. I hope you will become one soon.

—Angelica Lo Duca

Contents at a Glance

Contents

Introduction

What you're holding isn't just another book about the general concepts of data storytelling or a set of strategies for best visualizing your data. This book takes you far beyond the basics, equipping you with a proven framework borrowed from the world of cinema and literature—where stories captivate hearts and minds. Step by step, you'll learn how to craft data-driven stories that mirror the structure of great films and novels. You'll understand how to build characters (yes, even in data!), create a gripping plot, and arrange your narrative into a sequence that resonates with your audience. The inspiration for this book is simple: As data storytelling becomes increasingly essential in today's world, there's a pressing need for a guide that not only explains why stories matter but shows you exactly how to tell them. This is that guide.

I have always had a passion for stories, but until I met my Italian teacher in high school, I never knew how to organize and tell them following a logical structure. I remember feeling incredibly frustrated when I wrote stories that started and never finished or went on too long in the introduction and ended suddenly. I crafted very unbalanced stories. Even at school, the essays I did in class weren't that great. They had no structure; they talked about everything and nothing. Then, a flash of genius: My Italian teacher one day explained how to structure a story. From that day, I learned to write balanced, well-organized stories that follow a logical thread. I was only 15 years old. Many years have passed since then, but the desire to tell stories is still alive.

This book derives from the desire to share what I have learned with you, dear reader, to ensure that your data-driven stories are also structured, balanced, and follow a logical thread from beginning to end. Surely, you already know how to analyze data, and perhaps you also know how to present it appropriately. But have you ever thought about organizing your data precisely like a story with characters and a plot? Have you ever thought each story phase must last a certain time to be balanced? Have you ever thought that in order to make the audience listen to you while presenting your story, you must create a certain suspense? In one sentence, have you ever thought about designing your own data-driven story using the techniques that screenwriters, directors, or novelists use?

Well, in this book, you'll do just that: apply cinematic techniques to data storytelling! You will extract a hero from the data, a sidekick, and even an antagonist. You will build a plot based on the goal you want to achieve and structure it in three acts, just like screenwriters and novelists do. Each act will play a role in the story.

Throughout the book, I will use the story of rising temperatures in recent years as an example. I am not an environmental expert, so the example is only for demonstration. If you find any inaccuracies, please be patient and possibly report them to me through the contacts you see in this book.

So, are you ready to face this journey together?

What Does This Book Cover?

This book covers the following topics:

Chapter 1: Why You Need to Become a Data Storyteller

This chapter introduces the concept of data storytelling and explains why it is essential for communicating insights effectively. Data storytelling differs from data reporting and presentation in that it focuses on creating a narrative involving a "hero" and a "plot." Unlike simple data presentations, data storytelling constructs a coherent story around data points, highlighting the people, events, and transformations the data represents. The chapter emphasizes that stories are powerful because they resonate emotionally, creating a bridge between the storyteller and the audience.

Chapter 2: The Role of the Storyteller

This chapter explores the qualities of a great data storyteller, likening their role to a director who must make data the focus rather than themselves. It identifies three types of storytellers—apathetic, authoritarian, and authoritative—and emphasizes the importance of being authoritative by engaging, collaborating, and building trust with the audience. Essential skills for great data storytelling include humility, sincerity, vulnerability, empathy, flexibility, openness, and patience. The chapter also outlines three roles a storyteller can play—external, internal, or absent—and discusses synchronous and asynchronous storytelling methods.

Chapter 3: Making a Successful Data-Driven Story

This chapter delves into the "making" phase of creating a data-driven story, focusing on planning and structuring the narrative through three essential stages: preproduction, production, and postproduction. Preproduction requires selecting a theme, defining the subject, and planning scenes. Production is the story implementation and can be done using any tool. The final step, postproduction, refines and organizes the story by selecting and polishing scenes, ensuring smooth transitions, and enhancing visual and narrative clarity.

Chapter 4: First Act: Defining the Hero

This chapter focuses on the foundational aspect of data storytelling: defining the hero. A hero in data storytelling differs from literary heroes, as they emerge directly from the data rather than from the imagination. Heroes in data stories are characterized by their quest for an "object of desire" but face obstacles that hinder their journey. Unlike traditional storytelling, the hero in data storytelling must be grounded in real-world elements, either human-like (connected directly to people) or non-human-like (such as abstract concepts or phenomena).

Chapter 5: First Act: Defining the Sidekick

This chapter explores the role of the supporting character (i.e., the sidekick) in data storytelling, emphasizing that while the hero remains central, a well-crafted sidekick adds depth and resonance to the story. In data storytelling, a sidekick can serve several functions, from being a confidant who reveals the hero's inner thoughts to acting as a proxy for the audience, simplifying complex data.

Chapter 6: Second Act: Defining the Problem

This chapter centers on defining the problem in data storytelling, which is essential for crafting a compelling narrative. A hero's journey in storytelling only gains meaning with a clear problem that needs solving. Without a problem, there's no story—just a straightforward data presentation. This chapter explains the importance of the problem and describes how to identify and describe it.

Chapter 7: Second Act: Defining the Antagonist

This chapter defines the antagonist in data storytelling and structuring the story's second act. An antagonist in storytelling opposes the hero and heightens the story's conflict, making the hero's journey to achieving their goal more compelling. In data-driven stories, antagonists aren't just villains but can be forces, circumstances, or even internal conflicts that create obstacles for the hero.

Chapter 8: Third Act: Setting the Climax and Next Steps

This chapter delves into the structure and elements of the third act in data storytelling, which is critical for resolving the story's tension and providing a satisfying conclusion. Known as the climax phase, this act includes a series of steps to bring the story to its peak: the Dark Night, the Climax, and the Next Steps. Together, these elements provide closure, impact, and motivation for the audience to take action based on the story's message.

Chapter 9: From Making to Delivering a Data-Driven Story

This chapter discusses the transition from creating a data-driven story to effectively delivering it, focusing on crafting and adapting the story for the audience. With the story completed, the delivery phase involves tailoring it to the specific audience. The chapter emphasizes that while the story's core remains unchanged, its presentation and emphasis should adapt to the audience's expectations and knowledge level.

Chapter 10: What the Audience Wants and Knows

This chapter begins by underscoring that every audience is unique. Even a small group may consist of individuals with varied responses shaped by their personal beliefs and backgrounds. Therefore, effective data storytelling involves recognizing and respecting this diversity while striving to engage each person individually. This understanding is foundational to audience analysis, a critical skill in storytelling that involves identifying the characteristics, interests, and knowledge levels of different audience segments.

Chapter 11: What the Audience Thinks

This chapter continues the story adaptation to the audience. While the previous chapter focused on the audience's needs and knowledge, this chapter focuses on the audience's perceptions, which specify how the audience behaves after encountering the story.

Chapter 12: Retelling the Story

This chapter highlights the importance of repeating data-driven stories to overcome the forgetting curve, which causes most people to forget 90 percent of what they hear within a week. Retelling through varied channels and formats keeps the message alive, helps audiences internalize it, and broadens its reach. Techniques like spaced repetition ensure effective timing while adapting the context, and presentation maintains interest. The chapter emphasizes that data storytellers and audiences benefit from this process, potentially becoming new narrators who spread and enrich the story.

Additional Resources

Sprinkled throughout the book are featured sidebars that offer those extra bits of information that will enable you to further your storytelling.

Challenge: This resource is an excellent way to get you started in developing your story, as it provides challenging opportunities for you to complete your craft.

> **This sidebar will include general bits of information that will explain and aid you in understanding data storytelling.**

NOTE This sidebar includes notes on items of interest in data storytelling. Pay attention as you might just find more information to learn here.

How to Contact the Author

You can contact the author in the following ways:

- LinkedIn: `https://www.linkedin.com/in/angelicaloduca`
- Medium: `https://alod83.medium.com`

CHAPTER

1

Why You Need to Become a Data Storyteller

So, you have decided to become a data storyteller. You have probably already had several opportunities to present your data to an audience—either your boss, your teams, or even a large number of people—and you've likely had the impression of not being understood by those who listened to you. You've probably even had one big disappointment when few have listened to your words after working hard on your data. Not having had time to organize your speech at the time of presentation, you might have gotten lost in the details of this or that data, without giving a broader scope to your speech. Or, you've had plenty of time to organize the results of your data analyses, but in the end you simply didn't get the desired results, that is, having your data *used* for something.

I understand you. I also found myself in the same situation more than a decade ago. I was at a conference in Germany, in Bonn to be precise, presenting the preliminary results of exciting research on underwater networks. I had a minute available (yes, just one minute) to convince the audience to come and see the poster I presented. I had studied a lot to prepare that poster. For me, it was a really important moment. In the only slide I could use for the presentation, I had included many data visualizations describing the results of my analysis and had rehearsed the words to say on stage many times. But when my turn came, I slowly climbed the steps toward the stage and my mind went dark. I remembered all the tests I had done, the graphs of the results, and the software written. I wanted to collapse all the work done in that single minute. I began to speak quickly, describing all the data visualizations without any order, almost as if

I wanted to concentrate all my work into one minute. I talked about numbers, values, tests performed, and so on and so forth. The result: my presentation was an absolute disaster. I became lost in the details, and the minute flew by quickly. In the end, almost no one understood what my poster was about or came to see it. It was a real disaster. I returned home very disappointed, believing that I wasn't understood and thinking that the work I'd done wasn't as important as I had assumed. The real problem was that I presented the results of my analysis without a specific order, a central point, and an end. Probably, organizing my presentation as a short story would have persuaded the audience to understand the importance of my poster.

That terrible experience taught me a lot. Over the years, I have understood the power of stories and how telling stories makes a difference to the audience. In this book, you will learn to become a data storyteller so you will no longer be frustrated, disappointed, or messy in the presentation of your data.

To tell the truth, *you are already a storyteller*. You might not know it, however. Each of us is a storyteller, because telling stories is an innate characteristic of every human being. Think about all the times that you've told your friends or family about an event or fact from your life. Maybe you spoke about that time you went to the mountains for the first time or the time you flew with your children. Maybe you've never noticed it, but you've told many stories in your life. Likely, they were primarily stories about your life. When you told them, you felt emotions, not only yours but also those who listened to you. Throughout your story, you established a bridge between what you told and the people who listened to you. In some cases, sometime later, you still hear your friends or family talking about that story you told them sometime before.

Yes, a story can establish a strong bond between you and those who listen to you. A story can overcome the barriers of time and space. It can make you see with the eyes of your imagination what is heard with words. It can bring to mind the past and project toward the future. It can also make you navigate in space and take you thousands of miles across distances. Indeed, stories are powerful things.

The Need for Data Storytelling

If you want to become a data storyteller and even a *great data storyteller*, you must learn to tell other people's stories. You must understand the need for great data storytelling. A great data storyteller tells the stories of others—of people, of events, of situations, of concepts, of places—that hide behind the data. Data does not arise by chance and behind it there are people who have produced it with their behavior, with their situations. And these people are waiting for someone to tell their stories. Sometimes, these stories are of joy or of suffering;

other times they're business stories, stories of failed products, stories of sales, stories of success, stories of anything. But behind these stories are people. And you are the right person to tell their stories—the stories behind the data.

In this book, you will learn to become a data storyteller—someone who not only analyzes data but also knows how to look beyond and communicate it effectively to those who'll listen. A data storyteller is just that: someone who acts as an intermediary between the people behind the data and those in the audience. A data storyteller acts as the *bridge* between them. There's a gap between the data and the audience, and you have the task of filling this void. Kindra Hall, the author of many bestselling books in the field of storytelling, states in her book Stories That Stick that if you want to win the game, you must build the bridge that fills the void (Hall, 2019). This is precisely your job: building the bridge between data and audience. So, what are you waiting for? Off you go.

What Is Data Storytelling?

Let's start from the beginning. We are neither the first nor the last to tell stories. Since our origins, humans have told stories: stories to explain the origin of the universe or the causes of phenomena such as myths and legends, stories to entertain children such as fairy tales, stories to explain more profound concepts, and stories based on actual events. Stories of all kinds. *What is a story, and why is it so important to tell stories?* In his book *Building a StoryBrand: Clarify Your Message So Customers Will Listen,* Donald Miller states that a story is the most potent weapon we have to combat noise because it organizes information so that people are forced to listen (Miller, 2017). A story breaks barriers and places the storyteller and the listener on the same wavelength. A story makes us feel deeply human, with our strengths and weaknesses, our hopes and disappointments, and our feelings. Stories are an important part of the human experience.

Analyzing a Story

Let's analyze what a story is with a more formal eye. Note, not all stories are created equal; gifted raconteurs have been passing along their technique of storytelling over time. In this book I hope to do something similar for modern-day storytellers—to help you develop your storytelling technique.

A *story* is a narrative of events organized in a temporal sequence (Forster, 1927). These are not unrelated events but are rather organized in one intertwining narrative. The *plot* is the order in which events are presented. It is the first element that transforms a simple set of events into a story. Think about the last movie you watched or the last novel you read. Analyze it according to the previous definition: related events organized in a temporal sequence. Definitely, in the story, *something happened*. Several events occurred that followed one another over time and were related to each other. So, there was a *before* and an *after*. To have a story, therefore, there must be a change—a before and an after. Something must happen in the middle that messes everything up. Go back to your latest novel or film. What was it that changed everything? Probably an unexpected event—a complication that happened to someone, perhaps the hero. So, the second element, the hero, appears fundamental to the story. The hero is the one with whom the audience identifies. The hero, however, is only one of the characters in the story. There are others, such as the antagonist and the sidekick. But we will see this over the course of the book shortly. Now, all you need to know is that a story is a narrative telling about the change that the hero experiences. A story is described through a series of related events. Figure 1.1 summarizes the simplified structure of a story, with the plot and the hero.

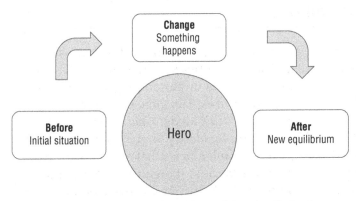

Figure 1.1: The hero's journey from an initial situation (before) to a new equilibrium (after) through a change (the plot), where something happens

So far, we have talked about the generic structure of a story. Thinking back to your last movie seen or novel read, it would just seem like it's the structure of a creative story. In reality, specific studies explain that any story, whether fiction or nonfiction, must have a plot and characters, including the hero, to be recognized as such (Rayfield, 1972). So, like it or not, if we're talking about data storytelling, we must have a plot and characters. Otherwise, those who listen to us won't think that we are telling a story but simply that we are presenting data. In fact, there's often confusion between data presentation and data storytelling, as the two terms are used interchangeably. In reality, when executing a data presentation, it is sufficient to present the data; when performing data storytelling, instead we have to tell a story.

Data storytelling is, therefore, telling a story based on data. Compared to novels or films, in data storytelling the subject of the story changes, which must be connected to reality—to events and facts contained in the data. Throughout the book, you will see how to extract characters and a plot from data. But for now, however, just know that data storytelling is not a simple presentation of data, and it is not even a data report. Figure 1.2 summarizes the difference between data reporting, data presentation, and data storytelling.

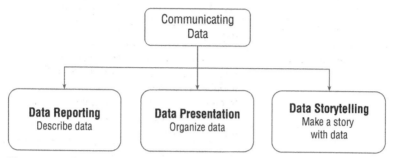

Figure 1.2: The difference between data reporting, data presentation, and data storytelling. All receive data as an input, but the produced output is different

All three are data driven. *Data reporting* describes the data; *data presentation* organizes it in a clear and visually comprehensible way; and *data storytelling* extracts a plot and characters from the data and tells them to an audience. Use data reporting to provide a comprehensive overview of the data without much interpretation. If you want to convey complex data through dashboards, instead use data presentation. Finally, to engage and persuade your audience, use data storytelling. The audience is the third central element of data storytelling. We will review the role of the audience in more detail later. For now, it's enough to know that when you tell a story, you always tell it to someone, and it's never about yourself. Table 1.1 shows when you should use each data communication form and its main pros and cons.

Challenge: Now, think about the last speech you listened to or a time you chatted with a friend that particularly impressed you. Was it a story, a report, or a presentation?

If we reflect on the previous challenge, we note that the impact of a speech often hinges not merely on its content but on its delivery and form. Whether it is a captivating story, an informative report, or a polished presentation, the way in which information is conveyed can significantly influence its reception by the audience. A speech that leaves a lasting impression typically possesses a combination of factors, including compelling storytelling, articulate delivery, and relevance to the audience. A well-told story has the potential to transport the audience into the narrative, making the message more memorable.

Now that you know that a data-driven story involves characters and plot, let's see how to build a story starting from data.

Table 1.1: Diverse Forms of Data Communication and Most Appropriate Usage of Each

	WHEN TO USE	PROS	CONS
Data Reporting	Reports without interpretation	Focuses on factual representation	May lack audience engagement
Data Presentation	Dashboards	Adds a layer of clarity and accessibility to the data	Can be difficult to extract a call to action
Data Storytelling	Presentations	Humanizes the data by contextualizing it within a narrative framework, making it more memorable for the audience	May sacrifice objectivity and accuracy in favor of narrative coherence

Understanding the Data Storytelling Process

Data storytelling is communicating the results of your data exploration/analysis process to an audience through a story. Transforming data into stories requires three fundamental steps, as illustrated in Figure 1.3.

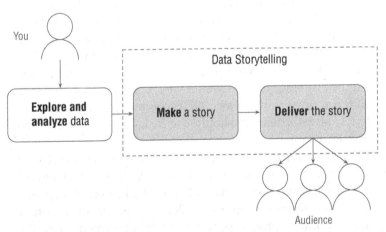

Figure 1.3: Transforming data into stories involves three phases: 1) explore and analyze data, 2) create a story, and 3) deliver the story. Data storytelling involves only making and delivering the story, although you might need to return to data exploration and analysis many times before finalizing the story

Let's break down the data storytelling process. First, you must *explore and analyze data.* I assume you already know how to do this and are an expert. I also assume you already know how to extract insights from your data, calculate statistics, etc. In addition, I suppose you know how to do it so well that it doesn't need to be the subject of this book. Second, you must *create a story*, starting from the data. Creating a story means precisely what it sounds like: creating a story with a plot and characters. But here, the situation is a little different. It's not about inventing a story, like a tale, but creating one based on facts, evidence, and data. There is a parallel thread to this, which is creative nonfiction, that aims to tell the stories of the people behind the facts (Gutkind, 2007). The term *creative nonfiction* might seem strange or even contradictory. In reality, according to its inventor, Lee Gutkind, creative nonfiction aims to capture and describe a subject so that even the most resistant reader is interested in learning more about it. It's not about making up stories based on facts but about presenting the facts in a more dramatic way, just like you do in creative writing. What is required of the creative nonfiction writer is a passion for the written word, a passion for research and observation to understand how things work in this world, and a passion for understanding their audience in order to tell the best story possible. Here, your job as a data storyteller is precisely this: to tell the stories of the people behind the data.

Returning to Figure 1.3, the third step is to deliver the story. Keep the making and delivery phases separated if you plan to tell the story several times to different audience types. Otherwise, transform the two into a single phase in which you think about the audience directly from the beginning. In this book, we consider the two phases separately to allow the same story to be told to multiple audiences. This is where contact with the audience takes place. *Delivering the story* doesn't necessarily mean going on stage and giving a brilliant presentation. There are also other forms of delivery, such as prerecorded videos, written documents, presentations, discussions, etc. In any case, the delivery can take place synchronously or asynchronously. *Synchronous delivery* requires that the storyteller and the audience are present simultaneously during the delivery. This simultaneity does not occur in the *asynchronous delivery*. You might think that synchronous delivery has greater audience engagement, but this is actually not true. Returning once again to Figure 1.3, you can see how data storytelling doesn't include the data exploration phase but only the creation of the story, beginning from the data and its delivery. However, this doesn't mean that the story creation process is linear, that once you have explored your data, it is set in stone. The process is iterative and dynamic in the sense that if, as you build the story, you realize that you need more data or more details, you can always go back to the exploration and analysis phase and gather what you need.

So remember: *Explore, Make, Deliver*. That is the secret to turning your data into stories. Now, let's explore in greater detail what making and delivering a story means, by beginning with making a story.

Making a Data-Driven Story

To better understand what making a data-driven story means, let's borrow the terminology of the field of cinematography. Not that you are creating films here; you won't invent stories, for goodness' sake, but you can think that the process of creating a story is similar in the two cases, in data storytelling and cinema. Why can this simile work? Because they both rest on visual elements. In the case of cinema, the *visual elements* are the moving scenes imprinted on the film. In contrast, in the case of data storytelling, the visual elements are the graphics and animations that accompany your story and that represent the analyzed data. Filmmaking consists of three fundamental parts (see Figure 1.4): preproduction, production, and postproduction.

Figure 1.4: The three phases of creating a film include 1) preproduction, 2) production, and 3) postproduction. Consider the process of creating a data-driven story like that of creating a film

Preproduction includes the definition of the *film script*, that is, the choice of theme, subject, and scenes, which involve the plot definition. The choice of theme also includes the message that the story wants to convey. Examples of messages can be general values, morals, and so on. Production concerns the moment in which the film is produced (that is, the cinematographic shooting), and postproduction includes the final *editing*, where the choice of the order of the scenes, the starts and cuts of the scenes, the soundtrack, etc., are decided upon. Don't worry if everything isn't clear to you now. We will return to this structure throughout the book. For now, it's enough just to know the three phases: preproduction (i.e., definition of the script), production (i.e., film shooting), and postproduction (i.e., editing) (Aimeri, 1998).

Similar to what happens in filmmaking, making a data-driven story includes these three phases (see Figure 1.5).

Figure 1.5: The three phases of creating a data-driven story include 1) preproduction, 2) production, and 3) postproduction

In the preproduction phase, the data storyteller defines the story's script. Starting with the data, the data storyteller extracts the story's theme, subject, and scenes from the data supplied. In the production phase, the data storyteller then writes the text and the accompanying visual elements. In general, the visual elements are graphs that, for example, show the trend of the data over time, the spatial distribution, etc. The text and visual elements represent scenes from the story. In the final postproduction phase, the data storyteller chooses the order in which to narrate the scenes and possibly eliminates some that aren't necessary for the narrative. I'll be diving deeper into how we do this in later chapters. The data storyteller can also decide to manipulate the scenes already produced for a better result. At the end of the postproduction phase, the story is finally ready. Now, it's time to tell someone about it.

Delivering a Data-Driven Story

When you create a data-driven story, you don't typically make it just for the sake of it but with a specific goal: you want to *communicate* the results of your analysis to your audience. For the audience to understand your story, you need to use their language; otherwise, they won't understand what you mean. Imagine having to speak about how the inclination of the earth's axis determines the duration of the hours of light and darkness during the various periods of the year. You will undoubtedly use a different language if you have to explain it to an audience of 10-year-olds versus an audience of scientists. This means the same story can be told in a thousand different ways, depending on the audience you have in front of you. Then, after you've created the story, you'll need to tailor it to your audience. In my poster example, this question should've come to mind: why not think about the audience right from the start and create a story directly adapted to my audience? Unfortunately, I didn't take into account who I was presenting to before I took the stage; thus, I didn't provide them with intriguing reasons in a language they could understand as to why they should specifically come see my poster. I rambled. Before I presented to them, I needed to understand who my audience was exactly, before I could relate why underwater networks should be specifically important to them. If you consider your audience early on, you create a story tailored *only* to that audience. If you create a generic story and then adapt it to your audience, you can tell it to different audiences each time, as shown in Figure 1.6.

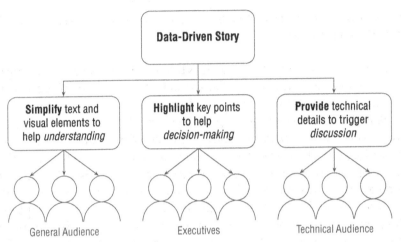

Figure 1.6: Once produced, a story can be adapted to various audiences, based on the objective to be achieved

Figure 1.6 illustrates three types of audiences: a general audience, an audience of executives, and a technical audience. The general audience doesn't know your data, so to make them understand the story, you need to simplify the text and visual elements as much as possible. Executives are those who know the data in broad terms. They're interested in making decisions based on your data, so you'll need to highlight the critical elements in your story. Finally, the technical audience knows the data in detail. They aim to understand all technical aspects, such as how the data was collected and processed. We'll look at the various types of audiences in more detail in Chapter 8, "Third Act: Setting the Climax and Next Steps."

To adapt a story to your audience, you need to use their language. Not only that, but you also need to understand what the audience wants: their desires, their problems, and what they care about most. One way or another, your story has to be of interest to your audience. You can't present a story about how many books a person reads in a year to an audience that isn't interested in reading. The audience must be interested in the change that the hero of the story experiences. If this doesn't occur, you must change the story.

The goal of your story is to communicate the results of your analyses to the audience so that they do something after engaging with your story. This "something" can be essentially anything, like making a decision, supporting one of your initiatives, etc. Therefore, behind every story there is a message defined during the making phase and a purpose being defined during this delivery phase. The end specifies the objective, or the *purpose*, of the story. Broadly speaking, we can define three purposes: to persuade, inform, and entertain the audience (Kelliher & Slaney, 2012), as summarized in Figure 1.7. Another type will be discussed soon.

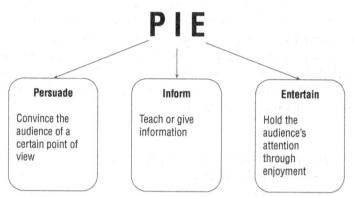

Figure 1.7: The three possible purposes of a story: 1) to persuade, 2) to inform, and 3) to entertain

Persuading the audience means you're convincing them of a particular point of view. *Informing* the audience means you're teaching or giving information. *Entertaining* means you're maintaining the audience's attention through enjoyment. In reality, there is also a fourth type of purpose, which is to explain, but you can aggregate it in the informing category. Consider again the example of presenting a story about how many books a person reads in a year to an audience that isn't interested in reading. Persuading that audience could involve using the book data to make them see why they should care. Then, if you've made them care, you can use real data to inform them. Finally, through entertainment, you can make the audience enjoy, capturing and holding their attention as you present the information and a relevant call to action.

Summing up what has been discussed thus far, we can say that making a story means defining its message and structuring it with characters and a plot. Delivering a story means defining its purpose and adapting it to a specific audience (see Figure 1.8).

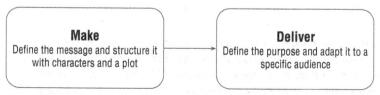

Figure 1.8: Making the story means defining the message. Delivering the story means defining its purpose

At this point, we are ready to analyze a simple case study.

Case Study: Solstices and Equinoxes

I recently read a beautiful example on how a graph can be created, starting from four simple points. In *Visual Analytics Fundamentals* by Lindy Ryan, the author shares that the four points are the dates of the summer and winter solstices and the dates of the equinoxes of the spring and fall (Ryan, 2023). Figure 1.9 is a simple graphical representation of these points, reworked from one of Dale Ward's lectures (Ward, 2017a), held as part of the *Weather, Climate, and Society* (ATMO 366) course in 2017 (Ward, 2017b). Ward is a lecturer on hydrology and atmospheric sciences at the University of Arizona.

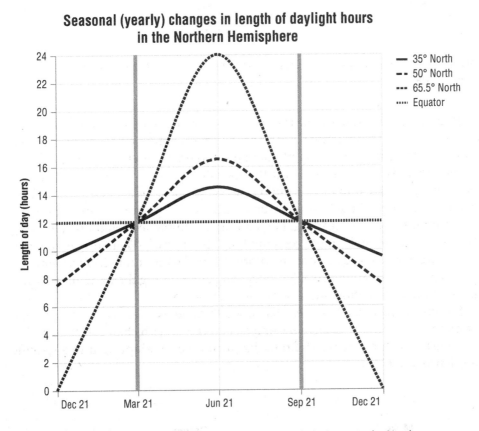

Figure 1.9: Seasonal (yearly) changes in the length of daylight hours in the Northern Hemisphere. At the equator, there are no seasonal changes. There are always 12 daylight hours throughout the year. At 35° latitude North, the longest day is 14.5 hours (June 21), and the shortest is 9.5 hours (December 21). At 50° latitude, the longest day is 16.5 hours (June 21), and the shortest day is 7.5 hours (December 21). At latitudes of 66.5° and higher, the longest day of the year is 24 hours, and the shortest day has 0 hours of sunlight

The book, however, stops at the simple visualization of data. Intrigued by this simple and attractive example, I considered how such a simple set of points could be transformed into a story. A first approach could be to explain what happens at each point, as described in Figure 1.10.

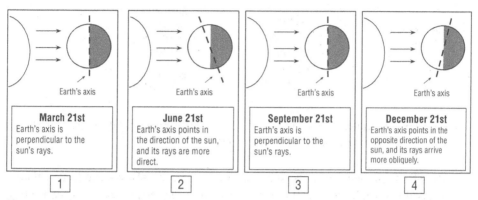

Figure 1.10: A sequence of four scenes explaining what happens to the Earth's axis at the equinoxes and solstices

I have defined four scenes, each of which describes what happens at each data point, with details relating to the position of the earth's axis with respect to the sun. Are you satisfied with this result? I'm honestly not. They seem like four figures to be included in a high school astronomical geography textbook. What's the deal with this sequence of scenes? The problem is that it's not a story: it doesn't have a hero, it doesn't have a plot, and it doesn't even reach a conclusion. It is simply a way of presenting data, of describing it, but it doesn't tell a story.

So, how can we tell a story with this data? Let's apply what we learned in this chapter. A story must have at least one hero and a plot. The whole story depends on the existence of these two elements. Who could be the hero in this particular case? Let's try to think. The four dates in Figure 1.10 represent the transition from one season to another, so our hero could be the *transition from one season to another*. Now, let's move on to the plot. To have a story, the hero must experience a change, which is usually caused by a problem. (We will learn more about this in the next chapter.) Let's reflect for a moment. What change does our hero experience? It's here that the search begins. We can look for the answer in the data (if necessary, returning to the exploration phase) or in reliable sources. In our case, I found a very interesting scientific article by Wang et al., which describes how over the years the length of the seasons is varying considerably due to climate change. By 2100 in the Northern Hemisphere of the globe, we will have very short winters and long and very hot summers (Wang et al., 2021). In our story, therefore, we can talk about this change, as shown in Figure 1.11.

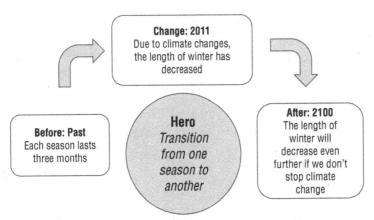

Figure 1.11: The sequence shows three scenes: 1) the initial moment in the past, 2) the change in 2011, and 3) the situation after the change in 2100

The story consists of three scenes. The first scene shows the hero *before the change*, otherwise known as the *initial moment in the past*; the second scene shows the *change*, or the reduction of the length of winter in 2011 due to climate change; and the final scene shows the hero *after the change*.

Now, let's take a step back. In our defined story, we implicitly included a message: climate change threatens our planet. Let's again look at the scenes in Figure 1.11. Is the message that the story wants to convey clear? If it seems clear to you, then you can proceed. Otherwise, go back to the story and try to modify it to help clarify the message. Assuming that the message is clear, let's try to go one step further. In defining the story, we acted a bit off the cuff because we don't have all the equipment to build a data story, yet. Over the course of the book, we will see how to systematize things and proceed with plotting. For now, the goal is to simply understand the difference between presenting data and telling a story. Up to now, we have worked on the preproduction phase, with the definition of the message (or theme), the characters, and the plot. Now, it's a matter of implementing the individual scenes of the story. Figure 1.12 shows a possible implementation.

The last part of the story creation phase is *editing*. We can decide whether to tell the scenes chronologically, exactly as shown in Figure 1.12, or to use other techniques. For now, let's be satisfied with the chronological order. We will see other story editing techniques throughout the book.

We have completed the making part of the story. Now, let's move on to delivering, which involves tailoring the story to your audience. Who do we want to tell the story to? To NASA scientists? To your grandma? To an audience of readers of online newspapers? To people who don't believe in climate change? Based on the answer we give, the way we tell the story will certainly change. For example, if we want to tell the story to NASA scientists, we will probably have to enrich each scene of the story with details interesting to

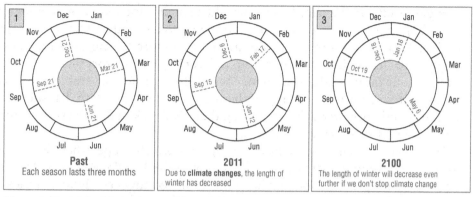

Figure 1.12: A possible implementation of the three scenes of the story described in Figure 1.10. Each scene consists of visual and textual elements

them, such as the techniques used by the researchers to make this discovery. If, instead, you tell the story to your grandma, a general version, without too many details, will probably suffice unless your grandmother is also a NASA scientist. However, if your grandma is an excellent cook and loves cooking zucchini, it might make sense to include references to cooking in the story, such as the effect that the reduction of the seasons has on zucchini cultivation. In summary, adapt your story to whomever is in front of you so that they can listen to you with interest.

You may ask why we didn't tailor the story to the audience from the beginning of your story, and we left the audience definition only for the delivery phase. The answer is simple but not obvious. This is because when you have defined the hero and the plot, you can tell the same story in infinite ways based on the audience's requirements.

The story doesn't end here, however. We must ask ourselves the crucial question: what do we want the audience to do *after* reading our story? In other words, what is the end of our story? Do we want the audience to respect the environment more? Do we want them to delve deeper into the topic? Whatever we choose as the end, let's say it clearly as the last scene of the story. I leave it to you to imagine what a possible final implementation of the story adapted to the audience of your grandmother, who loves cooking zucchini, would be like.

Challenge: Edit the story to suit an audience of your choice, such as friends, colleagues, or relatives. First, present the graph in Figure 1.9, then the presentation in Figure 1.10, and finally the story in Figure 1.12. Compare the results obtained in terms of audience interest and involvement in the story.

Understanding your audience is essential to effective communication. The challenge presented should help you understand that different ways of understanding the same topic may exist. You can take advantage of this as follows.

Use the results of this simple test to build a small pilot audience, segmented according to their preferences. This allows you to test your future data stories with specific profiles in your pilot audience, before telling the same story to your audience. In practice, before delivering a data story, start by identifying your target audience. Then, check if there is a comparable audience profile within your test audience. If there is, share the story with that subset of your test audience first. After gathering their feedback, refine the story before presenting it to your actual audience.

We have reached the end of this first chapter, in which I hope to have conveyed to you my passion for data storytelling. Using stories to tell your data helps you structure your presentation and keep the audience engaged. Telling stories is human, and, as Kindra Hall put it, stories don't just make us like others; they make us feel like others (Hall, 2019). Stories bring us into the audience and make us feel like one of them. Stories make us deeply human. In the next chapter, we will analyze how to construct a data-driven story in more detail.

Takeaways

- Data storytelling involves building and telling stories using data.
- For the audience to recognize a story as such, define at least a hero and a plot.
- The data storytelling process involves two phases: making and delivering.
- Making a story means defining the message and the story.
- Delivering a story means defining the purpose and adapting the story to various types of audiences.

References

Aimeri, L. 1998. *Manuale di Sceneggiatura Cinematografica: Teoria e Pratica*. Torino: UTET Libreria.

Forster, E. M. 1927. *Aspects of the Novel*. New York: Harcourt, Brace & Company.

Gutkind, L. 2007. *The Art of Creative Nonfiction: Writing and Selling the Literature of Reality*. New York: John Wiley & Sons.

Hall, K. 2019. *Stories That Stick: How Storytelling Can Captivate Customers, Influence Audiences, and Transform Your Business*. United States of America: HarperCollins Leadership.

Kelliher, A. & M. Slaney. 2012. Tell Me a Story. IEEE Multimedia 19(1), 4-4.

Miller, D. 2017. *Building a StoryBrand: Clarify Your Message so Customers Will Listen*. United States of America: HarperCollins Leadership.

Rayfield, J. R. 1972. "What Is a Story?" *American Anthropologist* 74(5): 1085–1106.

Ryan, L. 2023. *Visual Analytics Fundamentals: Creating Compelling Data Narratives with Tableau*. Addison-Wesley Professional.

Wang, J., Y. Guan, L. Wu, X. Guan, et al. 2021. "Changing Lengths of the Four Seasons by Global Warming." *Geophysical Research Letters* 48(6): e2020GL091753.

Ward, D. 2017a. "ATMO 336—Seasons; Seasonal Changes on Earth." Retrieved March 30, 2024. `http://www.atmo.arizona.edu/students/ courselinks/spring17/atmo336/lectures/sec4/seasons.html`

Ward, D. 2017b. "ATMO 336—Weather, Climate, and Society [Course material]." Retrieved on March 30, 2024. `http://www.atmo.arizona .edu/students/courselinks/spring17/atmo336/home.html`

The Role of the Storyteller

This chapter talks about you and your role in the story as a storyteller. If you remember correctly, in Chapter 1, "Why You Need to Become a Data Storyteller," I told you that you are already a storyteller whenever you tell your life stories to your friends and relatives. By choosing this book, you've already begun your path to learning about storytelling and how to become a *data* storyteller in addition to being a good one. In the chapters ahead, you will learn to build your story from data, from which you also extract characters and a plot and adapt it to your audience. At the beginning of the book, I made you a promise: to become not just any data storyteller but a great data storyteller. In this chapter, I will reveal how to become one. There is only one secret. Once I reveal it to you, you will have learned about all the qualifications that go into making a great data storyteller.

Imagine going to the cinema. You're sitting in the theater, ready to immerse yourself in the story, and when the lights dim, there isn't an actor, a breathtaking scene, or a memorable line in front of you. No, there is only the director, who tells you the story and shows you screenshots of the film, which are carefully organized exactly with the film's plot. All your enthusiasm suddenly vanishes. In the best-case scenario, you start to look at the director with a questioning look, while you probably get up from your chair to leave, thinking that you could have spent the ticket money differently. What is the reason for your frustration? The fundamental problem is that in films, the director is invisible.

You see only a name written in the opening or closing credits. Then, they never appear (except in some rare cases). Seeing them in the room telling the story is totally out of place. If you see the director in the story, something has gone wrong—everything must focus on the story, not the director.

The same rule applies to the data storyteller. Your role as a data storyteller is like that of a director: You must make the audience *see* and *feel* the heart of the story without realizing who is telling it. Building a narrative around data is a subtle art that requires a certain amount of invisibility. We are not at the center of the scene; it is the data that must speak.

Therefore, the secret to becoming a great data storyteller is to be invisible: the more invisible you are, the more the focus will be placed on the data and not on you. How can you be invisible? You will see it throughout this chapter, where, precisely, I will talk about the following:

- Who the data storyteller is
- Types of data storytellers
- Skills of a great data storyteller
- Role of the data storyteller in the story
- Possible scenarios in which to tell a story
- Examples of great storytellers

So, what are you waiting for? Let's begin with who the data storyteller is.

Who the Data Storyteller Is

The data storyteller is a data analyst who has developed the skills to communicate the results of their analyses. However, they don't communicate them in a standard way, that is, through simple presentations, dashboards, or reports, but rather through stories, which are organized in the same way that screenwriters organize films or novelists their novels. The fundamental difference between a director and a data storyteller is that the director has greater freedom because they can tell whatever they want, even about things that do not exist in reality. The data storyteller, on the other hand, has the task, the mission, and the duty to tell through stories *only* what emerges from the data. The data storyteller is faithful to the data. It all starts with the data, from which they extract an insight—something relevant, something worth talking about. In his book *Effective Data Storytelling*, Brent Dykes states that a good data storyteller must first have some knowledge of statistics to make simple calculations on the data, such as the mean, variance, and so on (Dykes, 2019). The data storyteller must also know the essential metrics of their work domain and how to calculate them.

In a word, the data storyteller must own what is called *data literacy*. Therefore, you can't imagine building stories based on data if you don't know how to analyze it. It seems like I told you something obvious, but it's always better to reiterate the point.

Another characteristic of the data storyteller, again according to Brent Dykes, is *data curiosity*, that is, being curious about the data. It is curiosity that drives us to investigate the data and want to understand what lies behind it. Without curiosity, you will always extract the same things from the data and have no desire to delve deeper into the topic.

You are probably already a data analyst with both data literacy and curiosity. But this isn't enough to be a data storyteller. With good data literacy and excellent data curiosity, you can become a great data analyst but not a great data storyteller.

To tell stories, you must start with data and then build a narrative upon them. A *data storyteller* is, therefore, the one who combines data literacy, data curiosity, and narrative skills to communicate what they have extracted from the data to the audience.

The data storyteller is the *bridge* between the data and the audience. In Chapter 1, you learned that you are already a storyteller, whenever you tell your friends or family something. Then, throughout the book, I will explain how to build a story starting from data (i.e., how to become a data storyteller). What you're probably missing is a little practice and a few secrets to turning your data into something profoundly memorable and engaging for the audience.

You might think you need to be a superhero when telling your stories or a knowledgeable professor who dispenses wisdom and presents data flawlessly without making mistakes. Honestly, the data storyteller is none of this. You don't have to wear a cape or fly around telling exciting stories about what you have extracted from the data. Rather, you are someone like the others in the audience. You act as a tour guide in a city with which the audience is unfamiliar. The audience might be disoriented, looking at the numbers as signs of another language. This is where you enter, with a clear map, simple explanations, and stories that make that data come alive and become meaningful.

You won't have to show off your skills as a data storyteller. You're not there to teach a lesson but to engage the audience and ensure they understand the data and can talk about it themselves. Make data accessible, engaging, and memorable for your audience. You are the facilitator—the bridge between the data and the audience. On the one hand, there is data, which speaks a complex language full of numbers, trends, outliers, and curves. On the other side is the audience who has questions, curiosities, and concrete needs. Your task is to build a dialogue between these two seemingly distant universes. It's not just about sharing information but about creating an emotional connection—a bridge of understanding.

Ultimately, your role as a data storyteller isn't to show how good you are at "handling data" but to ensure that those who listen or read cannot stop thinking about your story and, in turn, become a reteller of your story.

Three Types of Data Storytellers

Some time ago, I saw an image similar to Figure 2.1 on social media. The image showed four types of social values: reality, equality, equity, and justice.

This figure is self-explanatory, but it is worth saying a few words. In *reality*, some have a lot—more than necessary—and others don't have anything. In a system based on *equality*, everyone is given the same amount. The result, however, is that some still have too much, and others too little. In an equity-based system, everyone is given what they need. Finally, in a system based on justice, barriers are broken down, and no one needs to receive anything anymore.

Now imagine projecting Figure 2.1 to the data storyteller. Imagine that there is a barrier between the audience and the data, and your job is to make sure the audience can look beyond the barrier. You can leave things as they are, without intervening, like the example of reality, and therefore, those who already know the data understand it and those who don't remain excluded. Instead, you can tell a story that only some can understand, as in the equality-based system, or you can adapt to all audiences and make sure that everyone understands the data, as in the equity-based system. Finally, you can completely break down the barrier and ensure that a direct connection is created between the audience and the data, as in the justice-based system.

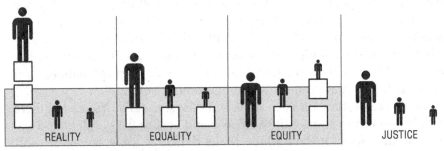

Figure 2.1: A graphical explanation of four types of social values

Leaving aside the first case in which you do not intervene at all in explaining the data, there are different types of data storytellers, but, in general, you can group them into three main types, as Figure 2.2 shows: the apathetic, the authoritarian, and the authoritative.

Let's look at each one individually, starting with the apathetic one.

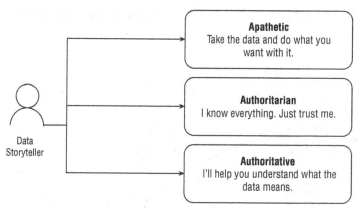

Figure 2.2: The three types of data storytellers

The Apathetic Data Storyteller

The apathetic, or passive, data storyteller presents data cold and detachedly, without instilling enthusiasm or involvement in the narrative. This type of data storyteller basically says, "Here's the data. Do whatever you want with it." They present the story as if it were a list of information to read, without worrying about creating a connection or making it attractive. They show no passion in the way they narrate. The underlying problem is that they don't even believe in the story they are about to tell. Their presentation may be objective and accurate, but it is sterile and uninvolved as if they don't care how the data is perceived or understood.

It might seem strange, but in my opinion, storytellers have all fallen into this category. We go through this phase every time we don't prepare our story and end up improvising something more or less sensible at the last moment. However, improvisation is a quality only of some professional actors. If a mere mortal like us tries to improvise, the result will be exactly what you expect: an improvised story that will leak everywhere. So, please prepare before telling a story. And if you say you don't have time to prepare, read Lea Pica's book *Present Beyond Measure*, and you'll realize that you have more time than you think (Pica, 2023).

The narrative of an apathetic data storyteller is flat, does not involve the audience, and has no interest in showing the importance of the results. An apathetic storyteller says things like, "These are sales numbers. Here, there is a decrease. There is an increase. Let's move on to the next slide." The result? Audiences quickly lose interest, as they lack guidance or an emotional connection that helps them see the data's value and meaning. The apathetic storyteller leaves it up to the audience to interpret, without offering any guidance or stimulus to understand the "why" or "how" behind the numbers.

In summary, the apathetic data storyteller has three characteristics, as shown in Figure 2.3.

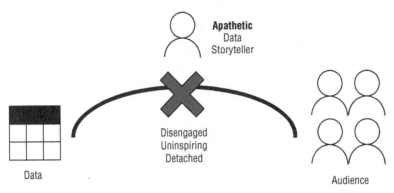

Figure 2.3: The apathetic data storyteller fails in building the bridge between the data and the audience because they are disengaged, uninspiring, and detached

The apathetic data storyteller is disengaged because they don't try to capture attention or involve the audience. They are also uninspiring because they lack enthusiasm or passion. They expose the data monotonously without bringing out relevant connections or elements. The effect is that the data loses meaning and appeal, no matter how accurate, leaving the audience indifferent or bored. Finally, the apathetic data storyteller is detached, because they present the data as a sterile list of information without considering the impact or value that this could have.

Although this type of data storyteller is the least compelling, it is undoubtedly the most frequent. At least, that's what I've seen in my experience.

Several factors can contribute to becoming an apathetic data storyteller (Millner and Price, n.d.). First is a fear of negative evaluation from the audience. Second is a lack of preparation, which can cause anxiety. Speakers may feel unprepared, leading to a lack of enthusiasm during delivery. Also, a nonstimulating environment or restrictive organizational culture can hinder enthusiasm and engagement in communication. Finally, psychological conditions like social anxiety disorder can lead to avoidance behaviors, resulting in apathetic communication.

The Authoritarian Data Storyteller

The authoritarian data storyteller wants to convey a message without leaving room for doubt. They own the truth, have complete control of the data, and expect the audience to accept them without question. An authoritarian approach often sounds like this: "The data says this is the trend. There is nothing to discuss. Point."

Imagine a company meeting in which the analyst presents a series of graphs on sales performance and, without much explanation, concludes that the team must follow their recommendations because "the data speaks clearly." There is no room for questions, alternatives, or interpretations. This style is very "textbook"—almost didactic—but it does not involve the audience in a dialogue. The audience may feel belittled, or worse, they may think that the data storyteller is there more to demonstrate their own superiority than to be helpful.

The authoritarian data storyteller uses imperative language and presents conclusions as definitive. They use a peremptory tone, which leaves no room for interpretation or doubt. They propose their solution as the only possible solution.

In summary, the authoritarian data storyteller has three characteristics, as shown in Figure 2.4.

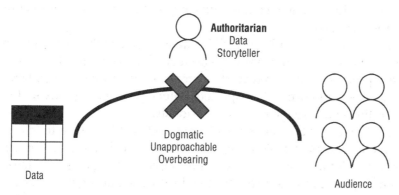

Figure 2.4: The authoritarian data storyteller fails in building the bridge between the data and the audience because they are dogmatic, unapproachable, and overbearing

The authoritarian data storyteller is dogmatic because they present the data as an undeniable truth, excluding any possibility of alternative perspectives. They provide a rigid interpretation of the facts, suggesting that there is only one correct way to understand the data, namely their own, leaving no room for critical or creative thoughts.

This data storyteller is also unapproachable because they create a distance from the audience. Their approach seems closed-minded, making the audience feel that their opinions or questions are not welcome, thus limiting shared understanding.

Finally, the authoritarian data storyteller is also overbearing because they impose conclusions decisively, using a peremptory tone that frames their point of view as the only valid one.

The problem with the authoritarian approach is that it risks alienating the audience, generating a sense of frustration or, even worse, mistrust. To be honest,

I have never encountered this type of data storytelling, and I hope it has never happened to you, either.

The Authoritative Data Storyteller

The authoritative data storyteller is the guide of the story. They aim to help the audience understand the data and act accordingly. Their expertise is visible but not ostentatious, and their approach is oriented toward involvement and trust. They show great enthusiasm and a passion for data and convey their curiosity to the audience. They are great motivators because they are motivated first. They explain what they've extracted from the data and why they think it's relevant but leave room for the audience to ask questions and share observations. Instead of saying, "We need to go this way," they'll say something like, "According to the data, sales have dropped in recent months, maybe we should explore why. Let's see together what could be behind it."

This approach works particularly well because it makes the audience an active part of the story. The authoritative data storyteller is not afraid to accept alternative interpretations. In this way, they create an atmosphere of collaboration and trust. The audience feels respected, valued, and more motivated to follow the narrative and take the messages seriously.

The authoritative data storyteller uses a balanced and inclusive tone and invites the audience to reflect. In essence, the authoritative data storyteller creates a dialogue and invites the audience to participate, acting as a facilitator, and not a commander. And, as a result, they build trust and gain a deeper understanding of the data.

In summary, the authoritative data storyteller has three characteristics, as shown in Figure 2.5.

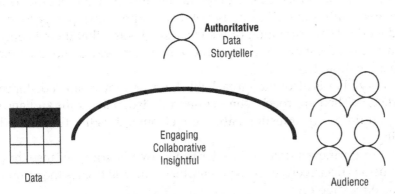

Figure 2.5: The authoritative data storyteller builds the bridge between the data and the audience because they are engaging, collaborative, and insightful

The authoritative data storyteller is engaging because they don't simply present the data but involve the audience, transmitting curiosity and passion for the content. They are also collaborative because they promote real collaboration with the audience, encouraging questions, observations, and even alternative points of view. Finally, they are insightful because they go beyond the surface level of data, explaining why they are relevant and what actions could result from them.

There are few authoritative data storytellers out there, and I hope you can become one of them. The most striking example of an authoritative data storyteller is Hans Rosling, a Swedish doctor and statistician. I'll talk about him at the end of this chapter. For now, let's look at the primary skills a great data storyteller must have.

Challenge: Reflect on whether you feel you belong to one of the types of data storytellers described.

The Data Storyteller Skills

To be a great data storyteller, knowing the data inside out is not enough. What really makes the difference are some personal qualities that enable you to create an authentic connection with the audience. To build this connection, the data storyteller must possess the following fundamental skills, as shown in Figure 2.6: humility, sincerity, vulnerability, empathy, openness, flexibility, and patience.

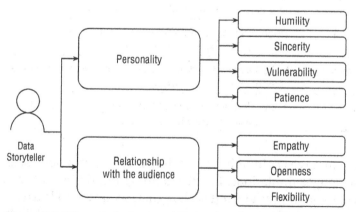

Figure 2.6: The most important skills a great data storyteller should have

Some of the skills described directly concern the data storyteller's personality, others concern their relationship with the audience. Let's look at them one by one, briefly.

Humility

As I mentioned at the beginning of this chapter, the best data storyteller is the one you can't see. To be invisible, you will have to acquire a certain amount of humility; that is, you will have to put yourself at the service of the story and not at the center. You will be a great data storyteller if you do not constantly try to draw attention to yourself but let the story take pride of place. Humility does not mean hiding your knowledge but putting it at the service of the story and the audience.

Humility pushes you to step back and think, "What is the simplest and clearest way to explain this data?" This approach makes the audience feel welcomed, not intimidated.

No one is born naturally humble, so don't be discouraged if you are not humble. However, you can work to become humble. There are several books that can teach you humility from various points of view and based on the culture and spirituality of reference. However, there are some general aspects you can work on to become humbler, as shown in Table 2.1.

Table 2.1: Strategies to Become Humbler

WHAT TO DO TO BECOME HUMBLE	A POSSIBLE WAY TO DO IT
Practice gratitude daily.	Take a few minutes each day (especially when you wake up or before sleeping) to reflect on what you're thankful for.
Seek feedback regularly.	Ask friends, family, or colleagues for honest feedback on your behavior. Listen without defending yourself.
Admit when you're wrong.	When you make a mistake, own up to it. Apologize sincerely and learn from the experience.
Celebrate others' successes.	Make it a habit to acknowledge the achievements of others without comparing yourself.
Recognize your limits.	Acknowledge that you don't have all the answers and it's okay to ask for help when needed.

Becoming humble involves cultivating a mindset that values others, seeks growth, and acknowledges limitations. Practice daily gratitude to shift focus from yourself to what you appreciate and seek regular feedback to learn and grow. Embrace mistakes and admit when you're wrong to foster accountability. Celebrate others' successes, recognize your limits, and reflect on your smallness in the broader context of life. Humility is a strength, not a weakness.

Sincerity

You will be a great data storyteller if you are sincere. Sincerity means speaking clearly about the data, even when it says something uncomfortable. The sincere data storyteller does not try to "fix" the data to make it seem better than it is, nor to hide problematic aspects. Sincerity means telling things as they are, with transparency. Sincerity sets you free because you are not forced to hide anything. With sincerity, you show your genuineness and attract the audience's trust and goodwill. My daughter Giulia manages to obtain people's goodwill precisely because of her sincerity.

Due to various life events, you may not be immediately sincere. But you can train yourself to be so by doing a little practice, as suggested in Table 2.2.

Table 2.2: Strategies to Become More Sincere

WHAT TO DO TO BECOME SINCERE	A POSSIBLE WAY TO DO IT
Be honest with yourself.	Reflect on your thoughts, feelings, and motivations to ensure you act and speak authentically.
Follow through on promises.	Do what you say you'll do. Consistency in words and actions builds trust and shows genuine intent.
Admit your mistakes.	Acknowledge when you're wrong or when you've hurt someone and apologize sincerely without excuses.
Avoid exaggeration.	Stick to the truth without embellishing facts to impress others.
Be transparent about your intentions.	Clearly communicate your motives and avoid hidden meanings.

To become sincere, start by being honest with yourself, reflecting on your true thoughts, feelings, and motivations. Follow through on promises to demonstrate integrity and reliability. Admit your mistakes openly, taking responsibility without excuses. Avoid exaggeration by sticking to the truth, ensuring your words align with reality. Lastly, be transparent about your intentions, communicating clearly and genuinely to build trust and authenticity in your interactions. Be sincere, and you will be a great data storyteller.

Vulnerability

You will be a great data storyteller if you also demonstrate your vulnerability. Nobody needs invincible heroes, and people want to see others with the same problems as themselves. If you show your vulnerability, the audience understands you are one of them. Through vulnerability, you create human bonds with others. Don't be ashamed of your vulnerabilities. They are what bring you closer to the audience. Later in this chapter, we will look at an example of a great storyteller, Brené Brown, a researcher and author who studies vulnerability and human connection.

Training yourself to show your vulnerabilities might seem absurd to you. In reality, showing your vulnerabilities to others makes you deeply human, so that you can share the burdens of humanity with others. Table 2.3 shows some aspects you can work on to be more "human," and therefore, implicitly show your vulnerabilities as strengths.

Table 2.3: Strategies to Show Your Vulnerabilities

WHAT TO DO TO SHOW VULNERABILITIES	A POSSIBLE WAY TO DO IT
Share personal stories.	Talk about challenges, failures, or insecurities you've faced to show your human side.
Express your emotions honestly.	Admit when you're feeling scared, sad, or overwhelmed.
Ask for help.	Reach out to others when you need support.
Admit when you're wrong.	Acknowledge your mistakes without being defensive.

Demonstrating vulnerability involves sharing personal stories to create connection and show authenticity. Expressing emotions honestly helps others understand your true feelings, fostering trust and empathy. Asking for help reveals humility and openness, showing you value others' support. Additionally, admitting when you're wrong demonstrates accountability and a willingness to grow, reinforcing sincerity and strengthening relationships.

Patience

Finally, patience is an often underestimated but crucial quality, especially when explaining complex data. Not everyone understands numbers in the same way and at the same speed. You will be a great data storyteller if you take the time to tell your story, answer questions, clarify doubts, and ensure that each person can follow the story without feeling lost or overwhelmed.

For example, if someone struggles to understand a complex graph, you will take a moment to review it together, perhaps using an analogy or simplifying it further. This approach helps the audience follow along better and demonstrates attention and respect for everyone's learning process.

There are different ways to practice patience, also based on various cultures and spiritualities. Personally, a technique that has helped me be more patient over the years is building castles with playing cards. I started this practice when I was about 10 years old, and I remember that at the beginning, it was complicated to build even a single-story castle because the cards fell, and I got angry. Then, I slowly realized that I had to stay calm to build a very tall castle. After many attempts and much patience, I managed to build a 12-story castle! If I hadn't gained patience, I wouldn't have succeeded.

Empathy and Openness

Empathy involves putting yourself in the audience's shoes and understanding their needs, expectations, and possible concerns. It means connecting with the audience and adapting the narrative accordingly. Empathy helps you choose understandable language, simplify complex concepts, and anticipate questions or objections that might arise.

In her essay "The Problem of Empathy," phenomenologist and philosopher Edith Stein underlines that empathy requires a capacity for openness toward others, the audience in our case: Empathy leads to feeling the same feelings and emotions as the audience, while remaining separate from them (Stein, 2018).

Openness is a mindset ensuring that personal biases or ego do not cloud the narrative. True openness involves embracing curiosity, actively listening to feedback, and being willing to adapt based on new insights. Openness and empathy are deeply connected because both involve stepping outside oneself to understand the audience's perspectives. Openness is being receptive to new ideas and feedback, while empathy enables a data storyteller to connect with the audience's emotions, needs, and experiences. Together, they ensure that a data storyteller not only shares insights effectively but also does so in a way that resonates and feels relevant to the audience.

You will be a great data storyteller if you are empathetic toward the audience and open to new ideas and points of view. Not all data interpretations are definitive; sometimes, the audience has observations that can enrich your analysis. Being open means listening and, when necessary, adapting your narrative to integrate the contributions of others as well.

Empathy is one of the most difficult qualities to develop because it requires putting yourself in others' shoes in their specific situations. However, with a little practice, you can become empathetic. Table 2.4 summarizes some possible strategies for becoming more empathetic and open-minded.

Table 2.4: Strategies to Become Empathetic and Open-Minded

WHAT TO DO TO BECOME EMPATHETIC AND OPEN-MINDED	A POSSIBLE WAY TO DO IT
Practice active listening.	Focus on what the other person is saying without thinking about your response.
Observe nonverbal cues.	Pay attention to the other person's body language, tone of voice, and other signs of emotion to sense their feelings.
Reflect on your biases.	Acknowledge any preconceptions you might have and work to set them aside when you talk to another person.

To become more empathetic and open-minded, practice active listening by fully focusing on what others are saying without interruptions or preconceived responses. Pay close attention to nonverbal cues, such as body language and tone, to understand emotions beyond words. Reflect on your biases to recognize and set aside personal assumptions, allowing you to approach conversations with openness and understanding.

Flexibility

You will be a great data storyteller if you know how to reshape your presentation based on the audience, the context, and the communication objectives. Each audience has its own level of knowledge, expectations, and language. Adapting means constructing the story in a way that is engaging and understandable for anyone.

As you tell your story, observe your audience's reactions. If you notice signs of disinterest, such as loss of attention or poor interaction, adjust your approach in real time. For example, if your audience doesn't respond well to overly complex data, simplify or use metaphors and visualizations to make it more accessible. Flexibility is a crucial quality to ensure that your message remains relevant and engaging, even in case of an unexpected response.

So far, you have seen the skills that, as a great data storyteller, you should have regardless of the story. But what could be your role within the story? *Challenge: Stop for a moment to think about which skills you already have, which ones you could develop with a little effort, and which ones would require a great effort.*

In summary, you will be a great data storyteller if you are humble, sincere, patient, empathetic, vulnerable, versatile, and always open to new perspectives. These skills will transform you from a simple data storyteller to a great data storyteller. Maturing these qualities requires time and a lot of work. But with some practice, you can become a great data storyteller, even learning from your mistakes. Nobody is perfect, but you can improve every day.

The Data Storyteller's Role in the Story

The data storyteller in the story plays the role of the narrator. There are three main types of narrators, as shown in Figure 2.7.

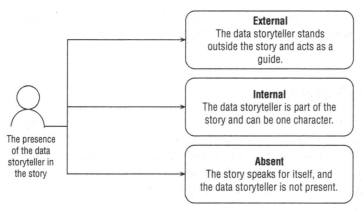

Figure 2.7: The presence of the data storyteller in the story

The External Data Storyteller

The *external* data storyteller tells the story from the outside, without entering the story. They move around the data and comment on them. When the data storyteller takes on an external role, it is as if they were observing the data from a certain distance, offering a broad and well-contextualized point of view. Consider Neil Halloran's *The Fallen of World War II* video (Halloran, 2016), a documentary that depicts the human cost of World War II, focusing on the scale of military and civilian casualties across nations. Through interactive graphics and storytelling, Halloran reveals the staggering numbers in a way that conveys both the enormity and tragedy of the loss, fostering a deeper understanding of the war's impact. Here, the narrator does not try to immerse the audience in the individual stories of the victims but provides an overall perspective. Halloran maintains a detached, almost "scientific" tone, but he directly brings out the tragedy's vastness. It's as if he's saying, "Here's the big picture, look what these numbers mean." This style enables the audience to understand the proportions and absorb the story through a broad perspective, often intensifying the message.

The Internal Data Storyteller

The *internal* data storyteller is a character in the story who experiences firsthand the drama they are telling. In extreme cases, the internal data storyteller could even coincide with the story's hero or the sidekick. For example, if the story's hero is patients in a hospital who suffer from diabetes, the internal data story-teller could share their experience if they also suffer from diabetes. This way, they could act as a sidekick to the story.

This type of data storyteller brings the audience into the story because they share their doubts and experiences. This approach is powerful when the data impacts individuals on a personal level, for example, when discussing topics like patient care or championing causes like climate change, education reform, or social justice.

The Absent Data Storyteller

In some data-driven stories, the data storyteller is *absent*. An example is *A visual tour of the world's* CO_2 *emissions*, which shows data on CO_2 emissions through animations and visualizations that speak alone (Vox, 2014). There is no voice, no face, only the data that transforms before the audience's eyes. It's a bit like going to a museum and looking at a work of art without a guide to tell you what you should see.

This type of storytelling works incredibly well when the data is powerful enough to tell a story without human intervention. However, it is a challenging choice: There is no room for clarification, and the audience must be able to draw their own conclusions. The narrator's absence can cause the audience to "discover" the meaning of the numbers independently, but it can also leave someone with unanswered questions.

Which type of data storyteller should you choose? It depends on what you want to achieve. If you want the audience to stop and think, use an external storyteller. An internal approach is ideal if you prefer to let the story live. And if you're confident enough that the data can speak for itself, the absence can be perfect. The important thing is that your chosen role is in harmony with the message you wish to convey, so that the story resonates deeply with the audience.

So far, you've seen the types of data storytellers, the skills you should have to become a great data storyteller, and your role in the story. But in what possible scenarios can you tell your story?

Possible Scenarios in Which to Tell a Story

There are two main scenarios to tell a story, synchronously and asynchronously, as shown in Figure 2.8.

Synchronously means live in front of your audience. Asynchronously means that first you prepare your story and tell it, and then the audience enjoys it. In the first case, you have direct access to the audience and see their reactions live. In the second case, you may never know the audience's reactions or even know who interacted with your story, as in the case of a data journalism article.

Usually, when you tell a story synchronously, you can use voice (e.g., in the case of a podcast), slides (e.g., in the case of a talk), or a video. There are two ways to tell a synchronous story: live or online. Presenting a story live is like staging a show, where the words, tone of voice, images, movements, and pauses are part of the narrative. In this context, you should involve the five senses to keep the attention high. The audience can "hear" the story not only with their ears but with their whole body. An alternative to the live presentation is the online one, which lacks many sensory elements, such as direct eye contact and the room's energy. The voice plays a key role: tone, rhythm, and pauses become crucial elements that keep the audience involved.

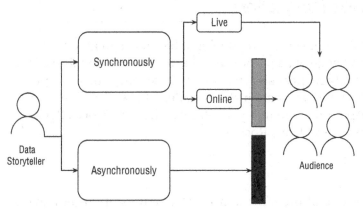

Figure 2.8: The two scenarios to tell a story: synchronously (live and online) and asynchronously. Only the live presentation gives direct access to the audience. The online presentation gives mediated access to the audience (through the medium [i.e., the computer]). The asynchronous presentation doesn't provide any access to the audience.

If you tell the story asynchronously, you cannot directly clarify the audience's doubts, so the story must be as clear as possible. For example, every sentence you write must make sense if you use written text such as a report. Each sentence represents a piece of a scene, so you have a duty only to write text that moves the story forward. Another asynchronous delivery method is a video that may contain data animations. You can use effects, colors, and music to emphasize the most touching or surprising moments, leading the audience to an immersive experience beyond the numbers. This is the ideal medium to give the data a powerful visual dimension that can remain imprinted in the viewer's mind.

Audio is a mode of story delivery that can be asynchronous and synchronous. In this case, you do not have any images available. You can use strategic pauses, an engaging tone of voice, and detailed descriptions to make your audience "see" essential elements. Furthermore, sounds and music become necessary tools for creating atmosphere and capturing attention.

Each scenario has its strengths and challenges, but the secret is knowing how to choose the one that best suits the message and the audience. A live presentation, for example, is perfect for telling stories that require immediate interaction and responses; a written article enables you to tell the story calmly and in detail, while audio is ideal for those who love listening to stories "with their eyes closed."

At this point in the chapter, I think you're almost ready to learn how to become a great data storyteller. You're only missing one thing: taking inspiration from the work of others. Let's look at this in the next section.

Examples of Great Storytellers

An additional secret that I haven't told you yet to become a great data storyteller is to watch how other great data storytellers tell their stories. In this section, I will introduce you to three great storytellers. Of these, only one is properly a data storyteller, while the others are just storytellers. However, their charm can help you gain inspiration in telling your stories. The three storytellers are Steve Jobs, Brené Brown, and Hans Rosling.

Steve Jobs

Steve Jobs is perhaps one of the most famous storytellers of our era, even though he was an entrepreneur and technological innovator, not a "traditional" storyteller. However, in every presentation of Apple products, Jobs demonstrated one of the most crucial storytelling qualities: simplicity. You can imagine simplicity as synthesizing all the skills I presented in Figure 2.6. He knew how to distill complex concepts into clear and accessible messages, speaking in a language anyone could understand.

Take, for example, the launch of the first iPhone (Protectstar Inc., 2013). Jobs didn't just present a list of technical specifications; he told the story of a device that would change our lives. As an external narrator, Jobs demonstrated the revolutionary features of the product, connecting them to moments of everyday life. He described a world in which the telephone would become an integrated part of our experience, and the enthralled audience saw in real time how technology could transform into an intimate and necessary component of our lives.

Jobs' secret? Knowing how to connect innovation to daily life. He knew how to capture people's imagination not by speaking in technical terms but by making them imagine the "why" of each function. It wasn't just a phone. It was a revolution in your pocket. With Jobs, technical data were tools to speak about a vision, and there was a promise of change in every one of his presentations.

What can we take from Jobs? Two things. First, his simplicity in telling things without frills. Second, care in preparing the presentation. He spent a lot of time preparing his presentations.

Brené Brown

Another extraordinary example of storytelling is Brené Brown, a researcher and author who studies vulnerability. Unlike Jobs, who described the data from the point of view of an external observer, Brown uses an internal and intimate approach: She brings the audience into the world of her research and her own life experience, creating an atmosphere of openness and honesty that involves emotion.

In her famous TED Talk, "The Power of Vulnerability" (TED, 2011), Brown explores data on human connections. Instead of presenting numbers and graphs, she tells stories that make the data part of our experience. It's as if she takes us directly to the heart of her research, showing us that there are people, emotions, and a universal desire to belong behind the data. She talks about her fears and weaknesses, showing a vulnerability that makes her message even more powerful.

Brown knows audiences don't just want to listen. They want to feel. Using her voice and personal experiences, she makes the message of her research tangible, ensuring people recognize themselves in her stories. This "internal" approach creates a very strong connection, transforming her presentation into a silent dialogue with the audience. Her words are not just data but invitations to look within and discover the beauty and power of vulnerability.

What can we take from Brown? Her sincerity and ability to engage the audience.

Hans Rosling

Hans Rosling was a true master of data storytelling and an inspiration to anyone who wants to tell stories through data. As a physician and statistician, Rosling knew how to use data to illuminate the most complex realities simply and visually arrestingly. His ability to make numbers accessible and meaningful is evident in his TED Talks, such as "Hans Rosling and the Magic Washing Machine" (TED, 2010), where he transforms seemingly dry statistics into living, dynamic, and engaging narratives.

Rosling used innovative visualization tools to depict changes over time and global comparisons, showing how the world was evolving and breaking widespread stereotypes about developing countries. For him, each graphic became a window into stories of progress, poverty, health, and hope, and with his enthusiasm, he dragged the audience on a journey into the reality of the world. His skill lay in the data and how he combined numbers and storytelling, highlighting the human impact behind the graphs.

With his passionate tone and creative use of visualizations, he knew how to make information memorable and easily understandable, even for those unfamiliar with statistics. Rosling demonstrated that data is never cold or impersonal;

it is the stories of people and societies in transformation. His approach teaches us that if narrated well, data can break prejudices and inspire new ways of thinking.

What can we take from Rosling? The importance of making data visual and accessible, and of describing it with passion. Like him, we can strive to convey our belief in the numbers and the stories they tell, knowing that clarity and excitement can make the data come alive.

These three great storytellers—Steve Jobs, Brené Brown, and Hans Rosling—show us multiple ways to tell a story and engage audiences, each suited to different contexts and types of content. With his simplicity and precision, Jobs teaches us that clarity and preparation are essential to capture attention and inspire. With her personal and authentic approach, Brown demonstrates that emotions and vulnerability can be powerful tools for creating a deep connection with those who listen to us. Finally, Rosling reminds us that if well visualized and told passionately, data can become living stories capable of changing perspectives.

Learning from these experts does not mean copying them but drawing ideas to develop a unique storytelling style capable of adapting to your content and audience. In data storytelling, your goal is not just to present information but to make data meaningful, accessible, and memorable. As these three examples teach us, a good data storyteller doesn't just communicate numbers but conveys a vision of the world that can inspire, move, and drive change.

Now, it's time to learn what makes a great data-driven story!

Takeaways

- The essence of a great data storyteller lies in invisibility—keeping the focus on the data, not the presenter. A great data storyteller acts like a film director, letting the data take center stage.

- There are three types of data storytellers: apathetic, authoritarian, and authoritative. The apathetic data storyteller presents data without passion, leading to disconnection with the audience. The authoritarian data storyteller imposes their interpretation on the audience, using a rigid approach that stifles collaboration. The authoritative data storyteller guides the audience through the story, using an inclusive and engaging approach that fosters trust and curiosity.

- Humility, sincerity, vulnerability, empathy, openness, flexibility, and patience are essential skills of a great data storyteller. These qualities enable effective communication of data insights and foster connection with the audience.

- A data storyteller can play one of three roles in a story: external, internal, or absent. The external storyteller narrates from a distance; the internal storyteller immerses themselves in the story, often sharing personal experiences; the absent storyteller lets the data speak for itself without a narrator.

- You can tell your data stories synchronously (live or online) or asynchronously (videos, reports).

- Examples of great storytellers are Steve Jobs, with his simplicity and precision; Brené Brown, with her sincerity and connection; and Hans Rosling, with his passionate visualization of data.

References

Dykes, B. (2019). *Effective Data Storytelling: How to Drive Change with Data, Narrative and Visuals*. New York: John Wiley & Sons.

Halloran, N. (2016) The Fallen of World War II. *Video* available at `https://www.youtube.com/watch?v=DwKPFT-RioU` (accessed October 31, 2024).

Millner, A. G., & Price, R. D. (n.d.). Classifying communication apprehension (CA). In: The Public Speaking Project (Chapter 11). University of Central Arkansas, University of Arkansas at Little Rock, University of Kentucky, and Southern Illinois University. Retrieved from `https://courses.lumenlearning.com/publicspeakingprinciples/chapter/classifying-communication-apprehension-ca` (accessed November 29, 2024).

Pica, L. (2023). *Present Beyond Measure: Design, Visualize, and Deliver Data Stories That Inspire Action*. New York: John Wiley & Sons.

Protectstar Inc. (2013). iPhone 1—Steve Jobs MacWorld Keynote in 2007—[Video]. `https://www.youtube.com/watch?v=VQKMoT-6XSg` (accessed October 31, 2024).

Stein, E. (2018). Zum Problem der Einfühlung: Das Wesen der Einfühlungsakte, Die Konstitution des psychophysischen Individuums & Einfühlung als Verstehen geistiger Personen. Prague: e-artnow (On the problem of empathy: The nature of Acts of Empathy, The Constitution of the Psychophysical Individual & empathy as understanding of spiritual persons. Prague: e-artnow).

TED (2010). The Magic Washing Machine. [Video]. `https://www.ted.com/talks/hans_rosling_the_magic_washing_machine` (accessed October 31, 2024).

TED (2011). The Power of Vulnerability. [Video]. `https://www.youtube.com/watch?v=iCvmsMzlF7o` (accessed October 31, 2024).

Vox (2014). A Visual Tour of the World's CO_2 emissions. [Video]. `https://www.youtube.com/watch?v=fJ0o2E4d8Ts` (accessed October 31, 2024).

Making a Successful
Data-Driven Story

Your journey as a data storyteller starts with data: data collected by your company, open data downloaded from institutions or government agencies, data extracted from whatever source. So, I assume that before reading this chapter, you had some data, analyzed it, discovered something exceptional, and now you want to communicate your discovery to someone through a data-driven story. After reading the first chapter, you know a good story should have a hero and a plot. Perhaps now you are wondering how you can extract a hero and plot using your data about sales trends, rising temperatures, comparisons between populations, and so on.

Don't worry. As your guide to becoming a data storyteller, I am here to lead you through this journey. Let's begin!

In the previous chapter, I noted that three phases are necessary to build a story:

1. Preproduction—writing the script

2. Production—implementing the scenes

3. Postproduction—editing

Let's analyze the three phases separately, starting with the first phase, preproduction. As a quick reminder, we won't focus on the audience in this chapter. Personally, I advise against inserting the audience at this stage, because you'll miss a great opportunity if you tell your story only once. The beauty of stories is that they can be told numerous times and adapted to various audiences.

It's human nature to tell stories, and if you have a portfolio of them ready and waiting, you can pull out a completed story every time.

Preproduction: The Data Story Script

This phase of *preproduction* consists of organizing the results of the data analysis, or exploration process, into a story. It transforms the data analyst into a data storyteller and is, therefore, the most difficult phase of the entire journey. Often, this phase is skipped altogether, and storytellers move directly to the next phase, *production*, with the implementation of the scenes through various data visualization techniques. The result, however, isn't a story but is a presentation of the data in a more or less organized way.

But if you want to tell data-driven stories, I suggest you implement the simple steps I will discuss here. Begin by sitting comfortably and thinking about each step to follow. Just to give you some context, the preproduction phase is pretty much the same in all areas of story writing (i.e., films, novels, comics, etc.). All share the same structure, so why not also apply it to data storytelling?

The preproduction phase requires these three steps:

1. Choose the *theme*.

2. Define the *subject*.

3. Implement the *script*.

Let's analyze each step separately, starting with the theme.

Theme

The *theme* is the central meaning of the story (McKee, 2010a). It must be as simple as possible—so simple that it can be summarized in a single sentence (McKee, 2010b). You can define a story's theme in several ways. In this book, the theme consists of three fundamental parts, controlling idea, message, and value, as illustrated in Figure 3.1.

Controlling idea	Message	Value
The main topic of the story, directly extracted from data	What we want to convey with the story	What is useful or important to the story

Figure 3.1: The three main elements define the theme of a story

First, the *controlling idea* is the main topic of the story, through which the message is conveyed. In a data-driven story, the controlling idea is the insight extracted from the data. Therefore, it is firmly anchored in the data and absolutely cannot be manipulated by storytelling.

> Describing how to extract insights from data is beyond the scope of this book. If you're interested in learning more about the topic, however, you can read several books on the subject, including *Effective Data Analysis* by Mona Khalil, or *Python for Data Analysis* by Wes McKinney if you use Python to carry out your analyses.

In short, each application domain has its analysis types. Table 3.1 lists some examples of scopes of analysis for relevant domains. Obviously, the table isn't exhaustive, but it certainly gives you an idea of the possible types of analysis.

Table 3.1:   Possible Types of Analysis for Different Domains

DOMAIN	TYPE OF ANALYSIS
Healthcare	Disease prevalence and trends
	Patient outcomes and treatment efficacy
	Health risk factors and their impact
Finance	Market trends and predictions
	Risk assessment and mitigation strategies
	Fraud detection and prevention
Marketing	Customer segmentation and profiling
	Campaign effectiveness and return on investment (ROI) analysis
	Product demand forecasting
Education	Student performance and learning analytics
	Efficacy of teaching methods and interventions
	Access and equity in education
Retail	Sales trends and forecasting
	Customer purchase behavior analysis
	Price optimization and dynamic pricing strategies
Social Sciences	Demographic analysis and population trends
	Socioeconomic disparities and inequality
	Public opinion analysis and sentiment tracking

Continues

Table 3.1 *(continued)*

DOMAIN	TYPE OF ANALYSIS
Environmental Sciences	Climate change impact assessment
	Pollution monitoring and mitigation strategies
	Natural disaster prediction and risk assessment
Technology	User behavior analysis for software and app development
	Cybersecurity threat detection and prevention
	Technology adoption trends and innovation analysis
Transportation	Traffic flow analysis and congestion prediction
	Public transportation usage patterns
	Vehicle routing optimization for logistics
Sports Analytics	Player performance analysis and scouting
	Game strategy optimization
	Fan engagement analysis

If you work in the healthcare domain, examples of analyses could be health risk factors and their impact, patient outcomes and treatment efficacy, healthcare resource allocation, and so on. If you work in the finance sector, examples of topics could be risk assessment or market trends and predictions.

Second, the theme's *message* is what you want to convey with your story. It's the takeaway you want to leave your audience with *after* the story ends. Each story ends with actions to be taken in the short term—the so-called *next steps*. These next steps, which are discussed in the following chapters in more detail, are practical actions. Instead, the message is something more profound and more lasting—it's the understanding you want your audience to gain at the end of the story. The message mustn't be transmitted in a moralistic way but via the mouth of the hero and events happening in the plot. They will be the ones that convey the theme's message. This message is never stated explicitly, because the audience will guess it from the actions described within the story. For example, if you want to convey the message "Respect the environment!" you shouldn't say it explicitly to your audience. Instead, you could show how the same controlling idea can convey different messages.

It's important to mention that a separate speech could be given on the use of data to manipulate the audience in transmitting propaganda or dishonest persuasion messages. I'm not going to elaborate on this aspect here but will simply note that the controlling idea is closely linked to the message that you want to convey.

To learn more about this topic, Google keywords like "disinformation," "fake news," or "propaganda," or simply read Ireton and Posetti's book, *Journalism, Fake News, and Disinformation: Handbook for Journalism Education and Training* (Ireton and Posetti's, 2018).

Finally, the theme's *value* is what is valuable, or important, to the story (Oxford Dictionary, 2024). In the literary field, each genre has its specific value, which is combined as a dichotomy between a positive and a negative element, as shown in Table 3.2 (Grahl, 2024).

Table 3.2: Values for Literary Genres

GENRE	VALUE
Action	Life/death
War	Honor/dishonor
Horror	Life/damnation
Crime	Justice/injustice
Thriller	Salvation/damnation
Love	Love/hate
Performance	Respect/shame
Society	Power/impotence
Status	Success/failure
Morality	Altruism/selfishness
Worldview	Sophistication/naivety

By reading a novel or watching a film of a specific literary genre, the reader expects to find a specific value. For example, in the literary genre of love, the value is the dichotomy between love and hate. In the thriller literary genre, value is described as salvation and damnation. Each literary genre has its own dichotomy of values, and you cannot betray those values. Otherwise, you'll betray the reader's expectations of them. For example, you cannot write a thriller whose value is the dichotomy between love and hate because this is specific to the love genre.

These same concepts can be applied to the field of data storytelling. In this case, instead of literary genres, reference domains, such as health, finance, education, and so on, are covered. Specific values are found in each domain, implemented through a dichotomy, as shown in Table 3.3.

Table 3.3: Values for Major Domains

DOMAIN	VALUE
Healthcare	Healing/suffering
Finance	Prosperity/poverty
Marketing	Influence/poverty
Education	Enlightenment/ignorance
Retail	Satisfaction/dissatisfaction
Social science	Understanding/ignorance
Environmental science	Preservation/destruction
Technology	Innovation/stagnation
Transportation	Mobility/stagnation
Sport analytics	Strategy/chaos

The list of major domains described in Table 3.3 isn't exhaustive but gives you an idea of the values for each domain. For example, if you analyze data in the education sector, the value manifests itself as a dichotomy between enlightenment and ignorance, while in the case of transportation, the values are combined as mobility/stagnation.

When defining your story's value, choose its domain and then decide on the type of story to implement. You can choose between a *prescriptive story*, which passes from the negative to the positive element of a value (e.g., from ignorance to enlightenment), or a *cautionary story*, in which you move from the positive to the negative element (e.g., from enlightenment to ignorance).

Now that the three main elements of the theme (controlling idea, message, and value) have been presented, let's look at a practical example. Imagine that you are a climate scientist and have witnessed the need to educate the public about the importance of respecting the environment, or you are a scientist working for a company seeking funding for your technology meant to mitigate climate change. Say you have a dataset on global temperature anomalies from 1860 to today (NOAA, 2023), as shown in the graph in Figure 3.2.

The temperature anomaly is a departure from a reference value. A positive anomaly means that the observed temperature was warmer than the reference value, while a negative anomaly means that the observed temperature was cooler than the reference value. Anomalies are provided with respect to the period 1901–2000, the 20th century average.

The controlling idea—the insight extracted from the data—is that temperatures have increased since 1977. The message associated with the controlling idea could be that *if eco-sustainable policies are not adopted, the planet's living conditions will worsen*. The value could be combined through a cautionary story if the final value achieved is destruction, which aligns with the message.

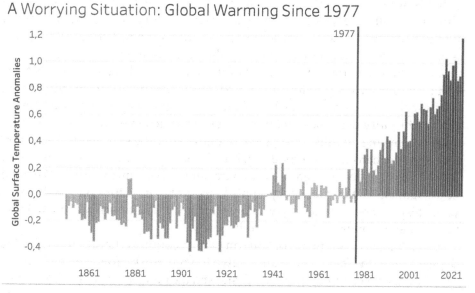

Figure 3.2: A chart showing the average temperature anomalies since 1860

To summarize, the theme is fundamental to ensuring that your story is coherent from beginning to end. Toss out anything from the story that isn't consistent with the theme.

Once you have defined the theme and its three elements (i.e., controlling idea, message, and value), you can move on to the next part, defining the subject.

Subject

The theme's subject (or *synopsis* in literary terms) is the summary of the story. It concisely contains the definition of the plot as it unfolds in chronological order. The best way to define a subject is to grab a pen and paper (or your computer screen and keyboard) and write what the story is about, filling a maximum of one page. The subject helps you understand what you'll need within the story.

The definition of the subject identifies three elements: the hero, the hero's object of desire, and the problem that arises between the two (see Figure 3.3).

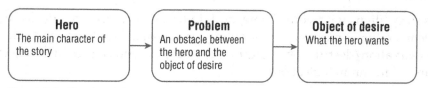

Figure 3.3: The three elements that make up the subject: the hero, the hero's object of desire, and the problem that arises between the two

In his aforementioned book, *Building a StoryBrand: Clarify Your Message. So Customer Will Listen*, Donald Miller states that a story begins with a character living an everyday life. Then, something disrupts them. The remaining story is about the hero's journey to return to the peaceful life they once enjoyed.

The hero wants to reach an object of desire, but an obstacle stands between them. This obstacle is possibly generated by an antagonist (i.e., the villain) who does everything to prevent the hero from reaching the object of desire. The final part of the story describes whether the hero has achieved the object of desire and contains the possible next steps to follow after the story ends. In a simple sentence, the hero wants something, but a villain prevents the hero from gaining the object of desire. Here, a new character has been introduced—the villain or antagonist—who is the story's anti-hero. Not every story has a villain, but your story will be stronger if you can write one in. The figure of the villain will be discussed in more detail later in this book.

Note, there is no single hero. You can extract countless heroes from the data, depending on the focus you want to give to your story. However, once you've identified the hero, the object of their desire and the problem are unique. Regarding the example of rising temperatures, the hero could be the temperature, and the object of desire could be to keep its average annual value constant. The problem that stands between them is rising values.

To help you write the subject, use the *three-act structure*, which you've already seen in the previous chapter:

1. *Start*—description of the initial situation and presentation of the hero
2. *Center*—description of the problem the hero encounters
3. *End*—solution to the problem and definition of the next steps

Using Figure 3.2's example of global temperature anomalies from 1860 to today, the subject could be the following:

Beginning: Until 1976, temperature kept its average annual value more or less constant.

Center: Since 1977, temperature has been facing a growing problem: rising global values caused by human activity and climate change.

End: To solve this problem, humans must take drastic measures to reduce greenhouse gas emissions, protect natural resources, and promote sustainable energy sources.

This story aligns with your theme, both in terms of controlling ideas (i.e., rising temperatures), message (i.e., adopting eco-sustainable policies), and value (i.e., preservation/destruction, a cautionary story). As you can see, the subject is organized in chronological order.

To write about a good subject, I suggest you implement the following techniques:

1. Start writing using the data and precisely what you learned from the results of your analyses and explorations. What did you discover? What insight emerges from your data?

2. Connect your discovery to a hero, which can directly be the subject of your data (e.g., temperature) or something more general (e.g., planet Earth).

3. Identify the object of desire—what your hero would like to achieve—and the problem that prevents him from achieving it. Both aspects must emerge from your data. You absolutely can't make them up.

To recap, the subject is the summary of the story and is organized into three acts—the beginning, middle, and end—all which are described in chronological order.

Now, you're ready to define the scenes that will make up your story.

Script Implementation

In this phase, you move directly to the script's *definition*, which contains a detailed description of the plot, sequences, and scenes that constitute the story's evolution.

The plot is an extended form of the subject and, therefore, contains the three-act structure defined in the subject in depth. Figure 3.4 illustrates the main structure of the plot.

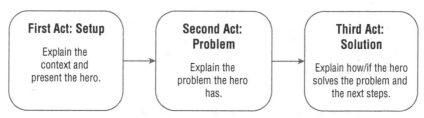

Figure 3.4: The three-act structure of the plot

The story's plot begins with the *first act*, which explains the story's context and introduces the hero. The *context* is the set of all the information necessary to frame the story. At this stage, you should enter as much of the information as possible. Then, during the delivery phase, you can decide whether to cut some details based on your established audience. You might think that if your story is aimed at only one type of audience, it would be better to immediately insert the elements necessary for that audience to understand the story in context. In reality, in this planning phase, you'll want to be as general as possible because you never know if you will have to present the same story to other audiences in the future. The first act ends with introducing the problem, or, in technical terms, the *first plot point*.

The *second act* defines the hero's real problem, or what is hindering the hero from achieving their object of desire. At the center of the second act is the *second plot point*, which describes the culmination of the problem.

Finally, the *third act* describes the final battle to resolve the hero's problem. This is where you decide who wins the battle and what to do after the battle is over. At this stage is the *third plot point*, which describes the maximum problem's manifestation. Starting from the next chapter, you will see extensively how to implement the plot. For now, just know that the plot contains all the story's details and moves it forward.

The *plot of a story* is the set of all the sequences within the story that define its evolution. A *scene* is a unit of place and time containing one or more actions. A set of consecutive scenes connected to each other by the same topic is called a *sequence* (Badino, 2021). Figure 3.5 shows a possible story divided into plot, sequences, and scenes.

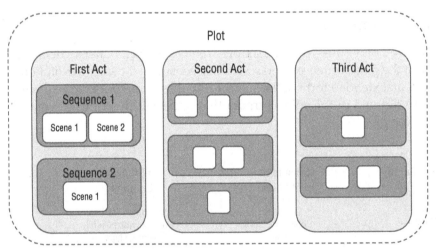

Figure 3.5: An example of dividing a story's plot into sequences and scenes

The number of sequences per act and the number of scenes per sequence can vary. For example, in Figure 3.5, the first act contains two sequences, the first with two scenes and the second with one; the second act contains three sequences, the first with three scenes, the second with two, and the third with one. Finally, the third act defines two scenes, one with one scene and the second one with two scenes.

There are four types of sequences, depending on the aspect highlighted in the scenes that constitute it (Kang, 2015):

- **Temporal sequences focus on change over time.** For example, they high-light the difference between Earth's temperature today and 50 years ago. This type of sequence is usually represented with timelines (i.e., graphical representations of events in chronological order) or trendlines (i.e., lines on a chart showing the general direction or pattern of data points over time). This detail, however, relates to the production phase, which we'll discuss later.

- **Spatial sequences highlight the comparison between two or more places.** You can make a comparison by starting from a small place and then going big, or vice versa. Alternatively, you can compare places of similar sizes. For example, you can analyze a phenomenon starting from one city (Rome) and then analyze the same phenomenon throughout Italy (from small to large), or vice versa, (i.e., starting from Italy and then focusing on Rome [from large to small]). Alternatively, you can also compare the phenomenon in Italy and France (i.e., places of similar size).

- **Relational sequences highlight relationships or differences.** For example, you can compare the temperature to a threshold or baseline value.

- **Cause-effect sequences show the factors at play in a story and describe their causes.** For example, you can show how the increase in Earth's temperature depends on human activity.

In the following chapters, types of scenes are examined in detail. For now, simply record their existence.

A dramatic scene keeps the audience engaged. One way to make a scene appealing and dramatic is to enrich it with details that the audience would not even imagine but help increase their interest and involvement in the story (Gutkind, 2007).

When thinking of a scene, always try to build suspense to make the audience curious to listen to you.

Let's now move on to a practical example. Consider the story about the anomalies in Earth's global temperature from 1860 to today again and proceed with the script.

First Act

Describe the situation before 1977. Use the following sequence with four scenes (see Figure 3.6):

1. Definition of the concept of temperature anomaly

2. Scene with temperature anomalies in 1860

3. Scene with temperature anomalies in 2023

4. The gap between today and 1860 (i.e., the first plot point)

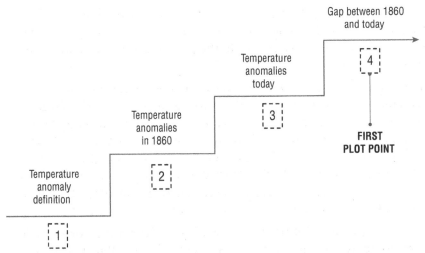

Figure 3.6: The first act of the story on global temperature anomalies from 1860 to today. We use four scenes, which slowly introduce the problem until we reach the first plot point, with scene 4

Second Act

Describe the problem with human intervention. To make your story more robust, you can include other data. In the context of the example, it's reasonable to think that you have additional data related to the environment, such as precipitation trends, CO_2 emissions, and so on. You might have downloaded them from open data provided by public institutions or collected them through sensors in your work in a meteorology department. Use a cause-and-effect sequence with these three scenes (see Figure 3.7):

1. The trend of temperature anomalies over time

2. The trend of CO_2 emissions over time (i.e., the second plot point)

3. Precipitation trend

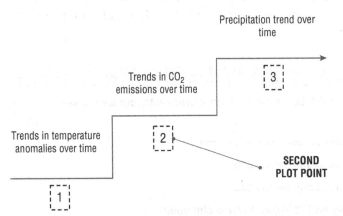

Figure 3.7: The story's diagram shows the second act of the story about global temperature anomalies from 1860 to today. We use three scenes, culminating in the center of the act with the second plot point

Third Act

Describe what happens if nothing is done. Use a sequence with these two scenes (see Figure 3.8):

1. Prediction of the temperature anomaly in the future (i.e., the third plot point)

2. Possible human interventions to mitigate the problem

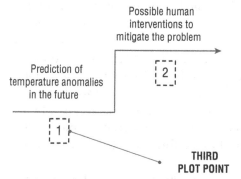

Figure 3.8: The third act of the story on global temperature anomalies from 1860 to today. Here, we use two scenes, which begin with the maximum problem's manifestation of the problem (i.e., third plot point) and then end with the possible solutions

The example just described illustrates a possible definition of scenes and sequences. Throughout the book, I'll discuss how to introduce other details to story planning.

Challenge: In the first act, you used a temporal sequence. Change the structure of the act to add a spatial sequence, such as comparing the temperature in two different places on Earth.

Once you are clear on what to describe in each act, you can add or remove sequences or scenes based on the level of detail you want to achieve, or the time available you have to tell the story. An important thing, however, is to maintain the proportion between the various acts, in the sense that, on average, you should dedicate a quarter of the time for the first act, a half for the second act, and a quarter for the third act. Otherwise, the audience risks losing the thread of the conversation. For example, if you have 80 minutes to tell your story, you cannot dedicate more than 20 minutes to the first act, 40 minutes to the second one, and 20 minutes for the third one. These aspects are covered in more detail later throughout the book.

With the description of the scenes, the preproduction phase ends. Undoubtedly, many things remained vague during the reading, and you likely have many questions. Don't worry, however. Beginning with the next chapter, you'll discover in detail how to define the preproduction phase with the three-act structure of the plot. For now, please settle for a general introduction to the topic.

Now, you're ready to move on to the next phase, the production phase, which you surely already know even if you don't know that's what it's called.

Production: Data Story Shot

The *production phase* consists of implementing the scenes. Your goal is to show the subject and theme in action, in each scene. You can implement a scene through a visualization (e.g., a chart), a picture, an image, audio, video, text, or even a combination of them.

Once you've conceptually defined what to represent in each scene, you can use your graphic skills to implement its contents. Begin by selecting the tools you want to use, which might include Tableau, Power BI, and Python libraries like Matplotlib or Altair. Note that this book doesn't cover how to implement individual scenes in such tools, as it depends on your preferences and skills. What matters, however, is to remain faithful to the three-act structure defined in the preproduction phase.

In the previous chapter, I distinguished between the making and delivering phases of the story. In the making phase, you planned the story, and in the delivering phase, you focused on its presentation. You need these phases to allow you to tell the same story to different audiences, even using various channels such as video, presentations, emails, etc. If, however, you plan to tell your story only once, you can combine the making phase with the delivering phase and think about the audience from the beginning, implementing the scenes directly addressed to the specific audience to which you are referring.

If you still think you'll tell your story only once to a single type of audience, it's best to think about the implementation details of the scenes, refined for your audience, already in this production phase. More details are given about the audience in Chapter 7, "Second Act: Defining the Antagonist," and include the concepts described in that chapter already in the production phase.

In this book, I adopt the distinction between "make" and "deliver." So in the production phase, you should implement only a basic version of the scenes, which you can then adapt to different audiences during the delivery phase.

To get an idea of how to implement the scenes, let's return to the example of global temperature anomalies from 1860 to today and try to implement the scenes in the first act. The first scene asks you to define the concept of a temperature anomaly. Very simply, think of descriptive text of this type:

What is a temperature anomaly?

According to the National Oceanic and Atmospheric Administration (NOAA) website, the term *temperature anomaly* means a departure from a reference value or long-term average. A *positive anomaly* indicates that the observed temperature was warmer than the reference value, while a *negative anomaly* indicates that the observed temperature was cooler than the reference value (NOAA, 2024a).

The second scene of the first act asks to show the anomalies in the temperature in 1860 (see Figure 3.9). You can insert a world map into your scene that indicates the anomalies in the global temperature in 1860 (NOAA, 2024b).

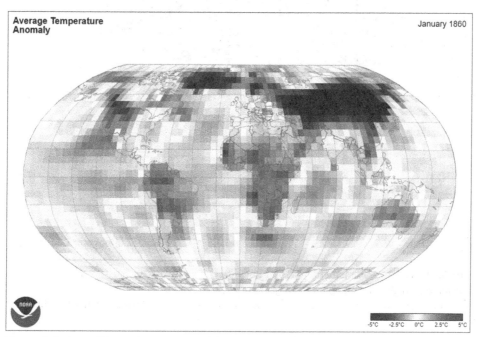

Figure 3.9: A possible implementation of the second scene of the first act shows the planisphere with global temperature anomalies in 1860
Source: NOAA / https://nauticalcharts.noaa.gov/data/data-licensing.html / Public Domain.

The third scene asks you to show anomalies in temperatures 2023. Again, select a world map that illustrates the situation in 2023 (see Figure 3.10).

Finally, the fourth scene asks to show the gap between now and 1860. For example, you can choose to use the following text that indicates the value corresponding to the gap:

1.36°C gap between January 1860 and January 2023

At this point, the first act has been implemented. In this example, I used maps that are freely accessible on the NOAA website (https://nauticalcharts.noaa.gov/data/data-licensing.html [NOAA, 2024b]). In most cases, however, you will implement graphs from scratch, using a tool of your choice. After implementing the first act, you can implement the other acts in a similar fashion.

Challenge: Implement the second and third act scenes using a tool of your choice. Remember to respect the structure that you defined in the preproduction phase. Do you find this way of proceeding easier than your usual method?

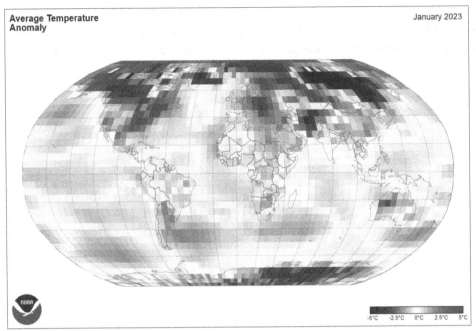

Figure 3.10: A possible implementation of the third scene of the first act illustrates the planisphere with global temperature anomalies in 2023
Source: NOAA / https://nauticalcharts.noaa.gov/data/data-licensing.html / Public Domain.

Following the story structure defined in the preproduction phase helps keep the individual scenes focused on a single topic and not overloaded with content. The idea is to show one concept for each scene to minimize the decision phase during the scenes' implementation.

After you have completed the production phase, you can move on to the last phase of story-making, the postproduction phase.

Postproduction: Data Story Editing

Your story is ready with all scenes implemented. Now, you can proceed with editing. The Cambridge Dictionary defines the editing phase as follows:

> ...the process of making changes to a text or film, deciding what will be removed and what will be kept in, in order to prepare it for being printed or shown.[1]

---

[1]https://dictionary.cambridge.org/dictionary/english/editing

In terms of data storytelling, during this phase, you proceed following three fundamental steps:

- **Review the choice of scenes to include in the story.** First, you should reexamine all the constructed scenes, from the first scene of the first act to the last scene of the third act. You might realize that some scenes aren't useful for your story, so you might decide to cut them. Mark Twain, the author of *The Adventures of Tom Sawyer*, said, "If I had had more time, I would have written a shorter letter" to underline the fact that it's much more difficult to be concise than to be long (Hall, 2019).

  In other cases, you might move a scene forward or backward within the story. One important thing is to note that *all* the scenes are useful to the story's progression. Cut any scenes that do not enrich the story with new elements, or bring it forward toward the conclusion. In his aforementioned book *Building a StoryBrand*, Donald Miller states that storytellers have filters to cut out the noise. If a character or scene doesn't serve the plot, it must go (Miller, 2017).

- **Further refine the scenes.** Refine scene layout, such as colors, fonts, and all aspects of scene layout. This phase also includes adding special effects, such as sound effects and animations (if they haven't already been implemented in the production phase). You can even think about adding images that reinforce the concept described within the scene. In any case, you mustn't exaggerate when filling the scene with new elements. Otherwise, the risk is of having the opposite effect: a scene that is too rich in details is poor in information content.

  Note, I don't dwell on scene refinement in this book, as I refer you to more specific manuals on the topic such as Kate Strachnyi's book, *Color-Wise* (Strachnyi, 2022).

- **Choose the connection between the various scenes.** Select the ins and outs from one scene to the next. By placing the scenes one after the other, you might realize that pieces are missing. This is why it becomes important to work on the transition from one scene to another. At this stage, you could add texts, images, or even less important graphics, which help the audience understand the transition from one scene to another.

Once the postproduction phase is complete, the making phase ends, and you're ready to move on to the delivery phase. As mentioned previously, in this book, the making and delivering phases are discussed separately to allow you to tell the same story to multiple audiences. If this point doesn't add up to you and you would like to think about the audience directly from the beginning, I hope to convince you over the next few chapters.

At this point in the reading, you may wonder how to organize your work if you work in a team and are not alone. How can the work be divided? Does everyone do everything? Or is there a more effective way? Let's see in the next section. Even if you work alone, I suggest you read the next section because it gives you an idea of the different profiles involved in the various phases.

Working in a Team

So far, you have learned how creating a story involves three distinct phases: preproduction, production, and postproduction. You can associate a different person or role with each phase. To understand which roles I am referring to, let's borrow the terminology from the world of cinema. In making a film, you'll find three central people: the screenwriter, the director, and the editor. The screenwriter deals with the preproduction phase, the director with the production phase, and the editor with the postproduction phase (see Figure 3.11).

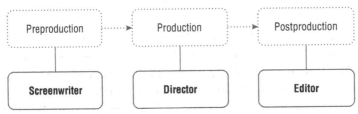

Figure 3.11: The three people involved in the creation of a film

Each person specializes in their specific sector but collaborates with the other people.

Like what happens in the cinema sector, even in a team of data storytellers, you can find three different people.

- **The screenwriter writes the story.** They could be the data analyst who analyzes the data, extracts insight, and builds the story. The screenwriter should have writing skills and be creative.

- **The director implements the individual scenes of the story with graphics and text.** The director corresponds to the technician or developer who has specific knowledge relating to a programming language or data visualization software, such as Tableau or Power BI.

- **The editor puts together the individual scenes (e.g., constructing a final report, a video, a presentation, etc.).** The editor should have knowledge of color theory and layout and know specific tools for assembling documents of various types, such as PowerPoint or tools for making videos.

You will also find the three people described in various contexts, such as data journalism, where there are the journalist (which corresponds to the screenwriter), the developer (which corresponds to the director), and the web designer (which corresponds to the editor). This shows the adaptability and versatility of these roles, instilling confidence in their applicability in different settings.

The three people described are typical of the story's making phase. If you also consider the delivery phase, you can add a fourth person, who must have communication skills to refine the story for the various types of audiences.

Summing up what has been covered in this chapter, the making phase allows you to design your story in the most generic way possible. Starting with the next chapter, I will go into more detail in the preproduction phase, defining the three acts of a story.

I would like to conclude this chapter with a thought taken from *Maria Carla Virzì's book, Gli strumenti dello storytelling*. Storytelling involves a transformation in the sense that the protagonist should change throughout the story. They can undergo an internal or external transformation, but in both cases, they are on a journey (Virzì, 2018):

I hope this short excerpt has intrigued you enough to turn the page and read the next chapter, which discusses heroes and how to extract them from the data.

Takeaways

- The making phase of a story consists of planning the story. It is composed of three steps: preproduction, production, and postproduction.

- Preproduction consists of organizing the results of the data analysis, or exploration process, into a story. It is the phase that transforms the data analyst into a data storyteller and is, therefore, the most difficult phase of the entire journey. Preproduction has three fundamental parts: the choice of subject, theme, and scenes.

- Production consists of implementing scenes using your favorite tool, such as Tableau, Power BI, Python visualization libraries, and so on.

- Postproduction consists of refining the story, refining the layout of individual scenes, and specifying the ins and outs with the transition from one scene to another.

References

Badino, Sergio. (2021). *Screenwriter profession. Structures and tools for writing stories*. Tuna.

Grahl, Tim. (2024). "Story theme: Definition and examples for a controlling idea." Retrieved on May 6, 2024. https://storygrid.com/story-theme

Gutkind, L. (2007). *The Art of Creative Nonfiction: Writing and Selling the Literature of Reality*. New York: John Wiley & Sons.

Hall, K. (2019). *Stories That Stick: How Storytelling Can Captivate Customers, Influence Audiences, and Transform Your Business*. HarperCollins Leadership.

Ireton, Cherilyn, and Julie Posetti. (2018). *Journalism, Fake News and Disinformation: Handbook for Journalism Education and Training*. France: UNESCO Publishing.

Kang, Martha. (2015). "Exploring the 7 different types of data stories." Retrieved on May 18, 2024. `http://mediashift.org/2015/06/exploring-the-7-different-types-of-data-stories`

Khalil, Mona. (2024). *Effective Data Analysis: Hard and Soft Skills*. Shelter Island: Manning Publications.

McKee, Robert. (2010). "Q&A: How to define your story in one sentence." Retrieved on May 6, 2024. `https://www.youtube.com/watch?v=E4RfpMHQHQE&t=59s`

McKinney, Wes. (2022). *Python for Data Analysis*. Sebastopol: O'Reilly Media.

Miller, Donald. (2010). *Building a StoryBrand: Clarify Your Message so Customers Will Listen*. [Kindle Edition. (p. 31)]. United States of America: HarperCollins Leadership.

National Oceanic and Atmospheric Administration National Centers for Environmental Information. (2023). "Global surface temperature anomalies". Retrieved on May 14, 2024. `https://www.ncei.noaa.gov/access/monitoring/global-temperature-anomalies/anomalies`

National Oceanic and Atmospheric Administration National Centers for Environmental Information. (2024a). "Background information—FAQ." Retrieved on May 20, 2024. `https://www.ncei.noaa.gov/access/monitoring/global-temperature-anomalies`

National Oceanic and Atmospheric Administration National Centers for Environmental Information. (2024b). "Climate at a glance: Global mapping". Retrieved on May 20. `https://www.ncei.noaa.gov/access/monitoring/climate-at-a-glance/global/mapping`

Oxford Dictionary. (2024) "Value". Retrieved on June, 29. `https://www.oxfordlearnersdictionaries.com/definition/english/value_1`

Strachnyi, Kate. (2022). *ColorWise*. O'Reilly Media.

Virzì, Maria Carla. (2018). *Gli strumenti dello storytelling*. Roma: Dino Audino Editore.

First Act: Defining the Hero

In a classical narrative, there are two types of heroes: those who do not change throughout the story and those who, instead, experience a change. The first are superheroes, like Superman and Spider-Man, who are performing already at maximum level and don't need to change. The latter, instead, are the common heroes with whom we tend to identify because they are like us, with continuous problems and conflicts. Even in superhero stories, something must change, even if it's not the superhero themselves. Instead, the world around them changes.

In this book, I only talk about heroes who experience change, leaving to your creativity the opportunity to deal with superheroes. To extract heroes who change from the data, the first step is to define their main characteristics and traits. As, in fact, Lee Gutkind, the inventor of creative nonfiction, says in his book *The Art of Creative Nonfiction*, that the audience sees the story through the eyes of the characters involved in the plot (Gutkind, 2007). This means the audience's involvement in the story also depends on the choice of the hero of said story because it will be your hero who communicates the message you want to convey to the audience. Designing a good hero is fundamental for the story because the audience will connect with the hero on a personal, emotional, and logical level. If you create a poorly done hero, you probably will damage the entire story and, thus, the message you want to convey. (Note, I will analyze the relationship between the hero and the audience later in the book.)

To complement the figure of the hero, there is the *sidekick*, who serves to strengthen the main character. (I'll talk about the sidekick in the next chapter.) This chapter and the next one focus on the First Act of the story, with this chapter highlighting the hero and, the next one, the sidekick.

In this chapter, I will analyze the following aspects related to the hero:

- Who the hero is
- How to extract the hero from the data
- Description of the hero

Let's analyze each aspect separately, beginning with who the hero is.

Who the Hero Is

In previous chapters, you learned that the hero is the story's main character who wants an object of desire but cannot have it because a problem or a villain stands between them and the desired object. This is immediately clear if you talk about a novel or a film. If you talk about data storytelling, however, the issue could become more complicated because the hero isn't just anyone, but someone who emerges from the data. You might be tempted to think that the hero is the audience or the person telling the story. This doesn't work in data storytelling, however.

Brent Dykes, one of the leading experts in the field of data storytelling, states that "most people don't want to be the focus of attention" (Dykes, 2019). This means that it isn't advisable to use the audience as a hero, as this could even generate embarrassment. Neither the audience nor the data storyteller is the story's hero because the hero must emerge from the data. You will read about the role of the audience and the data storyteller later in the book. For now, it's enough to know that the hero of your story is not you, nor even those who listen to you. As happens in novels, the hero of said novel isn't the author, nor even the reader, but an external character with whom the reader can identify and who the author can use to convey a message. In her book, Kindra Hall, a best-selling author of many books about storytelling says every story needs some characters the audience can identify with (Hall, 2019). Some examples of heroes extracted from data are products, trains, wars (in terms of journalistic investigation), etc. From the same data, more heroes and, therefore, more stories can emerge. Choosing one hero over another depends on what you want to say in the story. There is no wrong and right hero. It all depends on what story you want to tell.

A NOTE ON THE TERM *HERO*

Often, the main character of a novel or film is called a *hero*. In other cases, they are simply called the *main character*. In this book, I chose to use the term *hero* to indicate the main character because I believe that, in one way or another, there is always a hero at the center of a story, even if they do not perform sensational gestures or epic feats. The hero is someone who acts, while the main character could also be passive.

The term is also used in web design, which refers to the largest image on a page as the *hero image*—the one to which a user is likely to pay the most attention. Similar to what happens in web design, where the hero image is what you want the user to pay attention to, the hero of a data story is what the audience should focus on. The hero could be anyone. Each of us is the hero of their own life (Miller, 2017). You perform actions as a hero—the hero of your story—which is your life.

So, I like to imagine the main character of a story based on data as a hero who acts as a protagonist in an active way and doesn't simply suffer the world around them.

The hero makes sense if there is an *object of desire* to which they aspire. In the case of the product hero, their object of desire might be an increase in sales. In the case of trains, it's their punctual arrival; in the case of war, it's a desirable end. Every hero wants something. The goal of your story will be to describe whether the hero will get the object of desire.

Let's clarify this using novels and films. In most cases, the hero is always someone connected to humans or, in any case, with humanized traits. One way or another, they're connected to humans. This must also occur in data storytelling. Directly or indirectly, the hero in a data-driven story must be connected to humans. Compared to a novel or a film, in data storytelling, the hero must be real and not a fictional character. This is the biggest difference between fiction and data storytelling. According to Lee Gutkind, we can say that we must report only conversations that happened, and we can't modify them by adding details that didn't happen (Gutkind, 2007). This means despite being storytelling, data storytelling is *not* fiction, so you cannot invent your characters and attribute characteristics to them that they simply do not have.

We can, therefore, make a first classification of the heroes extracted from the data: humanlike and nonhumanlike (see Figure 4.1).

Humanlike heroes are heroes directly connected to people, while *nonhumanlike heroes* are heroes indirectly connected to people. Examples of humanlike heroes are patients facing illnesses, workers overcoming professional difficulties, or communities working together to solve social problems. Examples of nonhumanlike heroes are the global climate system, a face cream sold by a certain company, or ecosystems that react to environmental changes.

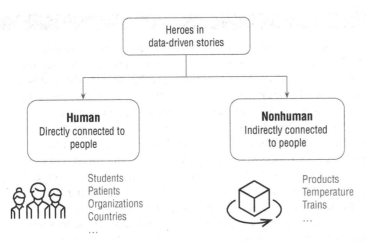

Figure 4.1: The two types of heroes in data stories: humanlike and nonhumanlike

An audience will hardly identify with the temperature, while they will most likely identify with people who suffer from problems linked to rising temperatures. However, extracting a humanlike hero from the data isn't always possible, so you will need to be satisfied with what you find. Indeed, the type of hero chosen must be as faithful as possible to the data to avoid moving too far from reality and ending up telling fictional stories or, worse, manipulated ones for objectives that aren't always immediately clear. In the next chapter, I will discuss how to associate human traits even with a nonhumanlike hero through the introduction of a sidekick.

At this point, I think it's clear who the hero is: someone who wants something but has a problem getting it. Now, let's see how to extract it from the data.

How to Extract the Hero from the Data

Extracting the hero from the data is the fundamental pivot around which your entire story will revolve. If you get the hero wrong, there will be an inconsistency between the graphics you show throughout the story and the story you tell. Therefore, it's essential to anchor the hero to the data and try to define their characteristics starting from data. If you don't connect the hero to the data, you will tell the wrong story and won't connect with the audience, who will be less likely to take action as I will discuss later in the book.

To understand how to extract a hero from data, you will use the *data–hero humanity matrix* and the *data–hero concreteness matrix*. Let's start by discussing the first matrix, the data–hero humanity matrix.

The Data–Hero Humanity Matrix

Earlier, you saw two heroes: humanlike, who was directly related to people, and nonhumanlike with nonhuman traits. The issue of humanlike and nonhumanlike returns theoretically, and perhaps off the cuff you can also identify whether your hero will be humanlike or not. However, the question arises spontaneously. Is there some less off-the-cuff criterion for understanding whether extracting a humanlike or nonhumanlike hero from the data is better? The answer is yes, and it is the *data–hero humanity matrix*. You've probably never heard of this humanity matrix because it is a totally new concept that I developed after deep reflection, and with the help of my boss, whom I sincerely thank. I've read many scientific articles about data storytelling, and the only one that inspired me to deeply reflect about how to extract the hero from the data was the one by Dasu et al. (Dasu, 2023). The authors of this paper analyzed different data-driven stories and extracted the story characters and the plot from them. Although the authors don't describe how to extract characters from data, their work inspired the new methodology I developed. The data–hero humanity matrix is a very simple concept, allowing you to understand from the data whether to use a humanlike hero or not. It is a matrix that combines types of data (qualitative or quantitative) and types of heroes (humanlike or nonhumanlike). I'm not here to dwell on the differences between qualitative and quantitative data. However, just to get an idea, quantitative data is measurable data, while qualitative data is not measurable. Examples of quantitative data are the trends of daily temperature over time, while examples of qualitative data are the responses to a survey on the satisfaction of a product.

Starting from the data type, you can extract the hero type simply using the matrix. Let's see how it works. Table 4.1 shows the data–hero humanity matrix.

Table 4.1: The Data–Hero Humanity Matrix

DATA/HERO	HUMAN	NONHUMAN
Qualitative	Experiences, opinions, perceptions, or behaviors of people	Description of objects, environments, events, processes, or systems
Quantitative	Performance measures, test results, or demographic statistics	Measurements of phenomena

You find the data in the matrix rows and the heroes in the columns. To use the matrix, start from the left column and look at the type of data you have. Is it qualitative or quantitative data? For now, ignore the case with both data types. I will discuss them later. Suppose you have qualitative data. At this point, check whether your data results from people's experiences, opinions, perceptions, behaviors, or concerns describing objects, environments, events, processes, or systems. Based on the answer you give, you will find the most suitable type of hero for your story. Put like this, it almost seems like reinventing the wheel, but I assure you that writing this thing down in black and white will help you make as few mistakes as possible when defining your character's typology.

Let's look at a practical example: suppose you have the usual dataset on anomalies in temperature trends over the last 50 years. This quantitative data measures a phenomenon for which it is better to use a nonhuman hero. (You will see later in the chapter how to choose a specific hero.) Another example is a dataset relating to the results of a questionnaire on a product's satisfaction rating. This is qualitative data, which describes people's opinions, for which the most appropriate hero is a human.

Consider now another example. Let's imagine you are a geologist who works at the United States Geological Survey (USGS), and you have data on earthquakes with magnitude greater than 4.5 from January 2024 to June 2024 (USGS, 2024). Map services and data are available from U.S. Geological Survey, National Geospatial Program. You have noticed that the earthquakes are concentrated more in the oceanic belt between Asia and Oceania and along the western coasts of South America, as shown in Figure 4.2.

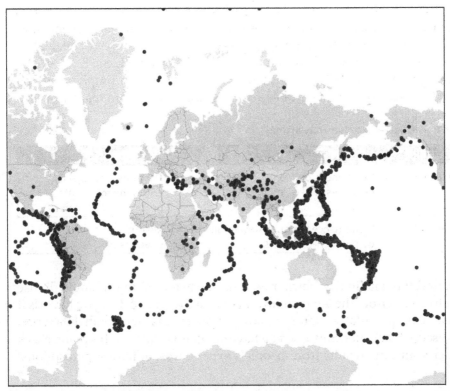

Figure 4.2: The geographical distribution of earthquakes with magnitude greater than 4.5 from January to June 2024

The map gives a very general overview of the places where earthquakes occurred. Each point represents an earthquake. The denser an area is, the greater the number of earthquakes that have occurred in that area. You're excited about your discovery and want to communicate your findings through a story. You need to choose your hero. Use the data–hero humanity matrix to identify it. Your data includes exactly the list of earthquakes in the considered period with a magnitude greater than 4.5. Your data is quantitative and measures a phenomenon, the earthquakes, so the matrix suggests you use a nonhuman hero. But what kind of hero would you choose if you also had the Did You Feel It (DYFI) results about the feeling people in those areas have from earthquakes? The DYFI data is also provided by USGS on a crowdsourcing basis and includes the number of people who felt an earthquake and signaled it to USGS using the online platform they provide. In this case, you still have quantitative data, as represented in Figure 4.3.

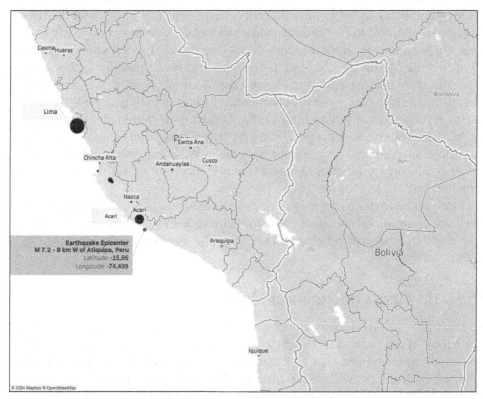

Figure 4.3: Number of DYFI answers in the different cities normalized to the total city population after the earthquake at Atiquipa, Peru, on June 6, 2024, at 5:36:37 a.m., at 28 km depth

Figure 4.3 shows the number of DYFI answers in the different cities in Peru normalized to the total city population in 2024 after the earthquake at Atiquipa,

Peru, on June 06. In this case, data are still quantitative but relate to demographics. If you had only this data, the data–hero humanity matrix would suggest using a human hero. However, if you consider both the data in Figures 4.2 and 4.3, the hero's choice is not obvious. It depends on the story you want to tell. If your focus is to discuss earthquakes as a phenomenon, use a nonhuman hero. Instead, if your focus is to discuss the effects of earthquakes on humans, use a human hero. Anyway, there is no correct hero and no wrong hero. The choice of the hero depends on the story you want to tell. Keep in mind that your story must have just one hero. One you have chosen yours, use the other data to support your hero.

Challenge: Think about the latest data you analyzed and try to identify the type of hero: humanlike or nonhumanlike.

If your data is extremely varied and you can extract both human and nonhuman characters, I suggest you build two different stories—one with humans as protagonists and the other without. Then compare them and see which works best.

One thing that can help you when choosing a hero is to check that the hero has a problem to solve. Just recently some students taking the exam in my Data Journalism course developed a story about diet issues. In their story they had identified the Mediterranean diet as the hero and being healthy as the object of desire. They also pretended to identify the Mediterranean diet as the Italian diet. According to them, the problem the hero had was that in reality eating habits in Italy were anything but healthy. Unfortunately, this identification of the hero is incorrect, as conceptually the Mediterranean diet is healthy and has no problems. A correct hero would have been Italy, and the problem would have been incorrect nutrition. From this experience, I suggest that you always remember to check if the hero has a problem.

Once you have defined the type of hero to use, you can then proceed with the more fine-grained choice of the hero themselves. You will use the *data–hero concreteness matrix*, which helps you to define the level of concreteness (or tangibility) of the hero.

The Data–Hero Concreteness Matrix

So far, you've seen that to determine whether to use a human hero you must look at the data. If in the data you find traces of test results, surveys, or statistical measurements that concern people, then use a human hero; otherwise, your hero will be nonhuman. Do you have results of a questionnaire (qualitative data) or the number of patients in a hospital (quantitative data)? Use a human hero. Do you have textual data on the description of earthquakes (qualitative data) or the number of earthquakes in the last 20 years (quantitative data)? Use a nonhuman hero. I think that up to this point the question is quite simple and clear. Use the data–hero humanity matrix to extract the type of your hero.

The problem now is understanding who the hero is. You know the type of hero, human or nonhuman, but you still need to figure out specifically who your hero is. I explain the concept first in an intuitive way, and then I formalize it. Suppose you have the results of a product evaluation questionnaire. This is qualitative data. Looking at the data–hero humanity matrix, you see that your hero is human. But who specifically is your hero? People in general? The people who bought your product? A group of people? To answer the question, look at the data and see how homogeneous it is. Who responded to the questionnaire? All the people in the world? In this case, you will have to use an abstract concept as a hero. Your hero will be the people in general. If, however, only a specific group of customers answered your questions such as those living in Italy, your hero will be more concrete—the Italians. Finally, if only people who visit a particular store where your product is sold answered your questionnaire, your heroes will be the store's customers. The concept is very simple. The more heterogeneous your data are, the more abstract your hero will be. I'll explain the concept of heterogeneous in a moment.

To make the explanation a little more formal, I use two matrices, the data–hero concreteness matrix and the mapping table between hero types and concreteness levels.

Let's start by deconstructing each type of hero, humanlike and nonhumanlike, to understand exactly what they are. Human-like heroes include (from the smallest to the biggest) individuals, organizations, and populations. *Individuals or groups* are single or collective entities with unique characteristics, needs, and behaviors. Examples include consumers, investors, patients, or community members. Think of them as the heroes of the everyday world, but instead of saving the universe, they're heroically navigating the complexities of grocery shopping, investment portfolios, and flu shots. *Organizations* are institutional entities that operate in different sectors, such as the public, private, or nonprofit sectors. Examples include companies, hospitals, government institutions, or nongovernmental organizations. *Populations* are larger groups of individuals who share characteristics or are in similar situations. Examples include specific market segments and demographic groups such as seniors or children or local communities.

Nonhumanlike heroes include (from the smallest to the biggest) elements, events, processes, and systems. *Elements* are goods, services, or measurements that satisfy needs or provide useful information to individuals. Examples include products, drugs, financial instruments, technologies, temperatures, or any other object, service, or data that addresses a specific need. Think of them as the gadgets that Batman relies on—whether it's the latest smartphone, a life-saving medication, or the reassuring 72-degree weather forecast—these elements swoop in to save the day, often with less fanfare and more precision. *Events* are specific moments that can influence data or situations in a certain context. Examples include product launches, advertising campaigns, natural events, or any other activity with a measurable impact. *Processes* are workflows or procedures that guide activities within an organization or system. Examples include decision-making and operational or administrative processes that directly influence the functioning of an organization. *Systems* are structures or environments in which human activities take place. Examples include natural ecosystems such as forests or oceans, urban infrastructure such as cities or transportation networks, or technological systems such as computer networks or industrial plants. Figure 4.4 summarizes the hero types just described.

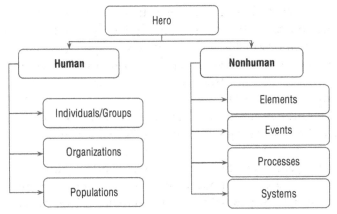

Figure 4.4: A more fine-grained classification of the various hero types

Whether human or nonhuman heroes, you can abstract the hero types into three levels of concreteness, ranging from the concrete to the abstract levels. Table 4.2 shows the mapping between the various hero types and concreteness levels.

Table 4.2: Mapping Between Hero Types and Concreteness Levels

	LEVEL 0 CONCRETE	LEVEL 1 MEDIUM	LEVEL 2 ABSTRACT
Human	Individuals	Organizations	Populations
Nonhuman	Elements	Events	Processes/Systems

Based on what you find in the data, you will define the level of concreteness of your hero. The *concreteness* of a hero describes how concretely you can define the hero based on the available data. The higher the level of concreteness, the easier it is to understand and visualize. A concept is more concrete the more specific, measurable, and tangible it is. When something is concrete, it's like a calming walk in the park on a sunny day. You can see, touch, and describe it easily. For example, imagine a friendly dog wagging its tail—you can picture its fur, hear its bark, and feel its playful energy. That's a concrete concept. On the other hand, abstract concepts are like gentle breezes—you know they're there, but they're harder to grasp. Think of happiness; it's a wonderful feeling, but it's not something you can touch or see. It's more like the warm, comforting glow you get from a beautiful sunset. So, as you work with your data, remember that the more specific and tangible your hero is, the easier it will be to understand and visualize.

You can extract the level of concreteness of a hero from the level of homogeneity of the data describing it. There are three levels of data homogeneity:

- **Homogeneous data:** This data is uniform and consistent in nature, coming from similar sources and measured using standardized methods. Examples include medical records and patients' demographics in the healthcare sector.

- **Semi-homogeneous data:** This data is similar but may come from various sources or have slightly different formats, requiring some degree of normalization or integration. Examples include clinical records, laboratory data, and textual descriptions of symptoms.

- **Heterogeneous data:** These data are very different from each other, coming from various sources, and are measured with different units or methodologies, often requiring significant transformations and integrations to be used together. Examples include medical records (e.g., diagnosis, treatments, medical history) and images of X-rays.

The more homogeneous the data, the higher the level of concreteness, allowing a clear and precise definition of the hero. On the contrary, less homogeneous data leads to a more uncertain and less concrete definition. Suppose you need to make a fruit smoothie. If you have only bananas available, the final taste will be bananalike, and it will be very easy for you to recognize the flavor. However, if you have bananas, apples, pears, strawberries, and cherries available, it will be more complicated to understand the final flavor of your smoothie. The same goes with data. If you have homogeneous data, it is quite easy to find the hero. But if you have heterogeneous data, the matter becomes complicated. Just like when you must recognize the taste of the macro smoothie from before!

To help you to establish the level of concreteness of the hero, use the data–hero concreteness matrix, which defines the mapping between the data's homogeneity level and the hero's concreteness level. The matrix might seem like an artificial mechanism for extracting the hero. I hope to convince you of exactly the opposite. Let's proceed in order. Table 4.3 shows the data–hero concreteness matrix.

Table 4.3: The Data–Hero Concreteness Matrix

DATA/HERO	LEVEL 0 CONCRETE	LEVEL 1 MEDIUM	LEVEL 2 ABSTRACT
Heterogeneous	X	X	V
Semi-homogeneous	X	V	X
Homogeneous	V	X	X

As with the humanity matrix, in the concreteness matrix, the data is in the rows, and the heroes are in the columns. To use the matrix, start from the data and try to understand if you are dealing with homogeneous, semi-homogeneous, or heterogeneous data. Then, choose your hero by looking in the matrix where you find the V symbol corresponding to your data type. For example, if you have several temperature datasets available and therefore have homogeneous data, your hero will be among the concrete ones. By looking at Table 4.2, you can choose your concrete hero type, for example, an element. Probably, in the example, your hero will be the temperature. In this case, the choice of the hero was very simple, so the data–hero concreteness matrix might seem useless to you.

Instead, consider heterogeneous data, which is concerned with different typologies. In this case, your hero must be abstract (see the V symbol in the data–hero concreteness matrix of Table 4.3). For example, suppose you have various data available on temperature, greenhouse gas emissions, rise in water levels, etc. In this case, you cannot group all heroes under one hat, so you can conclude that your data is heterogeneous. Looking at the matrix of concreteness, you will, therefore, have to choose an abstract hero among nonhumans. Using Table 4.2, you can choose a process or system. For example, your hero could be Earth or climate change. Finally, if your data is semi-homogeneous (i.e., somewhere between homogeneous and heterogeneous), you could choose a Level 1 hero (i.e., a hero that's neither too abstract nor too concrete). For example, if you have data on temperature and precipitation, this data isn't about the same topic but similar topics (both regard weather events). So, use a nonhuman Level 1 hero such as a weather event.

Let's investigate another example to better understand how to use the data–hero concreteness matrix. Consider again the example of earthquakes. Let's suppose that you have the data described in Table 4.4.

Table 4.4: Datasets for the Earthquakes Example

DATA TYPE	WHAT IT INCLUDES
Seismic	Magnitude, epicenter, depth, time and date, duration of the shocks
Real-time	Data streams from seismometers, seismic alarms
Geographical	Map of tectonic plates, topographic data
Historical	Register of past earthquakes, seismic catalogues
Impact	Structural damage, number of victims and injured, emergency responses
Meteorological	Weather conditions
Population	Population density, critical infrastructures
Economic	Damage costs, insurance

Given all this variety of data, imagine you want to define a hero. Given the majority of quantitative data measuring the earthquake phenomena, you decide to use a nonhuman hero. The next step is to decide who your hero is. First, you must establish if your data is homogeneous, semi-homogeneous, or heterogeneous. Group similar data and then generalize, as shown in Figure 4.5.

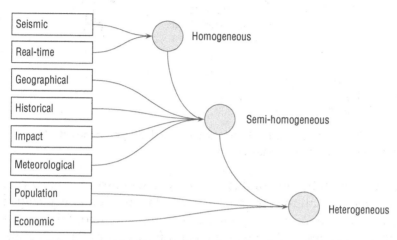

Figure 4.5: An example of how to group data related to earthquakes into homogeneous, semi-homogeneous, and heterogeneous

Seismic data and real-time data are both homogeneous data because they derive from the same source. Thus, if you had only these types of data, you could use a concrete hero (as derived from the V in the data–hero concreteness matrix in Table 4.3). In this case, you could use an element as a possible hero, such as an instrument that has detected something strange. Geographical, historical, impact, and meteorological data are semi-homogeneous data because they derive from similar sources. If you had only these types of data combined with the previous ones, you would use a medium-level hero, more specifically, an event, as explained in Table 4.2. For example, you could use a specific earthquake that happened somewhere in the world as your hero. Finally, if you had all the available data, including population and economic data, you would use an abstract hero, such as a seismic monitoring system, or Earth in general.

From the description just given, it is clear you should consider many factors. Figure 4.6 summarizes the workflow to extract the hero from the data, combining both the data–hero humanity and data–hero concreteness matrices.

Start with data and apply the data–hero humanity matrix to extract the hero type (human or nonhuman) and the data–hero concreteness matrix to extract the concreteness level (concrete, medium, or abstract). Then use the mapping between the hero types and the concreteness level to extract your hero.

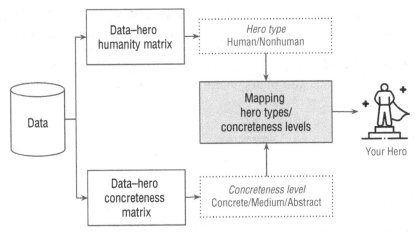

Figure 4.6: The workflow to extract the hero from the data, combining both the data–hero humanity and data–hero concreteness matrices

By the time you reach the end of this section, you will probably have your head confused between all the concepts of the data–hero humanity matrix, data–hero concreteness matrix, and human and nonhuman hero. Take a break to reflect on them. I suggest you prepare a good coffee, tea, or other drink that takes your mind off things and allows your brain to process these concepts.

Describing the Hero

I hope you followed my suggestion on reflection and are now ready to resume. The data–hero humanity matrix allows you to define, starting from the data, whether to use a human or nonhuman hero. A human and a nonhuman hero can be concrete, medium, or abstract. Use the data–hero concreteness matrix to figure out from the data whether to use an abstract, medium, or concrete hero. By combining the two matrices, define the traits of your hero: human/ nonhuman and abstract/medium/concrete.

You've finally extracted your hero from the data and defined their traits. Now, the next step is to *describe* your character. Grab a pen and paper and try to answer the following questions:

- Who is your hero, and what are their main characteristics?
- What is the object of your hero's desire?
- In what context does your hero live?
- When and what challenges or obstacles does your hero face?
- What are your hero's motivations and values?

Figure 4.7 summarizes the *identikit* of the hero you are creating.

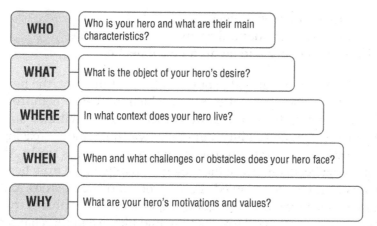

Figure 4.7: The hero's identikit is based on the answer to the five W questions

Note how the identikit is based on using the five W questions, typical of journalism. They indicate "the minimum information needed to certify the event" (the hero in our case; Papuzzi, 2003). Even if you're not a natural writer or journalist, force yourself to write at least half a page, specifying as many details as possible. The more precise you are in answering the questions, the more knowledge you will have about your hero. The point is understanding who your hero is and who you're dealing with. Only if you know them well will you be able to talk about them. "Of course, I know my hero!" you can tell me. "I've been working on the same hero for years!" All right, but have you tried to dissect their values—the motivations or beliefs that guide your hero? Have you tried to formalize what challenges and obstacles they encounter? Maybe, maybe not. Answering these questions in writing will only help you.

For example, consider the anomalies in the average annual temperature as the hero and answer these questions:

Who is your hero, and what are their main characteristics?
Name: Anomalies in average annual temperature
Features: Climate indicator, measured in degrees Celsius

In what context does your hero live?
It operates in all geographic regions and is influenced by natural phenomena and human activities such as CO_2 emissions.

What is the object of your hero's desire?
To stay within a sustainable range to ensure climate stability

When and what challenges or obstacles does your hero face?
Since the industrial revolution, there is an increasing level of emissions of greenhouse gases

What are your hero's motivations and values?
Motivations: Need to maintain natural balance and support life
Values: Stability, sustainability, and environmental health

The answers to the questions already contain a draft of the plot: the hero is someone who wants an object of desire, but a problem prevents them from obtaining it. In this example, the temperature wants to remain within a sustainable range to ensure climate stability, but global warming and increasing greenhouse gas emissions prevent them from doing so. The story is ready. All the discussions on the subject you saw in the previous chapter begin from here.

At the beginning of the chapter, I talked about heroes and superheroes, and I said that in this chapter I wouldn't talk about superheroes. And this is true from a data storytelling perspective. However, I would like to end this chapter on a personal note about superheroes. If you don't care about this, you can skip straight to the next section, or even the next chapter.

Since my childhood, my favorite hero has always been *Zorro*—the masked hero dressed in black—for his charm, ideals, and mystery. I was fascinated by his always being at the service of the poor, dedicating himself to their cause, with a heart full of compassion. Zorro wasn't just a masked hero; he was a symbol of hope and justice for those who had none. In Zorro, I saw not just a hero but a beacon of light in the darkness—a testament to the enduring power of human kindness and the relentless pursuit of justice. Just for fun, let's try to make an identikit of Zorro by answering the hero's five W questions, which we saw before.

Who is your hero, and what are their main characteristics?
My hero is Zorro, a man of courage and conviction, fighting for justice and the oppressed. His main characteristics include bravery, resourcefulness, and a deep sense of honor. His identity is a mystery to those he protects.

What is the object of your hero's desire?
The object of his desire is a just and equitable society where the poor and marginalized are protected from exploitation and oppression.

In what context does your hero live?
Zorro lives in a turbulent time and place, often set in colonial California during the early 19th century. This is a period marked by societal inequities, corrupt officials, and a struggling populace.

What are the challenges or obstacles your hero faces?
Zorro faces numerous challenges, including the constant threat of exposure and the danger posed by corrupt officials and their henchmen.

What are your hero's motivations and values?
Zorro's motivations stem from a deep-seated belief in justice and a desire to fight against oppression and inequality. He is driven by a sense of duty to protect the vulnerable and to challenge corruption wherever it arises. His values include honor, integrity, and compassion.

As you have probably noticed with the Zorro example, in the case of a fictional hero, it is much simpler to answer the five questions, but you will see, with a little practice, you will also be able to characterize your hero in the case of a data-driven story. Throughout this chapter, you learned how to extract a hero directly from the data. I hope to have convinced you that there is not a single hero hidden in the data. Instead, based on the message you want to convey and the insight you have extracted from the data, you can build different stories. The stronger the hero you build, the stronger the level of engagement of your audience with the story.

At the beginning of this chapter, I said there are two types of heroes—human and nonhuman—and that the audience prefers a human hero because they can identify with them more easily. I also said that a human hero does not always emerge from the data and that you must be satisfied with what is found in the data. What if you could find something human even for nonhuman heroes? Turn the page and read the next chapter, where I will discuss this topic, specifically, the hero's sidekick.

Takeaways

- The hero is the story's main character and must be anchored in the data. To extract them directly from the data, use the data–hero humanity matrix to understand if your hero is human or nonhuman and the data–hero concreteness matrix to understand the level of concreteness (or tangibility) of your hero.

- From the same data you can extract different types of heroes, based on the story you want to tell. However, any hero you choose must have a problem to solve and an object of desire to reach.

- Human heroes include individuals, organizations, and populations. Nonhuman heroes include elements, events, processes, and systems.

- Describe the hero by answering the five W questions: Who is your hero, and what are their main characteristics? What is the object of your hero's desire? In what context does your hero live? When and what challenges or obstacles does your hero face? What are your hero's motivations and values?

References

Dasu, K., Kuo, Y. H., & Ma, K. L. (2023). *Character-Oriented Design for Visual Data Storytelling. IEEE Transactions on Visualization and Computer Graphics.*30,(1):98–108.https://doi.org/10.1109/TVCG.2023.3326578

Dykes, B. (2019). *Effective Data Storytelling: How to Drive Change with Data, Narrative and Visuals.* New York: John Wiley & Sons.

Gutkind, L. 2007. *The Art of Creative Nonfiction: Writing and Selling the Literature of Reality*. New York: John Wiley & Sons.

Hall, K. (2019). Stories that Stick: How Storytelling Can Captivate Customers, Influence Audiences, and Transform Your Business. New York: HarperCollins Leadership.

Miller, D. (2017). *Building a StoryBrand: Clarify Your Message So Customers Will Listen*. New York" HarperCollins Leadership.

Papuzzi, A. (2003). *Journalist Profession*. Rome: Donzelli Editore.

United States Geological Survey (USGS) (2024) Search Earthquake Catalog. `https://earthquake.usgs.gov/earthquakes/search`

First Act: Defining the Sidekick

The hero is the main character of the story, but they aren't the only one. You can't think of building a compelling story with just one character. Every self-respecting hero has a *sidekick* to help them. Everything seems to be focused on the hero, but in reality, it's the sidekick who helps the hero carry the story forward and acts as an intermediary between the hero and the audience. The sidekick is so important in a story because they set the story's tone. Depending on how you build the sidekick, your story will have more or less a dramatic tone. Think, for example, of what Sherlock Holmes would be like without Dr. Watson or Mickey Mouse without Goofy. Surely you agree on the importance of the sidekick in a novel or a film, but in data storytelling, who is the sidekick? I believe the concept of a sidekick in data storytelling is quite new for the literature, and in this chapter, you will see how to shape a sidekick for your data-driven hero.

In the first part of this chapter, I'll analyze the following aspects related to the sidekick:

- Who the sidekick is

- How to add a sidekick to your data story

- How to extract a human sidekick from a nonhuman hero

In the second half of the chapter, I'll focus on presenting the hero and the sidekick in the first act of the story. Let's begin with the first part by analyzing who the sidekick is.

Who the Sidekick Is

In one of my youth novels (yes, I've always had a passion for narrative since I was a child), the hero was a certain André Violino, an 84-year-old man, and his sidekick was a dog named John (Lo Duca, 2009). A dog? Yes, you got it right. The sidekick can be anyone: a person, an object, a fictional character, or even an animal. So, unleash your brain and open up your imagination to figure out who could be the sidekick in your next story. But proceed slowly. To understand who the sidekick is, you must analyze their role in the cinematographic and novel fields.

The *sidekick* is a secondary character who accompanies the hero on their journey. Despite their secondary role, the sidekick is functional to the story for several reasons. According to Ron Buchanan, dean of Communications Technologies & Social Sciences at the Northern Virginia Community College, the sidekick should act as a confidant for the hero. (Buchanan, 2003). If, in the story, the hero is alone, they have no one to talk to and their thoughts remain in their head, and the only way to communicate with the audience is through their actions. However, if the hero has a confidant (i.e., the sidekick), they can also express their thoughts and let the audience understand what they think. The sidekick is *always* loyal toward the hero. They never betray the hero. In some extreme cases, the sidekick will even sacrifice themselves for the hero's cause to the point of giving their own life.

A second role the sidekick can play is to represent the audience. More specifically, the audience's thoughts. Indeed, the sidekick may have a slightly lower level of intelligence than the audience, to answer complex questions that the audience doesn't understand and to explain intricate situations. This allows the sidekick to be the link between the audience and the hero, because they reveal information that allows the audience to better understand the story. For example, in Sir Arthur Conan Doyle's famous novels, Dr. Watson brings the audience into the world of Sherlock Holmes and questions all his deductions on the audience's behalf.

Buchanan affirms this, stating that the sidekick should contribute to the hero's mission because they help the story's central cause to advance (Buchanan, 2003). Thus, the sidekick's contributions help to advance the plot and overcome obstacles. This active participation ensures that the sidekick isn't merely a passive follower but an integral part of the hero's journey. They often act as an advisor to the hero to help them make choices and overcome obstacles.

Another type of sidekick is the *enhancer*, the one who helps the hero be accepted by the audience. In fact, it may happen that the hero is too focused on their mission and, therefore, is a little distant from the audience. In this case, the sidekick mitigates this by providing a contrasting perspective, offering warmth, humor, or humility that balances the hero's more intense traits.

To summarize, the sidekick can play one of the following four main roles, as shown in Figure 5.1: confidant, audience proxy, active contributor, or enhancer.

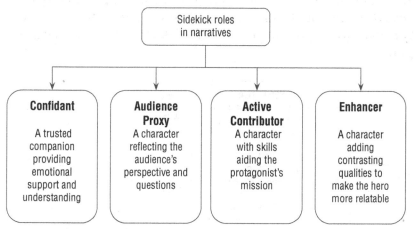

Figure 5.1: The four roles of a sidekick in narratives

Therefore, although the presence of the sidekick is not mandatory, every self-respecting story, in addition to the hero, should have a sidekick who helps them. If this is true for narrative and filmography in general, how can you apply these principles to data storytelling? I will discuss how to do so in the next section.

Adding a Sidekick to Your Data Story

Let one thing be clear: the protagonist of the story always remains the hero, never the sidekick, who is and must always remain a point of support for the hero. In short, the whole story must revolve around the hero, and the sidekick must help the hero in their mission. In the case of data storytelling, you might think of several possible sidekicks, but I personally believe that the best sidekick for any data story is only one. And it's always the same: a specific, tangible, and possibly human case. Let me explain better by using an example. Consider patients who suffer from diabetes as heroes. In this case, the sidekick is a particular patient who shares their testimony and brings the audience closer to the generic patient hero. Now, imagine that the hero of your story is the temperature, which has the problem of having increased in recent years. A possible sidekick for your story could be a person who witnesses the suffering due to this increase. Or imagine your hero is a product, experiencing a decline in sales. In this case, the sidekick could be a particular customer who complains about the product because it has some defects compared to the competition. The use of a specific, tangible case allows the audience to get closer to the hero without diminishing their importance.

In the first chapter, I said that a story can have three main objectives: to persuade, inform, and entertain. *Persuading* means convincing the audience of a certain point of view. *Informing* means to teach something or to provide information. *Entertaining* means holding the audience's attention through enjoyment. Based on your story's goal, three types of sidekicks are defined here, as shown in Figure 5.2.

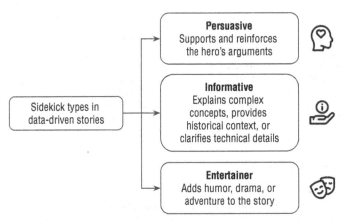

Figure 5.2: Sidekick types in data-driven stories

The *persuasive sidekick* is present in stories that aim to persuade the audience about something. This type of sidekick supports and reinforces the hero's arguments, offering additional evidence, testimonies, or viewpoints that reinforce the main message. They can represent the skeptical audience, asking questions or raising objections. In this way, the sidekick helps convince the audience of the hero's point of view.

In stories that seek information as their main goal, the *informative sidekick* plays a crucial role in stating the facts. This type of sidekick often acts as a sort of internal narrator, explaining complex concepts, providing historical context, or clarifying technical details. They facilitate the audience's understanding of the content by adding explanations that make the narrative more accessible and informative.

The *entertainer sidekick* is ideal for stories that aim to entertain the audience. This type of sidekick adds humor, drama, or adventure to the story, enriching the audience's experience. They can be a comic character who lightens the atmosphere. The sidekick entertainer makes the narrative livelier and engaging, maintaining the interest and attention of the audience through moments of fun and emotion.

Consider again the example of the temperature hero and the sidekick person who suffers from the temperature increase. Table 5.1 shows three examples of sidekicks, based on the story's objective.

Table 5.1:   Examples of Sidekicks

STORY OBJECTIVE	SIDEKICK EXAMPLE
Persuade	The sidekick is John Smith who describes how the summers have become unbearable, with temperatures regularly exceeding 40 degrees. He talks about how he had to install air conditioners throughout his house and how his energy bills skyrocketed. John also talks about his heat-related health problems, such as dehydration and heat stroke, to underline the seriousness of the situation.
Inform	The sidekick, Sara Jones, explains what a heat wave means and how you can protect yourself, suggesting staying hydrated and avoiding intense physical activity during the hottest hours of the day. Additionally, Sara could share personal experiences of how she took these preventative measures and the benefits she achieved, making the information more tangible and practical for the audience.
Entertain	The sidekick, Luke Reis, is a comical character who overreacts to rising temperatures. When the temperature rises, Luke constantly complains, trying in every way to cool down: by immersing himself in an ice pool or creating inventive but useless cooling devices. His antics create amusing situations and lighten the narrative, keeping the audience entertained and interested.

In all three examples, the sidekick has human traits but presents different facets based on the story's objective. The hero, however, is always the same: the temperature. Keep in mind that the sidekick should be a real person and *not* a fictional character. The ideal would be to have a real person who intervened to explain your situation. If it isn't possible to have a real sidekick in your story, it would still be advisable to interview them before inserting them into the story. Preferably, the sidekick should not be a generic profile built based on data, but a real person who experiences the same problem as the hero. However, if you can't find a real person to incorporate into your story, you can still use a generic profile extracted from data. Consider that a generic profile is less impactful than a concrete person. Figure 5.3 summarizes the process of extracting a sidekick from the data.

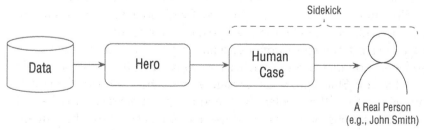

Figure 5.3: The process of extracting a sidekick from data-driven stories

Start from data and extract the hero, following the suggestions I provided in Chapter 4, "First Act: Defining the Hero." Then focus on a human case and, if possible, on a real person who can act as a witness, experiencing the same problem that the hero has.

In the case of a human hero, you can find a sidekick easily. You only must give concrete, specific, and tangible traits to the general hero and then find a real person representing the tangible traits that you have extracted. If your hero is a population, as a sidekick, draw a person representative of that population. Then, find a concrete person in that population, and let them tell their experience. Interviewing that person about the hero's problem will enrich the story with useful details that help the audience experience the same feelings of the hero. If you can't find a real person, you can still build a generic profile and use it as your sidekick. For any other human sidekick, follow the same approach.

How can you extract the sidekick in the case of a nonhuman hero? In the case of temperature, you probably used intuition and extracted a person experiencing the hot temperatures. However, what could you do in the case of a product, a train, an earthquake, or something that isn't human? Is there a more formal way to extract the sidekick in the case of a nonhuman hero? You'll discover how to proceed in the next section.

Discovering the Humanity of Your Hero

If your hero already has human traits, then you have no problem. It will be quite simple for you to use your hero with human traits to engage the audience. (Note, I detail this more later in the book.) If, instead, your hero isn't human, then you can associate them with something human, which isn't the hero themselves but something that strengthens them, the *sidekick*. To search for the sidekick associated with your nonhuman hero, identify the point of intersection between the data and the people; then extract a profile of a typical person associated with your data.

For example, if you have survey results, you can define the sidekick profile by analyzing the survey results and seeing if a typical profile emerges from them. If the answer is positive, you will have found your sidekick. Instead, if the answer is negative or you don't have questionnaire data, continue looking at the data. Who produced them? For example, if you have data on the sales of a product, your sidekick could be the average customer profile.

If nothing interesting emerges from your data, lift your head from the page of this book and look around. Do you work in a company? If so, try to see the people who work next to you. Start with your colleagues, even those who work in other departments, and analyze the problem from another point of view. Also, look at potential customers, friends, or relatives who use that product or one of the competitors. Do you work in the weather forecasting department instead? Try listening to experts in the sector. Open your mind and look around. Try to dissect your sidekick not only using data but also the people behind this data. You will surely discover traits of your hero that you didn't know about. In summary, analyze everything that revolves around your data, trying to understand who influences the hero, who is influenced by them, and who lives in the world around the hero. This will help you to build the ecosystem of potential sidekicks, as shown in Figure 5.4.

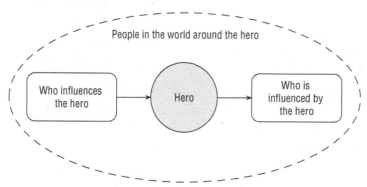

Figure 5.4: The ecosystem of potential sidekicks

For example, if your hero is the temperature and the problem it has is its global rise, then the typical person influenced by your hero could be the average citizen who suffers from the heat during the scorching summers, as I have already illustrated before in this chapter. But if your hero is a product and its problem is declining sales, the sidekick of your hero could be the people in the marketing department or those who influence the hero—the customers who buy the product.

Once you have defined the sidekick (from human or nonhuman heroes), you can give it a face, for example, through photographs, and a voice (Dykes, 2019), for example, by conducting interviews. Interviews? Yes, interviews. Real interviews, just like journalists do. Your goal is to understand the needs of the sidekick. You can use two types of interviews: interview *themes*, in which you interview someone about a given topic, and *personal* interview, where you interview someone as an important person or expert in their own right. In both cases, record the interview so you can listen to it again later and then insert it into the definition of the scenes of your plot. As Lee Gutkind put it, you should begin your research from home, and then reach the world (Gutkind, 2007).

In summary, to identify the sidekick, who is the human trait of your hero, first consider that all the data is produced by people, and then identify all the actors involved in the system you want to represent.

To give you a practical idea of what I'm talking about and to stimulate your creativity and reflection, Table 5.2 rounds up some heroes and possible sidekicks.

Pairing is not mandatory; you can always find new sidekicks for your heroes. What I propose are just some possible ideas.

Table 5.2: Different Examples of Association Between Data, Hero, and Sidekick

DATA	A POSSIBLE HERO	A POSSIBLE SIDEKICK
Student performance	Students	John, a student participating in interactive learning modules
		Mara, a teacher
Vehicle fleet and transit system	Bus routes	Sara, a passenger on a bus
		Joe, a bus driver
Water usage and infrastructure	Water management system	Linda, an environmental engineer
User behavior on an online platform	Users	Mark, a user
		Arthur, one of the platform's designers
Livestock productivity	Farms	Liam, a farmer

Note that the hero and the sidekick are always anchored to the data. They are never fictional characters.

Now it's time to summarize what was covered so far in this chapter and in the previous chapter. You have learned that there are two characters—the hero and the sidekick—both who are extracted from data. The hero is something strictly related to data—the temperature, a product, Earth, an earthquake, patients, a population, an organization, and so on. The sidekick instead is a specific human case related to your hero—a real person, if you can find them, or a generic profile extracted from data, if you can't locate a real person.

At this point you are ready to introduce the hero and the sidekick you have defined into your story, and precisely, you can present them to your audience in the first act.

Presenting the Hero and the Sidekick: The First Act

You have finally reached the writing of the first act of the story. If you remember, your plot is organized in three acts. In the first act, you present the hero. In the second act, you present the problem they have; and, in the third act, the solution and next steps. In this section, you will only learn how to structure the first act. In the following chapters, you'll discover how to organize the rest of the story.

Let's start with the structure of the first act in the world of novels and take inspiration from K.M. Weiland's book, *5 Secrets of Story Structure: How to Write a Novel That Stands Out* (Weiland, 2016). Figure 5.5 shows the timeline of the first act, which must last about a quarter of the entire story.

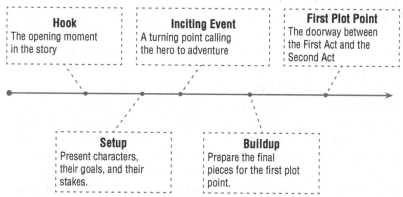

Figure 5.5: The first act timeline in novels

It all begins with a *hook*, which is the opening moment of the story that must attract the reader's attention. Next, there is *setup*, where the audience gets to know the characters, their goals, and the stakes. Then, there is an *inciting event* corresponding to the triggering event that prepares the hero's path toward adventure. Then, the *buildup* adds details to prepare for the last part of the first act, which is when the problem manifests itself. The *first plot point* is the point of no return. It's where the hero's life is definitively compromised, so they can no longer return.

Try to apply the same structure to data storytelling. Figure 5.6 shows the timeline of the first act in data storytelling.

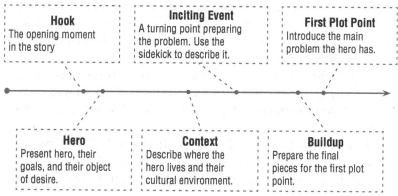

Figure 5.6: The first act timeline in data storytelling

I hope the figure intrigued you. I imagine your impatience in wanting to immediately see a practical example. However, to create a bit of suspense, first I'll explain the logic and then a practical example. Begin the story with a hook, which corresponds to the moment in which you attract the attention of your audience. In a data journalism article, for example, the hook could be the title. But if you tell stories around a product, it could be a question, an anecdote, a short story about the people your data impacts, and so on. You can include the sidekick presentation here as well. Then, introduce the hero, their goals, and possibly their human traits. Nothing new should be added; simply include everything you defined in the first part of this section.

Also, describe the context in which your hero exists. *Context* includes the physical places and cultural environment in which your character moves (Virzì, 2018). Next, introduce the *inciting event*, something that triggers the hero's problem, such as the opinion of an expert gained from an interview, a particular event that will trigger the problem, and so on. Complete the pieces with the buildup part in which you begin to present the data and, finally, move on to introducing the actual problem with the first plot point. Compared to a novel, you can also condense the inciting event, buildup, and first plot point parts into a single element. Or, if your problem requires a broader introduction, you can distinguish the three parts.

Remember that the hero and the context in which they live are only presented in this part, so be very clear. In the subsequent parts of the story, you will no longer return to these two aspects because you will assume that the audience acquired and understood them in the first act.

Also, remember to stick to what you say in the first act, as this is where you decide the story's tone, mood, and genre. If you start a story with an entertaining tone, you can't continue the story with a serious tone. You would lose credibility in front of your audience. Likewise, if in the first act you set the story with a serious tone, highlighting the seriousness of a problem, in subsequent acts, you cannot change the tone and start a joking tone. The effectiveness of the story and your credibility as a data storyteller depend on it remaining consistent. Also, use a different type of sidekick—persuasive, informative, or entertainer—to reinforce the tone of the story.

The basic structure of the first act has now been defined. You will see later that you might not follow this structure to the letter, but based on the audience, you might decide to skip some parts or reverse the order. For now, keep this chronological order.

To understand how to use the structure of the first act, let's review the previously discussed example of the temperature anomaly trend. In Chapter 3, "Making a Successful Data-Driven Story," we created a draft of the first act, which is resumed in Figure 5.7.

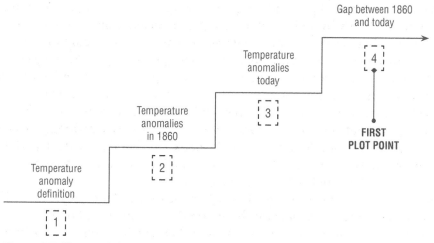

Figure 5.7: The story's first act on global temperature anomalies from 1860 to today, as introduced in Chapter 2.

Now, try to finalize the draft following the first act structure defined in Figure 5.6. Take a pen and a sheet (or a keyboard and a PC) and write down the structure of the first act. This is a design phase, so you don't need any specific tool for building charts or slides. Keep your data on the left and the sheet and the pen on the right and start writing. This is what I call the *writing and creative moment*, which I can ensure you is the best and most fun moment of the story creation process. If you don't agree with me, practice, practice, and practice, and when you discover the hidden writer inside you, you'll agree with me. And if you really can't find any hidden writer, consider the writing and creative moment as a pill you must take to recover from an illness.

As you can see from the structure of the first act, planning a story could take a long time. Often, however, you don't have all that time to extract characters from the data and organize a story out of them. Furthermore, if you have one minute to present your story to the audience, is it worth spending all that time preparing it? Take, for example, my case, the one with which I opened the book. I clearly said I didn't have time to prepare the one-minute presentation. Where could I find the time to organize the story into characters and plot? We are all in a hurry, and there isn't time for anything. The answer really isn't in the time it takes to extract characters from the data and organize them into a plot. The answer is to change your *mindset*, to open yourself to a new way of reasoning in which you organize your speech into a story. It is precisely the mentality of the storyteller who sees stories everywhere.

Of course, initially, creating the story from the data will take you time, practice, and why not, even mistakes. But once you have gained some experience, you will no longer need pen and paper. You will be able to imagine your story in your mind directly by looking at the insights extracted from your data, just as Michelangelo Buonarroti, a famous sixteenth-century Italian sculptor, saw the sculpture already in the marble before he even began to sculpt it. My suggestion is to, therefore, spend some time in practice, use pen and paper, and apply the suggestions written in this book, and when you have gained some experience, you will no longer need pen and paper, and perhaps not even this book. You will be so good that you will see stories everywhere. You will no longer be able to watch a film without thinking about the hook, the inciting incident, and the first plot point. And that's exactly what happened to me. And that's when you will have won. You will become a true data storyteller.

Returning to the structure of the first act, in the remainder of this section, I'll show you an example of what you should produce as an output of the writing and creative moment. The output is *short* and *clear* text describing exactly what you should include in your story.

The Hook

The *hook* grabs your audience and commands their attention. You can use different types of hooks as you write your first act, such as the following:

- **A personal anecdote:** I remember a summer in my childhood when the heat was so intense that it seemed impossible to find relief. I now understand that it wasn't just a particularly hot summer but part of a larger climate change.

- **A provocative question:** What would happen if global temperatures continued to increase at the current rate? We could face unbearable summers and snowless winters. This is the reality of temperature anomalies.

- **A surprising fact:** Did you know that global temperatures have risen by more than 1 degree Fahrenheit/Celsius since 1860? This may not seem like much, but the consequences are devastating. Here's how temperature anomalies are changing the world.

- **A powerful quote:** As climate scientist [X] said, "We are in a planetary emergency situation." This alert concerns temperature anomalies, a threat we can no longer ignore.

- **A vivid display:** Imagine a future where coastal cities are submerged, tropical forests have disappeared, and summers are unbearably hot. This future is not that distant, depending on the temperature anomalies we observe today.

The Hero

After you've presented your hook in the first act, you can present your hero. Using the previous weather example, your hero in this situation is the anomalies in average annual temperature. Answer the following questions:

- **Who is the hero?**
  Name: Anomalies in average annual temperature
  Features: Climate indicator, measured in degrees Fahrenheit/Celsius

- **What is your hero's object of desire?** To remain within a sustainable range to ensure climate stability

- **What challenges does your hero face?** Global warming and increasing emissions of greenhouse gases

Once you have defined your hero's identity card, you are ready to introduce them in your story. Use one of the following possible strategies:

- *Visual representation*, which can create a lasting impression on your audience. In the case of the temperature anomalies, this does not make much sense. But in the case of a product, show a photo of your product.

- *Descriptive language*, which provides information about your hero. For example, use the following text: *The temperature anomalies, an indicator of our planet's health, fluctuate each year. Measured in degrees Fahrenheit and Celsius, their ultimate desire is to maintain a balance that ensures the longevity and stability of our global ecosystem.*

- *Action*, which gives an idea of how the hero behaves. In the case of temperature anomalies, it doesn't matter. Think, instead, about earthquakes. It could be interesting to show a short video about an earthquake and what happens to people, buildings, and objects when they occur.

The Context

Setting the context means identifying all the surrounding information needed by the audience to understand your hero. Try to identify all the possible information your audience may require, covering scientific, historical, sociocultural, and other backgrounds. This phase is mostly based on research. Be as scientific and accurate as possible. There is no place for creativity here. Search for accurate sources of information and do your research. Don't underestimate the search for context, because it's at this stage that you demonstrate the validity of your work—where you show that you aren't talking about a work of fiction but about something real that you have worked on. It's also where you demonstrate your knowledge of the topic. At this stage, you can also briefly explain how you worked, where you collected the data from, and the type of research you conducted. It's also where the audience decides whether or not to trust you. Your credibility as a data storyteller is at stake at this stage.

Continuing the weather example, the context might include the following aspects:

- **Scientific context:** Explain how you performed your research and analysis, which kind of data you analyzed, and its source. In the example, you can simply say that you have collected data from the National Oceanic and Atmospheric Administration (NOAA), but if you have more datasets, list all of them.

- **Historical context:** Explain information related to the past, which can be useful for your audience to understand the problem. In the example of temperature anomalies, describe the weather conditions, from the beginning of Earth up to the moment before your historical data started. This could include glacial areas and special events that influenced the temperature increase, such as the 1883 eruption of Krakatoa. Just for curiosity, in the year following the Krakatoa eruption, average Northern Hemisphere summer temperatures fell by 0.4°C (0.72°F) (Bradley, 1988).

- **Sociocultural context:** Explain which categories of people are involved in your story, including the social and cultural environment where they live. In the example, all humanity is involved in temperature increase, so you can skip including this type of context. However, if, instead, you are talking about an earthquake that happened in Peru, it could be useful to illustrate the sociocultural background in which the population in Peru lives.

- **Other contexts:** Explain other relevant sectors that may help the audience to understand the subject you are discussing, such as economy, politics, and healthcare. In the case of the temperature increase, for example, explain that it can affect agricultural yields, labor productivity, and energy costs.

- Analyzing the context requires time because you need to study and search. You might wonder if it's worth spending all this time conducting thorough background research. My answer is yes. Serious and accurate work requires in-depth knowledge of a topic. You can't communicate something effectively if you don't know it. My suggestion is to build all facets of your context, including all the types of contexts just discussed. Then, depending on the type of audience to which you will present your story, from time to time, you will choose whether to omit some or discuss them all.

- Returning to the topic of lack of time, in this case, a suggestion for optimizing the time spent searching for context is this. If you always work on the same data, organize a document, a folder, or even a sheet of paper, in which you write all the context related to your data. Try to keep it updated as much as possible. Whenever you discover something new about your data, add it so you always have context ready to use.

The First Act's Inciting Event

So far in the story, you have presented the situation before the problem occurs. You have presented the hero and the context in which they live. The inciting incident is the irreversible action that changes the hero's life. Use the sidekick to introduce your inciting event. Define a different sidekick based on the tone you want to give to your story. Use Table 5.1 as a possible reference to define your sidekick in this specific example of temperature anomalies.

What can you do if you don't find anyone to work as a sidekick for your story? An alternative sidekick I haven't mentioned so far is *using the audience themselves* as the sidekick. In their book *Making Numbers Count*, Chip Heath and Karla Starr say that people tend to forget the stories they read or listen to. Instead, they can better remember what they see and even more what they experience. (Heath and Starr, 2022). I'll deepen this topic later in the book, but, for now, I'll show just an example to give an idea.

Imagine that you are in a room full of people and you want to talk about the temperature increase. Your hero still remains the temperature, and you decide to use the audience as a sidekick. Imagine that you have agreed with the room managers to manipulate the room temperature. After introducing the hero and the context, you gradually increase the temperature in the room up to the first plot point, when the temperature will be at its maximum, making the audience *experience* the problem. I can already imagine the audience starting to sweat and getting to the heart of the problem! This is fine for a live presentation and if you reach an agreement with the managers of the room where you present. In the other cases, use your creativity to make your audience *feel* and experience the problem the hero has. If you don't present your data story live or your creativity doesn't suggest anything, search for a real person as a sidekick or, in the worst-case scenario, introduce a typical profile of a person suffering the warm temperatures.

The First Act's Buildup

During this phase, increase the level of engagement of your audience by providing further details that prepare the problem manifestation. For example, you can add one of the following examples:

- A *specific event*, splitting the hero's life into two parts: before and after the event. In the case of the temperature anomalies, explain what happens in 1977, the year when the temperature starts to increase.

- *Expert opinion*, who can help the audience understand the gravity and legitimacy of the hero's experiences. In the case of temperature increase, the expert explains the science behind the temperature increase, discussing the importance of keeping the temperature steady over the time.

- *Recent news* on the subject, which creates a sense of urgency and relevance, showing that the hero's struggles are part of a larger, global issue.

The First Plot Point

Now it's time to reveal the hero's problem in all its gravity and urgency. Use one of the following strategies to structure the first plot point:

- A *question*, which sets the stage for the hero's urgent quest to find solutions. It underscores the gravity of the situation. In the case of the temperature example, the question might be: *How much has the temperature increased in recent years?*

- A *shocking revelation* is a dramatic and unexpected piece of information that alters the hero's understanding of their current situation. This revelation often serves as a pivotal moment in the narrative, creating a sense of urgency and escalating the stakes. It typically involves uncovering hidden truths, secrets, or previous unknowns. In the case of temperature anomalies, show the gap in anomalies between 1860 and today.

- An *ultimatum or deadline* involves setting a specific time limit or presenting a non-negotiable demand that the hero must meet or address. This element serves to propel the plot forward by forcing the hero to take decisive action, often leading to heightened tension and conflict. For example, you could say that beyond this deadline, the temperature rise will become irreversible, leading to catastrophic consequences such as the collapse of ecosystems.

- A *critical failure* is a pivotal moment where the hero's efforts to achieve their object of desire result in a significant setback. This setback reveals the complexity and scale of the problem, emphasizing that simple solutions won't suffice. One example could be a failed policy initiative.

At the end of the first act, you have set the story, and ideally you have raised the audience's interest. Compared to the structure of the first act described in Chapter 2, you have now added more details, including the hook, the hero description, the context, and the inciting event. Consider that the first act duration must be a quarter of the total story's duration, so rather than compressing everything to fit the time you have, remove some parts and focus on the most important ones. Which ones you should consider important depends on your data story flow. Later in the book, you will see how to adapt the data story flow based on the audience and the time available.

You have reached the end of this chapter, which covered how to define the sidekick of your story and how to introduce them in the first act. In the next chapter, you will learn how to describe the hero's problem you have introduced in the first plot point.

Takeaways

- The sidekick is the hero's companion. There are three main types of sidekicks: persuasive, informative, and entertaining. Use a different sidekick based on your story objective. The presence of the sidekick is not mandatory. However, it reinforces the hero's point of view.

- To have more impact on an audience, even a nonhuman hero must be associated with something human. Look for the intersection between data and people to understand who your hero's human sidekick can be.

- Introduce your hero and the context in which they live in the first act of your story. Remember that the first act is the only time the hero will be described, so they must be presented clearly and memorably.

- Start your story with a hook—something interesting that captures your audience's attention. Then, describe your hero and the context in which they live. The first act then moves on to preparing the problem, with the definition of the first plot point.

References

Bradley, R. S. 1988. The explosive volcanic eruption signal in Northern Hemisphere continental temperature records. *Climatic Change*, 12(3), 221–243.

Dykes, B. 2019. *Effective Data Storytelling: How to Drive Change with Data, Narrative and Visuals*. New York: John Wiley & Sons.

Gutkind, L. 2007. *The Art of Creative Nonfiction: Writing and Selling the Literature of Reality*. New York: John Wiley & Sons.

Hall, K. 2019. *Stories that Stick: How Storytelling Can Captivate Customers, Influence Audiences, and Transform Your Business*. New York: HarperCollins Leadership.

Heath, C. and Starr, C. 2022. Making Numbers Count. London: Penguin Random House.

Lo Duca, A. 2009. *Il Violinista*. Castrovillari: Edizioni il Coscile.

Miller, D. 2017. *Building a StoryBrand: Clarify Your Message So Customers Will Listen*. New York: HarperCollins Leadership.

Papuzzi, A. 2003. *Professione Giornalista*. Rome: Donzelli Editore.

Virzì, M.C. 2018. *Gli strumenti dello storytelling*. Rome: Dino Audino Editore.

Weiland, K.M. (2016). *The 5 Secrets of Story Structure: How to Write a Novel That Stands Out*. PenForASword Publishing. `https://www.kmweiland.com/wp-content/uploads/5soss.pdf`

Second Act: Defining the Problem

Some time ago, I had the idea to write some stories with my children. I would write the text, and they would draw the various scenes. A story for each child. However, the idea had to come from them.

The first question I asked them both was "Who is the hero of your story?" "The ants," replied the older one. "The bees," replied the younger one. Then I asked them a second question: "And what problem do they have?" The older one immediately replied, "They can't bring a piece of cake to the anthill." Great, I thought. My little boy got dark and started thinking, but he didn't answer me. After a while, very happily, he said to me, "Mom, I found the problem with the bees in the story: they produce too much honey!" Brilliant! Both had found a problem to write about in their stories!

Using this brief personal experience, I want to tell you that every hero has a problem to solve to achieve a certain goal. After all, even in daily life, each of us has goals to achieve, and a problem almost always comes between us and our goal. Without a problem, there is no action, and without action, there is no story. The presence of a problem is what distinguishes a simple data presentation from a data-driven story. If you haven't found a problem to talk about in your data, then it doesn't make sense to talk about data storytelling. Present your data, organize it in some way, and that's it—no story can be written. However, if your data has a problem or some conflict, then you can tell a story.

The problem is the controlling idea that I discussed in the second chapter. It is the dominant idea of the story. It's why a story is worth telling. Try to answer this question: what happened that's worth telling a story about? If you find even the slightest conflict in your data, that's where your story begins. All stories arise from a problem that the hero has—a more or less small, more or less complicated, problem. But still, there is always a problem.

In this chapter, you will learn about the following aspects related to the problem that the hero faces throughout the story:

- What the problem is
- Various types of problems
- How to describe the problem
- How to communicate the problem

In this chapter, you will not see how to structure the second act of the story, where we describe the problem. Instead, that discussion is postponed to the next chapter, where I also introduce another concept that has been hidden so far. I'll reveal it to you in the next chapter. For now, keep the suspense and curiosity and read this chapter. Let's begin by discovering what the problem is.

Introducing the Problem

In previous chapters, you learned that you can summarize the structure of a story with this simple sentence: *the hero wants to reach an object of desire, but a problem stands in the way*. The problem is exactly what makes the story alive and gives it movement and action. It is the moment in which the story explodes, in which things change (Hall, 2019). Something big or small can happen, but to have a story, something must happen to interrupt everyday life.

Given the importance of the problem in the story, you will need to take special care of it. In previous chapters, you learned that in a data-driven story, the problem is the insight extracted from the data and the controlling idea of the story (i.e., the main topic of the story). Later in this chapter, I will cover what it means when the problem is the insight extracted from the data. For now, let's try to discover, on a theoretical level, what the problem is and its importance in the story.

Introducing the problem into the story corresponds to revealing the maximum knowledge of the universe that is being told (Aleandri, 2020). The *universe* is everything you know about the data and derives from the *data exploration* phase. In this book, I don't focus on data exploration, but consider deepening your focus on this topic if you are not sure about that. In data terms, revealing the problem is showing the most knowledge you have about the data.

Therefore, revealing the problem means expressing your data discovery to the audience, making them identify with the hero and feel the problem is theirs. The insight, problem, or controlling idea—whatever you want to call it—is completely different from the raw data. It's what you discovered when you analyzed your data. So, don't think of showing the audience a simple raw graph that shows a trend without any explanation. As the same data can have multiple heroes, the same hero can have multiple problems, in the sense that you might extract different insights from the same data. However, my suggestion is to focus on a single problem at a time: each story must contain just one problem. If your hero experiences multiple problems, tell multiple stories based on the message you want to convey. Imagine that Zorro—my preferred superhero, as I mentioned previously in the book—must intervene to save a farmer falsely accused of a crime, fight a corrupt magistrate, and defend himself from the attacks of Sergeant Garcia and Captain Monasterio, who suspect that there's a connection between Don Diego and Zorro all in one episode. The result would be a very complicated plot that the audience would hardly be able to follow. Similarly, don't try to solve multiple problems in the same data-driven story.

The problem is closely linked to the hero. Different heroes will experience different problems, so you should pay attention to the hero you choose. Remember my students who chose the Mediterranean diet as their hero and identified the fact of not being healthy as a problem. Obviously, this was a false problem. The Mediterranean diet is recognized as being healthy and does not have such a problem.

The revelation of the problem divides the story into two parts, as shown in Figure 6.1 (Virzì, 2018).

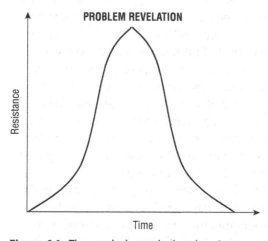

Figure 6.1: The graph shows the hero's resistance to the problem over time. Resistance is at its greatest at the point of manifestation of the problem. Afterward, the resistance begins to decrease to release new values.

Before the problem is revealed, the hero lives with old values and shows some resistance to change. After the problem is revealed, the hero acquires new values and is willing to change. It's by facing the problem that the hero begins to experience change. This is also true when you face a problem in your life. The moment a problem arises, your first reaction is aversion or resistance. Then, slowly you accept it and experience a change. The problem changes you; you are no longer the same as before, and after you have solved it, you will have changed in some way, for better or for worse. That's how life is. The same thing happens when the hero of the story is data because, after all, behind the data, people can always be found.

You might think that the graph in Figure 6.1 fares best in the final stage of the story, when there is the final fight—the *climax* of the story. In reality, the graph doesn't show the level of problem's severity but the level of resistance of the hero to the problem. This means that during the final fight, which usually takes place in the third act (as you will see better later), the hero no longer resists the problem. Indeed, they are determined to go all the way. In the second act, instead, the hero initially does not accept the problem. Then, they change their attitude and begin to accept it.

Let's take an example to better understand the concepts. Consider the usual hero of anomalies in temperature change. Your problem might be a gradual increase over the years, which produces reduced crop yields or increased energy costs during summer. The first reaction to the problem is refusal, or, even worse, denial. The hero doesn't want this problem; they want temperature values to remain constant over time. After the initial negative reaction to the problem, however, the attitude changes: what can we do to solve the problem? So, from resistance, the hero moves on to the release of new values: how to solve the problem. At this stage, you don't propose the solution to the problem yet. You only introduce the problem. For the solution, there is time. Your objective here is to make the audience aware of the problem. To better understand the problem, I'll list some other examples. If your hero is the earthquakes, their problems could be the damage they cause. In the case of patients, the issue may be how many die each year from a disease. In the case of a product, the decrease in sales, and so on. Find a problem for your hero, and you'll have your story in hand. In addition, your audience will also follow you. It's just like when you can't tear yourself away from a good novel, in which you want to know if the protagonist manages to solve their problem and reach the object of desire.

Stop and think for a moment. In reality, the problem of rising temperatures (or whatever problem) is perhaps also *your problem too*, and not just for the hero. If the answer is yes, then I'll reveal another clue: the problem isn't just the hero's but also the audience's. The problem is why the audience listens to you; it is something that the audience cares about. The broader scope of the problem is to understand the human experience under challenging situations (Gutkind,

2007). However, to avoid being big and vague, the problem should focus on a particular aspect of a general experience (Hall, 2019).

The problem is something interesting, so it's worth hearing the whole story. If in your data there is no conflict or discovery, there is no point in telling a story. Show a flat graph and the story simply ends there. There's no point in embarking on one if there isn't something to resolve. Indeed, the problem is even more important than the object of desire. Film director and producer Alfred Hitchcock stated that the object of desire can also be a gimmick, a cop-out, a trick—what he defines as a *MacGufffin* (McCarron, 2023). The best MacGuffin is the emptiest—the most abstract. Think of many action films in which the hero searches for a mysterious object. The object can be anything. What gives life to the story is the problem it generates.

For example, consider the graph of a product's sales trend, shown in Figure 6.2.

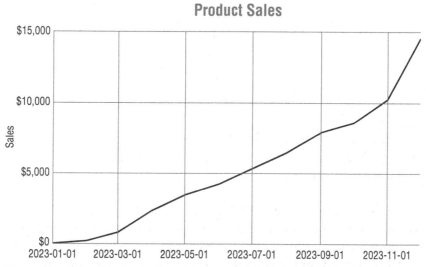

Figure 6.2: The graph shows a steady increase in product sales. Because there's no problem, this graph isn't suitable for telling any story.

The graph shows that sales are increasing. In this case, the hero could be the product and its object of desire, the increase in sales. Is there something that stands between the hero and the object of desire? No. Then there is no story. Show the graph and send everyone home. If, however, sales decrease at a certain point and then increase again, as shown in Figure 6.3, then the problem arises there. That's where you can tell a story. A totally different situation could arise if the graph in Figure 6.2 showed the solution to a previous problem. Suppose that at time 0 (2023-01-01) you opened a business, following a previous problem, such as the failure of a previous business. Then sales begin to increase little by little. You definitely have a story to tell: the product success story. But the graph you are showing is completely inappropriate. It doesn't mention any problems. To have a story, you should show what happened before time 0 and the time of failure of your previous business. In that case, you would have a story to tell. So, when you look at the data, you need to understand where the problem is, and that's where you can start working.

Figure 6.3: The graph shows a decline in product sales during June and July 2023. This could be a problem, so this graph could tell a story.

We said that the problem is the controlling idea of the story, around which it will have to revolve entirely. Closely linked to the controlling idea is the message that the story conveys. When you reveal your story's problem, you need to ensure that you also reveal the story's message. As previously mentioned, the message should never be stated openly; otherwise, your story runs the risk of appearing too moralistic. The message, however, must be understood by describing it through the hero's actions and the revelation of the problem. I will talk about the importance of the message later in this book. For now, be satisfied with what I have told you, and be patient.

Now that you have identified the problem, it's time to learn about the various types of problems.

Problem Types

The problem is the insight extracted from the data. But what types of insights can you extract? The answer to this question is complex because it depends on the domain you are analyzing.

> **NOTE** *Insight* is the result of data analysis, which goes beyond the discussion in this book. For more details about insight, I suggest you read Mona Khalil's book, *Effective Data Analysis*, which I personally found brilliant because the author concentrated on the most important data analysis concepts (Khalil, 2024).

Your insight can be both qualitative and quantitative, depending on the type of data you have available. In Chapter 4, "First Act: Defining the Hero," you saw the data–hero humanity matrix that divided data into qualitative and quantitative. Just as the hero can arise from both types of data, so, too, can the insight be both qualitative and quantitative. Consider, for example, the temperature anomalies increase over the years. Imagine that you have collected qualitative data through surveys and interviews, where people describe how they feel and how the heat affects their daily activities. A qualitative insight you could extract is that, during the month of July, people reported feeling more uncomfortable and sleeping less well due to high nighttime temperatures. Now, imagine that you have collected quantitative data on the sales of air conditioners. From the analysis of your data, you discovered that in July, the average nighttime temperature was 27°C (80,6°F), with a peak of 30°C (86°F) on several occasions. This increase in night temperatures led to a 15 percent increase in sales of air conditioners compared to the previous month. Even if you started from different types of data (qualitative and quantitative), in both cases you have extracted an insight.

To extract insight from data, three fundamental factors are needed: *knowledge* of data analysis techniques, *experience*, and *curiosity*. For the first point, study. For the second one, practice. For the third, be passionate about the work you do, and you'll be increasingly interested in finding out what the data tells you. In any case, always start with a question you want to ask your data. Use various data analysis techniques to extract answers to your questions from the data. And if your data doesn't contain the answer you're looking for, look for more data.

Think about the type of analysis you'd like to do, or you could potentially run into a roadblock. Just to get an idea, let's group the types of data analysis into the following five categories (Anderson, 2015):

- **Descriptive:** Shows what happened in the past through an analysis of historical data. Extracting a problem by conducting this type of analysis could mean capturing a different trend than in the past, such as the increase in temperatures in the last 50 years.

- **Comparative:** Compares data to highlight similarities, differences, strengths, and weaknesses. One problem this type of analysis could extract is the difference in temperature anomalies between urban and rural areas over the past 20 years.

- **Inferential:** Derives general conclusions from sample data through statistical techniques. In this case, a problem could be to discover that the measurement of the temperature increase in Antarctica can be generalized to the whole Earth.

- **Predictive:** Predicts what might happen in the future through statistical or machine learning models. An example would be to predict that temperatures over the next 30 years will increase by a certain number of degrees if CO_2 emissions continue growing at their current rate.

- **Diagnostic:** Explains why the phenomena related to the data happened. In this case, a problem might be discovering that the causes of the temperature increase are increased greenhouse gas emissions, deforestation, and changes in land use patterns.

Figure 6.4 summarizes the various types of data analysis.

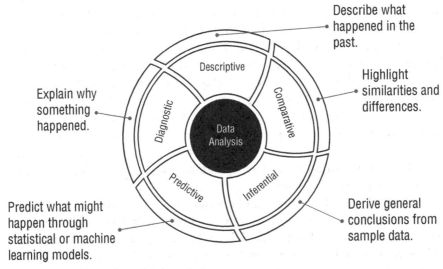

Figure 6.4: Various types of data analysis

Starting from the descriptive analysis and moving clockwise in Figure 6.4, the level of difficulty increases. The most complex analysis is the diagnostic one, as it is very difficult to understand the causes of a phenomenon. The fact that data is analyzed doesn't necessarily lead to the identification of a problem. In other words, data analysis is a necessary condition for discovering something interesting in the data but not sufficient. More elaboration is needed.

Challenge: Think about the last data you analyzed. What types of problems or insights have you extracted?

Looking at your data, you might have noticed that you extracted several types of problems and not just one. So, what to do in your story? Should you tell them all? Select just one? The right answer depends on the story's context and the needs of the audience (Nussbaumer Knaflic, 2015). Personally, I believe that to have a clear and easily understandable story, there must be only one problem;

otherwise, the audience won't be able to focus on it well. My suggestion is, therefore, even if you extract many types of problems from your data, focus on the *most important* one that will likely summarize all the others, and consider it as the main problem of the story. Then, if you really can't live without the other problems, consider them minor and give them less importance throughout the story. Remember, only one problem for one story. I talked about the *most important problem*. But what is actually more important? Certainly, more important is not referring to you but to your hero. What is the biggest problem your hero has in achieving their object of desire? That will be your problem. Consider the temperature example again. Different insights may emerge from the analysis of your data about temperature: outliers in values in some areas, increases in others, even areas experiencing a decline, colder years, below normal, and so on. What is the most important problem here? It depends on the object of desire that your temperature hero wants to reach. If the object of desire is to remain stable, its most important problem is the increase in the last 50 years. However, if your hero is the temperature in zone A and is experiencing a drop unlike the rest of the world (outlier case), then your problem will be the drop. Choose the most important problem based on your hero.

Summarizing what has been said so far, you can extract different problem types from the different types of analysis. Choose the most important one and tell it in your story. Use any other problems as support for your main problem.

Once you've described the main problem, you're ready to introduce it into your story. Let's see how in the next section.

Describe the Problem

There are three ways to describe a problem. The first way is to describe the problem as it presents itself. This is usually what you do when you present a graph. You describe what the graph contains, such as "The following graph shows an increase in temperatures over the last 50 years, with a peak in July 2023." Personally, I find this technique quite boring because it adds nothing to the graph. It simply describes what the audience is already viewing. It's not even a comment on the graph. To understand what it practically means to describe a problem in this way, try to think of an adventure novel where the hero experiences a series of sensational events in which they escape from an enemy. Imagine reading the following excerpt:

> In the heart of a dense forest, James ran through the trees. Behind him, his enemy pursued him.

The text simply describes the scene—no more or less. Now, read this other version of the same story:

> In the heart of a dense forest, James ran through the trees. He could feel the branches whipping at his face and legs, but he couldn't afford to slow down. Behind him, his enemy advanced quickly, his heavy, menacing footsteps echoing in the stillness of the forest. James jumped to the side to avoid a large fallen log. The sweat dripping down his forehead was proof of his mad dash for survival.

Do you notice a difference between the two descriptions? Yes? While the first version describes the scene, the second describes the action that takes place in the scene. Surely you imagined the scene and saw James running through the forest, sweat dripping down his forehead. Here's another version:

> In the heart of a dense forest, James ran through the trees, his heart pounding in his chest. Behind him, the enemy was chasing him. Fear tightened his chest like a vice; every shadow among the trees seemed like a threat. Sweat poured down his forehead and he felt his legs burning from the effort, but he couldn't stop. Every branch that scratched his face and arms increased his anxiety, but he had to keep running.

In this last case, James's feelings emerge. Among the three clips, the third is the one that likely involved you the most because it describes the emotions that the protagonist experiences while being chased by the enemy. Let's put things in order. There are three ways to describe a problem, as shown in Figure 6.5.

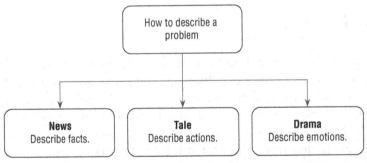

Figure 6.5: The three ways of describing a problem

The first way is the *news*, which describes the hard facts as they happen. News reporting isn't telling a story but simply reporting the facts as they are. When you use the news to describe your problem, you risk being too specific, formal, and broad. News is fine for describing a journalistic fact, but in the case of data storytelling, it is better to put it aside. Yet, how many graphs are accompanied by news, which is more or less an in-depth description of what happens in the graph? Having put aside the first way of describing a problem, let's move on to the second, the *tale*, which explains the actions that occur in the story. An action is an event that happens in time and space. In a story, there can be three types of actions (Pizzo, 2023):

- **Dramatic action:** The actions that the characters perform
- **Narrative action:** The actions that the narrator of the story takes to advance the story
- **Audience action:** The action of the audience when the story is interactive

All three action types move the story forward, each with its own characteristics.

The third way of describing a problem is the *drama*, which describes the feelings that the characters experience when carrying out actions (Pizzo, 2023). This narration type allows the audience to connect their experience to what is described until the boundary between the story and the audience dissolves (Hall, 2019).

To understand the differences between the three types of problem descriptions, let's look at some examples, in which you imagine having to summarize the associated problem with a single sentence. Depending on the type of description you choose, you will use a different phrase. Table 6.1 shows five examples and the possible associated sentences based on the type of description chosen (news, tale, or drama).

Table 6.1: Five Examples Using the Different Types of Problems

EXAMPLE	NEWS	TALE	DRAMA
Monthly Sales Performance	Company ABC's Monthly Sales Surge by 15% in June	The Month That Turned the Tide for Company ABC	From Despair to Triumph: Sales Team's June Journey
Annual Rainfall in Region Y	Region Y Records Highest Annual Rainfall in a Decade	A Year of Downpours: How Rain Transformed Region Y	Caught in the Storm: Families and Farmers Weather the Wettest Year
Student Performance in National Exams	National Exam Scores Show a 10% Improvement Across Schools	Breaking Barriers: The Year Students Excelled in Exams	Against All Odds: The Stories Behind This Year's Top Exam Scores
Hospital Patient Satisfaction Ratings	Hospital Z Achieves Highest Patient Satisfaction Rating in Q2	The Journey to Excellence: How Hospital Z Improved Patient Care	Healing Hearts: Patients Share Their Stories of Care and Comfort at Hospital Z
Energy Consumption Trends in City W	City W Reduces Energy Consumption by 20% in 2023	A Greener Future: How City W Cut Down on Energy Use	Powering Down: Citizens and Businesses Unite to Save Energy in City W

As you can see from the examples, all news contains descriptions of the problem, tales describe what happened (the actions), and dramas describe the emotions connected to the problem. Of the three modes, drama is the one that involves the audience the most because it allows them to experience firsthand the problems that the hero has.

Let's now return to data storytelling and try to understand how to use what I just covered. Consider the graph of increasing temperature anomalies over the last 50 years shown in Figure 6.6.

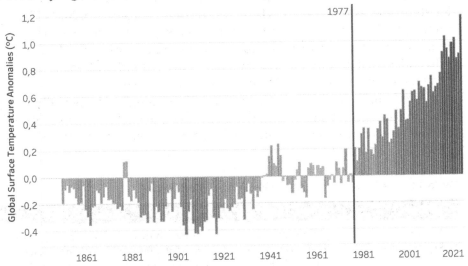

Figure 6.6: A graph showing the average temperature anomalies since 1860

If you want to simply describe your graph, use the following news phrase:

From 1977 to today, temperatures have increased by approximately 1.2°C (2.5°F).

Here, you are describing simple news, which highlights the problem but adds nothing to the graph you are showing. Imagine removing the graph from your presentation and simply stating the previous news sentence. The audience will receive the same exact message. Perhaps adding the graphic stimulates the visual channel of your audience as well as the auditory one, but ultimately you are conveying the same message through two different senses. And this could be a waste of energy for both you and the audience. Now, transform the news into a tale:

From 1977 to today, temperatures have increased by approximately 1.2°C (2.5°F). The air that was once cool and crisp now carries with it an oppressive heat. The seasons mix, with milder winters and hotter summers. The change is palpable:

Glaciers are retreating, leaving behind lands once hidden under layers of eternal ice. Rivers shrink, vegetation suffers, and the animals that depend on these ecosystems struggle to adapt.

Compared to the previous case, the hero of the story—the anomalies in the temperature—experiences the problem, which materializes and becomes a real problem understandable by the audience. You have described actions.

Now, consider the last type of description, the drama:

From 1977 to today, temperatures have increased by approximately 1.2°C (2.5°F). The world has begun to change before our eyes, the heat grips the Earth like a vice. Every day brings new evidence of this change: Sweat drips down our foreheads as we feel the planet burn. The days, once pleasant and warm, have become oppressive and muggy, forcing us to seek relief in the shade or in the air conditioning.

In the latter case, the problem—the increase in temperatures—becomes a problem not only for the hero but also for the audience.

Return to the graph shown in Figure 6.6. Accompany it with a tale or a drama to make both the graph and the rest indispensable.

To sum up, if you want to describe your hero's problem to generate suspense in the audience, use a story that describes the action. However, if you want to engage your audience emotionally, use drama. You will read later in this book how to manage the audience. For now, just know that the way you present the problem to the audience will generate a different effect on them.

Challenge: Think about the last data you analyzed and the problem you extracted. Can you describe it as a short tale or as a drama?

Describing a problem as a tale or as a drama isn't easy and requires some practice. An ancient saying says, "No one is born already wise." Wisdom matures with practice and experience, so if you don't get it perfect at first, practice. Practice, practice, practice. In time, you will learn. And if you really can't, in the age of artificial intelligence (AI), ask for help from generative AI tools, which my boss calls "augmented intelligence." And if you're a purist who wants to avoid help from external tools, assume I didn't tell you anything.

Once you have learned how to describe the problem, you can understand how to communicate it effectively.

Communicate the Problem

Communicating the hero's problem means making it understandable to those who interact with the story. You can use two strategies to communicate the problem effectively: *simplification* and the *use of the five senses*, as shown in Figure 6.7.

Let's look at the two strategies separately, starting with simplification.

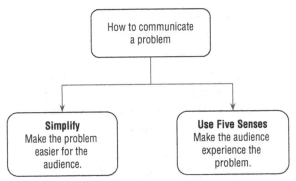

Figure 6.7: Two strategies for communicating a problem

Simplification

Simplifying means making a concept easier so that the audience's brain doesn't struggle to understand. I haven't actually talked about audiences yet, but you don't have to be a scientist to realize that it's easier to understand a concept if it's explained in a simple way. Even if your audience is made up of scientists, it doesn't mean that you will need to use complex concepts or unnecessary details, because scientists are also human beings, and their brains are more likely to understand concepts explained in a simple way than in a complex way.

Let one thing be clear: explaining things in a simple way does not mean trivializing them at all. In fact, just the opposite is true. The more simply something is described, the more work has gone into simplifying it. When you are faced with a clear and concise explanation, what you often don't see is the enormous amount of work that went into simplifying to that level of clarity. Simplifying does not mean trivializing or omitting important details, but rather being able to distill the essence of a complex concept, eliminating everything that is super-fluous and maintaining what is fundamental. Behind every simple explanation, there is a process of reflection, synthesis, and revision that demonstrates the communicator's ability to make information accessible and meaningful. It's like when you enter a completely clean house. You don't think about the effort that went into dusting furniture and furnishings. You see the house as clean and that's it. However, if you enter a house and find it dirty, you immediately notice. You start looking at everything that's wrong: the spiders in the corners of the walls, the dust on the furniture, and so on. This is how a problem is: if it is explained in a simple way, you don't look at the effort that went into simplifying it. You just understand it.

If you're still not convinced, I'll try to explain myself better with another example. Consider the following complex expression:

$$\cos(\pi) + 3 = \sin\left(\frac{\pi}{2}\right) + 1$$

It might seem like a refined way of communicating, but it does not communicate a concept effectively. Imagine using this expression as an example in your presentation. I doubt that after your presentation anyone in the audience will come up to you and repeat your exact words. However, if you use the same simplified expression as an example in your presentation, everyone will probably remember it. Do you know what the simplified expression is? Simply 2 = 2! Everything can be as complicated as you like, but once you reach a certain point, you can no longer simplify.

Your goal in communicating the problem behind your data is just that: to simplify it as much as possible so that it is understandable and memorable. Don't be afraid of appearing less intelligent if you show things in a simplified way, because this isn't true. I remember many very technical presentations I've attended in which the presenter seemed like a very intelligent person, describing detail after detail, but so many details that no one asked him any questions in the end. Personally, I believe that the audience felt lost, and no one had the courage to ask questions on a topic they didn't understand. The point is not to show off your knowledge, but to put yourself at the service of the audience, to help them understand what you, too, have understood by analyzing your data. You will learn about the role of the data storyteller later in this book, but I believe that putting yourself at the service of the audience is the right attitude to communicate a message. You might even undergo some training in effective communication if you want to learn more.

At this point, you might wonder if an excessive simplification of the data could lead to their manipulation and, therefore, to various types of ethical problems. In this book, I do not delve into the ethical problems related to data manipulation, because I assume you are a responsible and serious person, faithful to the data, and willing to reveal what they contain. So, I'm assuming the manipulation problem isn't your problem. And if it ever were a problem for you, I don't think I would convince you with a few words written in this book. However, simplifying doesn't mean deceiving. Simplifying means explaining a concept so that the audience can understand it. In their book *Making Numbers Count*, authors Chip Heath and Karla Starr state, for example, that the human mind reasons better by relating everything to simple and more intuitive concepts rather than using numbers (Heath and Starr, 2023).

Let's return to our data storytelling. How can you simplify the problem to communicate it effectively? Again, authors Chip Heath and Karla Starr help. According to them, you can use at least three strategies to simplify the problem. The first strategy is to *avoid numbers*. It might seem absurd to you, given that I'm talking about data, which are made up of numbers, but I agree with Heath and Starr on this. Once you extract a problem from data, you don't need to use numbers and data to describe it. Think about the case of the increase in temperature anomalies. Once you understand that temperatures have risen, you don't need to provide the audience with precise temperature numbers. The point is that temperatures have increased about 1.2°C (2.5°F). That's all.

The second strategy is to use the *power of one*, which is reducing large numbers to the dimension of one. For example, if you have 100,000 out of 500,000 inhabitants, simplify and reduce that number to 1 in 5 inhabitants. It might seem like reinventing the wheel, but pointing out this may help.

Third strategy: round up. No one will remember a temperature increase of 1.23456°C (2.222208°F), but everyone will remember a temperature increase of 1°C. You might object by saying that by simplifying everything, you lose the accuracy of the data. This is certainly true but remember that your goal in data storytelling isn't to build a report but to ensure that your audience understands the data. If someone is particularly interested in your data, they will read your report, in which you will have to be very precise and accurate. But if you want to communicate something, you must use simple and clear language.

Let's now move on to the second data communication strategy: the use of the five senses.

Use of the Five Senses

Usually, when talking about data, I only use two senses: sight to look at graphs and presentations and hearing to listen to the voice. However, senses are much more. You can use them to make your audience *experience* your story. Stop for a moment and focus only on your hearing. What do you hear around you? Maybe silence, if you're reading at night and everything is quiet. Maybe the background of the television, or maybe the children screaming from the nearby umbrella, if you're at the seaside. Or maybe the birds singing, if you are in the park. Now, focus only on the sense of smell. What do you smell? Your neighbor's perfume? A bad smell? Coffee fresh out of the machine? Now, focus on your hands. Do you feel the smoothness of this book's pages? If you're reading this on the tablet, do you feel the smoothness of the screen? Not to mention taste. Do you taste the sweetness of a good donut or the bitter taste of a lemon? Each sense produces different experiences in you, and you can use all of them to communicate the problem that your hero has.

For example, suppose you need to tell your audience that temperatures have increased by 1.2°C (2.5°F) in the last 50 years. We already said in the previous section to round 1.2°C to 1°C (however, if you are using °F rounding to 2.5°F is not appropriate because it is already a simple number to remember). Simply saying that the temperature has increased by 1°C might seem trivial and not alarming to your audience. After all, 1°C is a small value. Try transforming this information into something that involves the five senses, as described in this excerpt:

Imagine you are in the shower. The water flows at a pleasant 37°C (98.6°F), as it always does. Suddenly, the temperature starts to rise. Just 1° (2.5°F) more. Your skin starts to burn, the heat becomes unbearable. You desperately want to turn off the water, but the knob is broken. You can't do anything. You are trapped in this torment. Now imagine that this is not just happening to you but to our entire Earth. Even just 1°C (2.5°F) more can turn comfort into a nightmare, bringing with it devastating consequences.

This is an example of a vivid problem description, using the sense of touch to relate an abstract problem to a practical experience.

While using the senses of sight and hearing may be simple, using the other senses may be more challenging. However, it is precisely the use of all five senses that transforms a description of a problem into an experience of the problem. You can follow these tips to use the five senses to describe the problem:

- **Sight:** Describe what the problem looks like. For example, imagine seeing a lush forest slowly transforming into an expanse of dead trees and scorched leaves, the bright green replaced by dull browns and grays. Use photos or images to reinforce this concept.

- **Hearing:** Imagine hearing the sounds that accompany the problem. You might describe the deafening roar of a storm, the wind howling with increasing force, the eerie silence that follows a natural disaster, the sound of ice melting and breaking, or the sound of waves crashing violently on the eroded coasts.

- **Smell:** Smell can evoke strong emotions and memories. Describe the smell of smoke-filled air during a fire; the pungent sulfur odor that accompanies volcanic eruptions; or the acrid, stagnant odor of polluted water. These odors can make you physically perceive the problem.

- **Taste:** Although less immediate, taste can also be evocative. Imagine the unpleasant taste of contaminated water, which leaves a feeling of dryness and bitterness in the mouth, or the taste of the salt of tears that fall during a crisis, a symbol of suffering and loss.

- **Touch:** The sense of touch can make discomfort palpable. Describe the feeling of burning skin under the relentless sun; the sharp cold freezing your toes during a cold snap; or the roughness of the dry, parched earth beneath your feet. These details can make the problem physically felt.

To help you use the five senses, transform the abstract problem into a concrete one that can make the audience understand what you are talking about. In Heath and Starr's book, they suggest "translating your problem from the abstract domain of numbers to the concrete domain of senses." Use comparisons and metaphors that are immediately clear to the audience.

Challenge: Think about the last data you analyzed and the problem you extracted. Try to simplify it, using a concrete example that involves the five senses.

It takes work to simplify a problem. Perhaps the main reason for the difficulty isn't so much the problem itself but your way of thinking. Often, it's believed that using simple concepts is childish or diminishes importance. Your goal isn't so much to appear intelligent or as a know-it-all but to make the audience understand what you're talking about. The more invisible you are, the more important the story becomes. Do you see the screenwriter or director who created and produced the film? Of course not. The same goes for you, the data storyteller. Change your mentality. You don't have to prove anything to anyone, neither does your intelligence or your skill. Focus on the audience, not on yourself. Simplify and win the game.

With this kind of exhortation to humility, this chapter ends. You saw how to develop the problem of a story through concepts of simplification and use of the five senses. There is also a third wheel, in addition to the hero and the problem who is known as the antagonist, who up to now I have talked about vaguely. In the next chapter, I will talk about him and will call him a *villain*, precisely because I like strong terms, like *hero*.

Takeaways

- A story, whether data-driven or not, can be summed up as a hero who wants an object of desire, but an obstacle comes between them. Without a problem, there is no story.

- The problem, or conflict, is the insight extracted from the data. Use different data analysis techniques to extract insight.

- There are three ways to describe an issue: news, tale, and drama. The news describes a problem without adding any details. A tale describes actions, and drama describes emotions.

- Communicating a problem means simplifying it and using all five senses to involve the audience more.

References

Aleandri, S. and Moliterni, R. 2020. *Fare un Documentario*. Roma, Italy: Dino Audino Editore.

Anderson, C. 2015. *Creating a Data-Driven Organization*. Sebastopol: O'Reilly Media.

Gutkind, L. 2007. *The Art of Creative Nonfiction: Writing and Selling the Literature of Reality*. New York: John Wiley & Sons.

Hall, K. 2019. *Stories That Stick: How Storytelling Can Captivate Customers, Influence Audiences, and Transform Your Business*. Nashville: HarperCollins Leadership.

Heath, C. and K. Starr. 2023. *Making Numbers Count*. Dublin, Ireland: Penguin Random House.

Khalil, M. 2024. *Effective Data Analysis*. Shelter Island: Manning Publications.

McCarron, G. 2023. *Cultural Theory in the Films of Alfred Hitchcock*. London: Anthem Press.

Nussbaumer Knaflic, C. 2015. *Storytelling With Data: A Data Visualization Guide for Business Professionals*. John Wiley & Sons Inc.

Pizzo, A., V. Lombardo, R. Damiano. 2023. *Interactive Storytelling: A Cross-Media Approach to Writing, Producing and Editing with AI*. Oxfordshire: Routledge

Stanford. 2015. Steve Jobs' 2005 Stanford Commencement Address. `https://www.youtube.com/watch?v=UF8uR6Z6KLc` (Accessed July 25, 2024).

Virzì, M.C. 2018. *Gli Strumenti dello Storytelling*. Roma, Italy: Dino Audino Editore.

Second Act: Defining the Antagonist

When I was little, neither of my parents told me stories, much less read them to me. They bought me several books but left me there to read them alone. It was my grandmother who told me ancient stories with great heroes who'd battle evil and fearsome ogres. I remember sitting around the lit fireplace, as she told the same stories. A great storyteller, my grandmother brought the story to life, as you became the characters in the stories. You really felt the ogre's wickedness via the grotesque voice mimicked by my grandmother. You experienced its power when my grandmother spread her arms wide, illustrating how big that bad ogre was. There was no need for any video projection or any other means of support to view it, and no special effects needed to hear it. My grandmother's mere presence was enough to bring the story to life. Everything materialized in that room, thanks to her great skill as a storyteller.

It is precisely from these childhood stories that the image of the antagonist was born. For every hero, there is an antagonist. Every self-respecting story has an antagonist, someone who opposes the hero. The stronger the antagonist, the greater the merits of the hero in their journey toward the object of desire. Even if the presence of the antagonist isn't mandatory in a story, I strongly advise you to add them to increase the audience's interest in the events narrated during your story and to increase the audience's sympathy toward the hero. The more powerful the antagonist, the greater the audience's sympathy toward the hero. This is a golden rule. If you want to convince someone of your hero's importance, pair them with a very strong and powerful antagonist. The antagonist isn't just any character. They are someone who's surprisingly strong, capable of causing serious problems for the hero. Like the hero, the antagonist also has their own reasons for acting, and, in some cases, their behavior may even be understandable (even if not relatable) for the audience.

Think, for example, of Batman, one of the most famous superheroes, and his archenemy, the Joker. Remove the Joker from all Batman stories now. What remains? Batman without the Joker would probably be a less tormented and obsessed character, but one who's also potentially less deep and complex. The Joker is fundamental to Batman's story. The same is true in your data-driven stories. Find an antagonist, and your story will be more complete and interesting.

However, what if you can't find them? In this chapter, I will explain how to find an antagonist for your story. To proceed in order, I've divided the chapter into two parts. In the first part, you learn how to answer the following questions:

1. Who is the antagonist?

2. What are the various types of antagonists?

3. How can I extract the antagonist from the data?

4. How can I add the antagonist to the story?

In the second part, you will learn how to structure the second act of the story. So, what are you waiting for?

Who Is the Antagonist?

So far, you have seen that a story can be summarized in this sentence: the hero wants to achieve an object of desire, but a problem stands in the way. Now, add a piece to the story: the hero wants to achieve an object of desire, but a problem *caused by an antagonist* comes between the hero and the object. The antagonist is precisely the cause of the problem. More formally, the antagonist is the situation or people obstructing the hero from achieving their goal.

The antagonist is, therefore, the *cause* of the problem that the hero has in reaching their object of desire. How do you insert a good antagonist into the story? Let's start by using an example from the cinematic world. Jerry B. Jenkins, author of 21 *New York Times* bestsellers, reveals five tricks for creating a complex antagonist, as shown in Figure 7.1 (Jenkins, 2022).

First, the antagonist must *have a realistic and sympathetic backstory*. A convincing antagonist must have a backstory that explains their actions and motivations. If the audience can understand why the antagonist behaves in a certain way, they certainly understand them better even if they don't justify their actions.

Consider the example of temperature anomalies described in the previous chapters. The antagonist could be CO_2 emissions. The backstory of this antagonist is very strong. It has its roots in the Industrial Revolution, when the massive

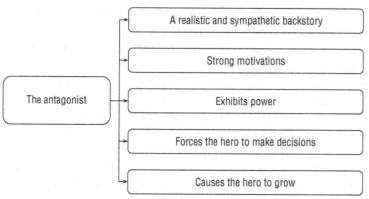

Figure 7.1:   Five tips to build a complex antagonist, according to bestselling author Jerry B. Jenkins.

use of fossil fuels for energy and industry fueled economic growth and global infrastructure development. The historical dependence on these energy sources and the late awareness of the environmental impacts have made the transition toward more sustainable solutions difficult. Explaining this within your data-driven story helps the audience better understand why humanity has come to emit so much CO_2 into the environment: there is a strong past linked to progress. When we see all the industrial development today, it is because, in the past, a large quantity of energy was produced from highly polluting sources.

Second, the antagonist must have *strong motivations*. An effective antagonist doesn't simply act for the sake of it. The antagonist has clear goals and a specific reason for carrying out their actions. When the antagonist's motivations are credible and strong, the conflict with the hero becomes more intense and meaningful. In the temperature example, the antagonist has their own motivations: producing energy for heating, transportation, industrial processes, and economic growth, along with energy-intensive consumption habits. Inserting these motivations into the story helps the audience understand why the antagonist acts a certain way. Indeed, as a result, you may have a split within the audience, with some even going so far as to share the antagonist's viewpoint. Explaining the antagonist's motivations, therefore, can become a crucial point in the story if you want to spark a discussion or debate within your audience.

The third characteristic of the antagonist is that they must *exhibit power*. To be a true threat, the antagonist must possess a certain degree of power. This might be physical, intellectual, political, financial, or otherwise. A powerful antagonist creates greater tension in the story because they pose a real risk to the hero. In the case of CO_2 emissions, they could exhibit their power by contributing to climate change and causing global warming, extreme weather events, and melting glaciers. Furthermore, CO_2 emissions influence energy and geopolitical policy, reshaping the global balance of power and posing economic challenges for the transition to a sustainable economy.

The *urgency* to solve the problem and fight the antagonist is closely linked to this aspect of power. The stronger the power of the antagonist, the greater the urgency to fight them as soon as possible. Show the audience an almost invincible antagonist if you want to arouse in your audience the need to solve the hero's problem as soon as possible. Think, for example, about a product's drop in sales. The hero is the product, the problem is the drop in sales, and the antagonist is the cause of the drop in sales, for example, a better competitor product. If you want your team to work on improving the product right away, showcase the strengths of your competitor's product. The more strengths of the antagonist you show, the more urgent it will be to modify your product to solve its problem of declining sales.

In addition, the antagonist must *force the hero to make difficult decisions*. A good antagonist places the hero in situations where they must make difficult and often painful decisions. This not only increases the tension of the plot but also enables the reader to see the true character of the hero. Difficult decisions might involve personal sacrifices, complex moral choices, or dilemmas that test the hero's values and beliefs. An antagonist who pushes the hero to the limits of their abilities creates a compelling and dynamic narrative. In the CO_2 emissions example, the hero isn't human (it's the temperature), so they cannot make decisions independently. However, the antagonist forces governments and communities to make difficult decisions on how to adapt to climate change and reduce emissions through energy policies and investments in resilient infrastructure. Furthermore, issues of equity and climate justice must be addressed, balancing economic growth with the need for a transition to a sustainable economy.

The last aspect of the antagonist is that they *cause the hero to grow*. Through the challenges and difficulties imposed by the antagonist, the hero must evolve, develop new skills, strengthen their determination, and often review their beliefs. In the case of the temperature example, the temperature hero isn't human, so they cannot grow directly. However, the antagonistic CO_2 emissions push humanity to develop clean technologies, adopt sustainable policies, and promote international cooperation to reduce emissions. This process stimulates innovation, environmental education, and global movements pushing for a more sustainable future.

You have seen five characteristics that a good antagonist should have. Obviously, it isn't certain that the antagonist has all five characteristics; they could have only one or even none. However, I suggest you include at least one in the story to build a compelling story for your audience.

At this point, you are ready to proceed to the next step, which is analyzing the various types of antagonists.

Various Types of Antagonists

In their article titled "Character-Oriented Design for Visual Data Storytelling," Keshav Dasu et al. explain two types of problems in stories: *external* and *internal*. In internal problems, the hero struggles against their desires and beliefs. In external problems, instead, the hero fights against something external (Dasu et al., 2024). Generalizing what was said by Dasu et al., there are four types of antagonists, as shown in Figure 7.2 (Masterclass, 2021): the villain, the conflict creator, the inanimate forces, and the hero themself. The first three cause external problems, and the last one causes internal problems.

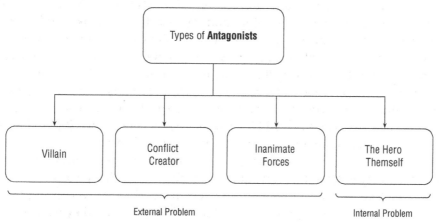

Figure 7.2:   The four types of an antagonist in a story

The *villain* is the classic *bad guy*, who contrasts with the *good guy* in the story. Obviously, the good guy is the hero of the story. The villain is the one who creates the conflict in the story and, therefore, hinders the hero because they're (morally) corrupt or, more generally, because they have bad intentions. In his book *Building a StoryBrand*, Donald Miller states that the stronger and more evil the villain is, the higher the audience engagement (Miller, 2010). Let's use an example from data storytelling to understand better. Suppose you have data on deaths caused by COVID-19 over time in a given city, say, Rome, Italy. Your hero is the people in Rome. Their object of desire is to stay alive; the problem is death caused by the pandemic, and the antagonist is the coronavirus. Even if it doesn't have strictly human traits, you might consider the coronavirus a villain precisely because it has bad intentions. In summary, the villain is an antagonist who creates problems for the hero because they are bad, ill-intentioned, or morally corrupt.

The *conflict creator*, on the other hand, is someone whose objectives conflict with those of the hero but who isn't necessarily a bad guy. The conflict creator simply has opposite interests to the hero. For example, if the hero is a sunscreen product and its object of desire is to increase sales, the conflict creator could be another competitor's sunscreen. This isn't the bad guy of the story, but its interests compete with those of the hero. Consider our usual example of temperature anomalies. The conflict creator in that case could be CO_2 emissions. These, in fact, create conflict in the story; that is, they hinder the temperature hero in maintaining its stable values over time.

The antagonist doesn't necessarily have to be a human. It can also be an *inanimate force*, which, for the purposes of the story, must have human traits. This antagonist type causes the problem for the hero unconsciously; that is, their goal isn't to hinder the hero, but as a side effect of their powerful action, they cause problems for the hero. For example, consider the efforts to limit damage caused by earthquakes as the hero of the story and the object of desire is to reduce the earthquake damage as much as possible. Here, the antagonist could be the earthquakes themselves, understood as inanimate forces. Returning to the coronavirus example, you could also classify it as an inanimate force and not necessarily as a villain. But be careful. Depending on how you choose to classify the antagonist, the perspective in the story changes. If you choose to classify the coronavirus as villainous, then its wickedness will have to emerge from the story. If you choose to classify it as an inanimate force, its power will have to emerge.

I'm sure what I just conveyed has certainly raised many questions for you. Be patient. I'll clarify everything soon. First, check out the fourth type of antagonist, which is the *hero themself*—for example, their insecurities or something from their past. This type of antagonist causes the problem because they believe in a *lie* (Weiland, 2016). The lie is what is wrong with their story. The hero wants the wrong object of desire, which is connected to their lie, but they really need to achieve another object of desire. In the case of the product hero, such an antagonist could be the product itself in the past. Here, it would be worth making a comparison, for example, between product sales today and a year ago. One example of a lie here would be that the product wants to increase sales without improving its quality. Table 7.1 summarizes the described examples for each type of antagonist, showing the hero, the object of desire, the problem, the antagonist, and how the antagonist enhances the hero's journey.

As you can see from the last column of the table, each type of antagonist poses new challenges to the hero, making the story more compelling. Indeed, each type of antagonist has particular characteristics that determine different reactions in the audience. Even if you haven't yet seen in detail how to refine the story based on your audience, it is worth seeing the effect of the various antagonists on the audience here. Table 7.2 details the four types of antagonists, their characteristics, and audience reactions.

A morally corrupt and evil villain arouses a strong aversion and desire to see the hero prevail. If you use this antagonist type, the audience will develop a certain empathy for your hero, creating a clear contrast between good and evil

Table 7.1:   Antagonist Examples

ANTAGONIST TYPE	HERO	OBJECT OF DESIRE	PROBLEM	ANTAGONIST	HOW THE ANTAGONIST ENHANCES THE HERO'S JOURNEY
Villain	People in Rome	To stay alive	Death caused by the pandemic	Coronavirus	The hero must find ways to survive and combat the pandemic.
Conflict creator	Sunscreen product	To increase sales	A decrease in sales	Competing sunscreen product	The hero must improve its features or marketing.
Inanimate force	Efforts to limit earthquake damage	To reduce earthquake damage	Destruction caused by earthquakes	Earthquakes	The hero must develop new strategies to reduce destruction.
The hero themself	The product	To increase sales	Past bad performance	Product poor quality in the past	The hero must find out what is wrong with their past activity.

Table 7.2:   Four Types of Antagonists in a Story, Their Characteristics, and the Audience's Reactions

ANTAGONIST TYPE	WHY THEY CAUSE THE PROBLEM	MAIN CHARACTERISTIC	AUDIENCE REACTION
Villain	They want to cause harm to the hero.	Evil, moral corruption	Strong aversion and desire to see the hero prevail
Conflict creator	They have opposite interests to the hero.	Opposition, contrast	Challenge and tension
Inanimate force	The problem is a side effect of their action.	Strength, power	Sense of helplessness and vulnerability but also a strong empathy for the hero
The hero themself	They believe a lie.	Interior conflict	A deeper understanding of the hero

and generating suspense and tension. A conflict creator generates a dynamic of challenge and tension that pushes the hero to overcome obstacles and difficulties. The audience might feel frustration at the constant impediments but also curiosity and interest in seeing how the hero will resolve conflicts. This type of antagonist often stimulates critical thinking and analysis of the strategies adopted by the hero. An antagonist represented by an inanimate force, such as a natural disaster or disease, causes a sense of helplessness and vulnerability. The audience tends to feel a strong empathy for the hero, creating a deep emotional bond. This antagonist type often evokes reflections on human frailty.

When the hero is their own antagonist and travels through internal conflicts, fears, or personal weaknesses, the audience is pushed into introspection and develops a deeper understanding of the character. This type of antagonist generates empathy and identification. The audience feels emotionally involved in the hero's personal journey, supporting them in their process of growth and self-discovery.

Challenge: Think about the latest data you analyzed and try to identify the antagonist. What type of antagonist did you find? Villain, conflict creator, inanimate force, or the hero themself?

You might find multiple causes for the problem that the hero has, or you might not be able to find any. So, the next question is, how do you extract the antagonist—the cause of the problem—from data? I break this down in the next section.

How to Extract the Antagonist from the Data

In his book *The Seven Basic Plots*, Christopher Booker states that storytelling is about the terrifying, life-threatening, seemingly all-powerful monster the hero must fight with to keep them alive (Booker, 2004). Booker even goes so far as to call the antagonist a monster, to give an idea of how strong and powerful the antagonist must be. In the case of data storytelling, the antagonist doesn't necessarily have to be a monster. The important thing is that they hinder the hero from reaching their goal.

In data storytelling, the antagonist more precisely is the *cause* of the problem. Discussing causes in data means knowing the problem well to identify its causes. These skills go beyond storytelling skills. It's about analyzing the data in depth, conducting experiments, and understanding the problem's root cause. Of course, the cause depends on the type of data you have, the hero you extracted, and the problem you identified. For example, if your hero is a product and its problem is declining sales, the antagonist could be a defect in the product, a better product than the competition, a worsening of the product compared to the past, and so on.

Surely, as a good data analyst, you already know how to extract the antagonist from your data, that is, the cause of the problem. And if you really can't, ask the experts in that sector. Get help by broadening your horizons. Ask your colleagues, both inside and outside your department. Ask experts who live on the other side of the world. Ask anyone who can help you. Don't be alone in your data analysis. Expand your network. Thanks to collaboration with others, you will feel less alone in your work, and you'll learn to love it even more. Don't forget that every discussion with experts and colleagues can lead to new perspectives and innovative solutions, enriching not only your analysis but also your professional experience. Collaboration will enable you to face challenges with greater confidence and creativity, transforming every obstacle into an opportunity for growth and continuous learning.

To give you an idea on how to extract the antagonist from your data, I'll briefly describe seven techniques known in the field of problem management for identifying the cause of a problem. For further information, read *Problem Management: A Practical Guide* by Jim Bolton and Buff Scott III (Bolton and Scott III, 2016). Figure 7.3 illustrates the seven techniques for identifying a problem.

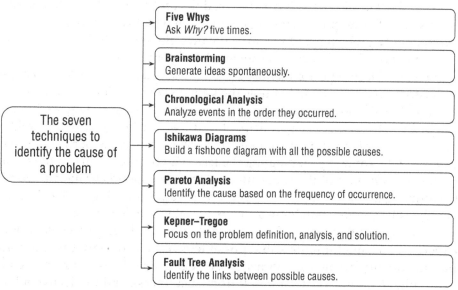

Figure 7.3: The seven techniques for identifying a problem

As an example, I will describe only the first two techniques. If you are interested in the topic, you can learn more by reading Chapter 3 of Bolton and Scott's *Problem Management* mentioned previously. The first technique is that of the *five whys*, which consists of asking yourself five (or more) times *why* something happens. Children are the most excellent experts in this technique. They use it to understand how the world works and to provide answers to their count-less questions. When adults provide an answer, they immediately ask another question, and so on. The five whys technique works just the same as how children use it. For example, suppose the hero of your story is a product and its problem is declining sales. Here, I'll show you a possible way to proceed to extract the antagonist, and thus the problem cause, using the five whys:

1. Why have product sales dropped? Because customers are buying the product less.

2. Why are customers buying the product less? Because they received bad reviews online.

3. Why did the product receive negative reviews? Because many customers have encountered quality problems with the product.

4. Why are there quality problems with the product? Because during produc-tion, some key components are defective.

5. Why are some key components defective? Because the supplier changed the material used without informing the company.

Using the five whys, you have identified the root cause: The decline in sales is caused by the supplier changing the material of critical components, which led to quality problems and negative reviews. So, the material of the critical components of the product is the antagonist of your story.

The second technique for identifying the cause of a problem is *brainstorming*, an unstructured technique that uses the knowledge of various people to iden-tify a problem's root cause. One way to organize a brainstorming session is to use sticky notes, where each participant writes a possible cause of the problem on a note. After having discussed all the possible causes, the participants then proceed with voting by eliminating the least-voted causes. Finally, they come to the identification of the root cause, which corresponds to the antagonist. Consider again the example of sales drops for a product. Figure 7.4 shows 12 possible sticky notes containing as many possible problem causes.

After a careful analysis of the available data and/or a discussion with experts, you can eliminate some possible causes until only three remain: product quality problems (confirmed by negative reviews), price perceived as too high (confirmed by feedback from customers), and ineffective adver-tising campaigns (confirmed by market analyses). Among these three possible causes, who will be your antagonist? It depends. You can choose to have all three causes as the antagonist, or you can focus on the one that makes the most sense for your story.

Just for completeness, I'll quickly report the other five techniques here. *Chro-nological analysis* represents all the involved events chronologically. The objective here is to understand which events triggered other events to re-build the problem.

Figure 7.4: Twelve possible causes relating to the decline in sales of a product

This should help you to understand the root cause. The *Ishikawa diagram*, also known as fishbone diagram) is a structured way of brainstorming. First, draw a line representing the fish spine and the problem. Then, define the broad categories of the possible causes to the problem and add each of them as a rib to the spine. Next, add each possible cause as a branch of the related rib. Finally, proceed as in the brainstorming strategy, by removing the less probable causes. *Pareto analysis* shows for each possible cause its number of occurrences. Then, sort the causes based on the cumulative percentage to identify the top causes. The *Kepner–Tregoe methodology* first describes the problem, and then it identifies the possible causes and tests them to verify if they really determine the problem. Finally, *fault tree analysis* aims to identify the links among possible causes using Boolean logic.

The techniques just described underscore the importance of understanding the cause of the problem that emerges from the data. Only if you identify the cause of your problem will you know how to solve it. And the cause of the problem is precisely the antagonist of your story. Here, however, a question arises. What if I can't find any convincing cause, despite the efforts and support of leading experts from all over the world? In this case, the problem is very serious, and the antagonist becomes an even more powerful force—something mysterious—which makes the story even more complex. You can still talk about an antagonist, although in this case the antagonist will not have any well-defined traits.

Table 7.3 provides some possible stories based on data. Each story details the data used, the hero, the desired object, the problem, and the antagonist. Feel free to draw inspiration from this table!

Table 7.3:   Examples of Stories Extracted from the Data

DATASET	HERO	OBJECT OF DESIRE	PROBLEM	ANTAGONIST
Air pollution levels in different cities	Air quality	Become clean	High levels of pollution	Polluting industries
Blood sugar levels of diabetic patients	Patient health	Maintain normal sugar levels	Blood sugar spikes	A diet high in sugar
Number of road accidents in a city	Road safety	Reduce accidents	Increase in road accidents	Distracted and careless driving
The trend in university enrollments in recent years	University	Increase enrollments	Decrease in enrollments	Increase in university fees
Energy consumption of a city	Energy sustainability	Reduce energy consumption	Increasing energy consumption	Inefficient use of resources

The examples described always show a problem in the negative form. The concept of antagonist, in fact, is linked to a negative experience. If, however, you have positive situations in your data, such as an increase in product sales or university enrollments, you no longer have an antagonist in the story but simply a cause. You can still tell a story with that, provided you can organize it as a conflict.

Once you have extracted the antagonists from the data, the next step is to add them to the story.

How to Add the Antagonist to the Story

One thing I haven't told you so far but that is widely developed in cinema, is that even the antagonist has a supporter. Just as the hero has a sidekick, so, too, does the antagonist. This supporter is usually called a *henchman* or *minion*, a term taken from a famous film series. Unlike the sidekick, minions serve only to generate noise in the story and are usually ineffective. In the case of data storytelling, you can consider including minions in your story, for example, if your goal is to entertain the audience. Otherwise, you should avoid including them. In any case, if you really do want to include them, you can associate a human trait with them, just as you did with the sidekick. The difference is that the minions must act as supporters for the antagonist, while the sidekick is a supporter for the hero. Be careful, however, not to add too convincing minions; otherwise, the audience could side in favor of the antagonist!

Now let's return to our discussion of the antagonist and how to add them to the story. The goal isn't to show the antagonist alone but to always show them in relation to the hero of the story. The antagonist's presence in the story must increase the audience's interest and *urgency* to stop them from solving the problem (Bergstrand and Jasper, 2018). In the cinematographic field, antagonists are constructed so powerfully that they inspire the audience with the urgency to fight them and even kill them (Booker, 2004).

Think about how many films you have seen or books you have read in which the antagonist dies at the end. In none of them did you feel compassion for the antagonist. Yet, they are a person who dies. The audience is so taken by the hero's problem that they actually hope that the antagonist dies at the end of the story. I might present an exception, however. Personally, I have never liked the stories where the antagonists die at the end. In fact, in one of my youth stories, I designed antagonists who recognized their wickedness and evolved to become good at the story's end (Lo Duca, 2014). Unfortunately, that wasn't a good idea. One reader, in particular, criticized this antagonist's positive transformation, saying that the antagonist should remain the antagonist. And, he was right. Character theory states that each character has a very specific role, which they must necessarily follow. Otherwise, the story doesn't work, and the audience is disturbed (Bergstrand and Jasper, 2018). So, if you have found an antagonist in your story, they must remain an antagonist throughout your story. That the antagonist is eliminated or even killed at the end of the story is not necessary. This depends on how the story is constructed, depending on whether the hero or the antagonist wins. What matters is that the antagonist remains the adversary from start to finish.

So far, I have talked about the hero and antagonist as two opposing figures, which is fine. Throughout the story, the two characters have to clash directly sooner or later. This means there needs to be a specific scene or sequence (i.e., a series of scenes) in your story where the "fight" between the two takes place. I remember with regret two of my students who presented a very interesting data journalism project related to the topic of reading. Their hero was reading; the problem was the decline in readers, especially among young people, and the antagonist was the increased entertainment available on tablets and cell phones. My students had done a very interesting study, in which they discovered, by analyzing various data sources, that young people spend on average about six hours a day on the Web compared to about an hour a day reading. The story sounded fantastic. Its only flaw was that nowhere did they directly confront the hero and antagonist. No graph was provided showing the two trends over time. Sin! It would've been a fantastic project if only they'd added one additional scene—the crucial one of the confrontation between their hero and antagonist. It would've been wonderful to see that the decline in reading corresponded to an increase in entertainment located online.

You must include the fight between your hero and antagonist at some point in your story. In the context of data storytelling, if you really don't want to talk about combat, at least show a comparison between the two. You have two options, depending on whether you have supporting data about your antagonist. If you do have supporting data about your antagonist, display it, preferably in combination with data about your hero, as shown in Figure 7.5.

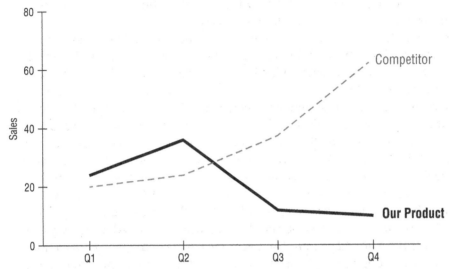

Figure 7.5:   An example of a scene with a direct confrontation between the hero and antagonist, with data available on the antagonist

Figure 7.5 graphs a direct comparison between our product (the hero) and that of the competitor (the antagonist). From the figure, it is clear who the hero is (indicated with a bolded line).

If you don't have supporting data, you can still show the cause of your problem using a comment, callout, or annotation, as shown in Figure 7.6.

In this case, the hero is the product, while the antagonist is the deterioration in product quality. Although no antagonist data is shown in the figure, the cause of the problem is clear.

To summarize what has been said, if you have data relating to the antagonist, display it, combining it, if possible, with that of the hero's data. If you don't have data about the antagonist, add annotations, callouts, or comments in the scenes where you show the hero's problem to make it present and visible to the audience.

After learning who the antagonist is and their role in the story, let's move on to the final part of the chapter, which describes how to structure the second act of the story.

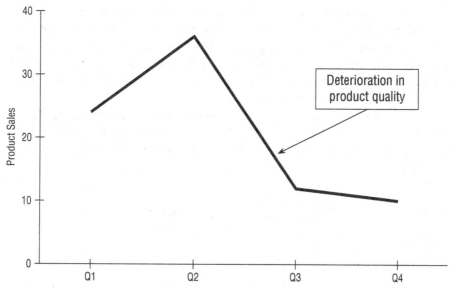

Figure 7.6: An example of a scene with a direct confrontation between the hero and antagonist, with no data available on the antagonist

Presenting the Problem: The Second Act

In the story's second act, you present the problem and antagonist. If you remember, your plot is organized in three acts. In the first, you present the hero; in the second, the problem they have; and in the third, the solution and next steps. In previous chapters, you learned how to structure the first act. In this section, you will learn how to structure the second act.

Just for a quick recap, Figure 7.7 shows the structure of the first act.

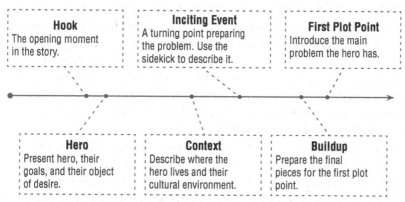

Figure 7.7: The first act timeline in data storytelling

Start your story with a hook, something that raises interest. You'll see later in the book that you can change the hook based on the audience interests.

For now, define a general hook, which is suitable for a generic audience. Next, introduce the hero, their goals, and their object of desire. Also, present the context where your hero lives. As a following step, show the inciting event, a turning point preparing the problem. You can use the sidekick to introduce it. Prepare the final pieces to introduce the first plot point, which is the main problem the hero must face with throughout the full story.

With the first plot point, the plot enters the second act, where the problem is further developed and deepened. Figure 7.8 illustrates the timescale of the second act in novels and cinema, which must last about half of the entire story (Weiland, 2016).

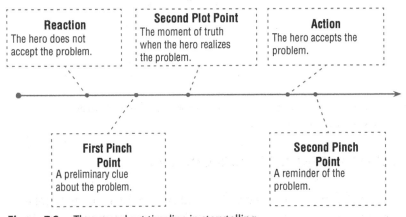

Figure 7.8:   The second act timeline in storytelling

The second act begins with the hero's resistance to the problem. As you saw in the previous chapter, the hero initially doesn't accept the problem but reacts to maintain their old values. Subsequently, something new happens, the *first pinch point*, which corresponds to the first trace of the problem, culminating with the *second plot point*, where the problem manifests itself in all its fullness. After the second plot point, the hero changes their attitude toward the problem, becoming active. The hero then finally accepts the problem and becomes willing to face it. At the end of the second act, to reinforce the problem, a second event occurs—the *second pinch point*—opening the doors to the third act.

Let's apply this same structure to data storytelling. Figure 7.9 displays the timeline of the second act in data storytelling.

If you remember correctly, the first act ended with the introduction of the problem. Now, the second act begins by reinforcing the problem, exhibiting additional data related to the problem. Here, the objective is to cover the effects caused by the problem. Then, the story moves on to the first pinch point where you introduce the antagonist, explaining their motivations and everything that the audience needs to understand them. If necessary, you can also introduce the henchmen or minions here. Then, you move on to the second plot point, which

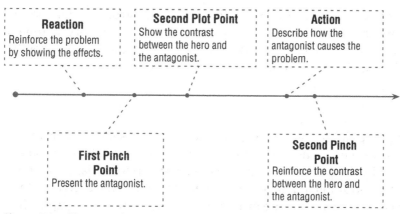

Figure 7.9:   The second act timeline in data storytelling

is the exact moment you show the comparison/contrast between the hero and antagonist. This moment splits the story into two parts:

■ Before the second plot point, the audience doesn't really know the cause of the problem.

■ After the second plot point, it becomes clear who to fight against. It's here where you describe how the antagonist causes the problem (i.e., action) to support the second plot point.

Finally, introduce the second pinch point, in which you reinforce the contrast between the hero and antagonist. This moment can also open up new scenarios, which will then be described in the third act.

To understand how to use the structure of the second act just described, let's use our usual example of the temperature anomaly trend. In the second chapter, I created a draft of the second act, which I'll now resume in Figure 7.10.

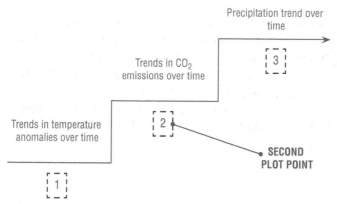

Figure 7.10:   The second act of the story about global temperature anomalies from 1860 to today. Three scenes are used, culminating in the center of the act, with the second plot point.

Now, let's finalize the draft, following the second act structure defined in Figure 7.9. Remember that at this stage you are designing your story, without any focus on a specific audience. The objective here is to build the plot. You'll see how to tailor the plot to an audience later in the book.

Reaction

After the first plot point in the first act, the audience was shocked that there was a data problem. Now is the time to reinforce the concept detailing the other effects produced by the problem. If you have data to support this, show it. If you have no other additional data, use your hero's sidekick to strengthen the issue. In the case of the temperature example, you can show, for example, the following data that reinforces your problem:

- Trends in land and sea surface temperatures, sea level, etc.
- Changes in plant-flowering times and fruiting
- Migrations and changes in the habitats of species
- Increased energy consumption for cooling, for example, for the use of air conditioning

These are just examples of data that you can use to strengthen your case. Remember that, at this stage, it's important to show the effects of the problem, not the causes.

First Pinch Point

Ideally, at this point, your audience is interested in understanding who's causing all these problems. This is where you introduce the antagonist. Reserve a place of honor for the story's antagonist. Give them time to exhibit all their ferocity and strength.

In the case of the temperature anomalies example, your antagonist could be CO_2 emissions. Describe your antagonist using Jenkins' five tips presented at the beginning of this chapter. Explain to the audience the motivations of your antagonist so that the audience understands why the antagonist behaves in a certain way. Explain that CO_2 emissions aren't the result of an evil action, but rather of humanity need to generate energy, following an ever-increasing demand. If possible, also include examples of who emits these CO_2 emissions in the environment, such as industries, cars, and so on.

Second Plot Point

It's time to show the direct confrontation/clash between the hero and antagonist. The audience is ready and can't wait for anything else. Show one or more scenes in which the hero, temperature, and the antagonist, CO_2 emissions, collide. A simple graph with a trendline indicating the two trends should be sufficient. An increase in one should correspond to an increase in the other.

Action

Explain how the antagonist causes the problem; that is, why do CO_2 emissions produce an increase in temperature? If your sidekick is an expert, you can involve them in explaining the phenomenon. If you don't have an expert, however, you will be the one who explains the causes directly. For example, clarify details relating to the greenhouse effect and how CO_2 emissions contribute to increasing it.

Second Pinch Point

Having reached this point, your audience has a clear picture of the situation and is finally ready to fight the antagonist. If you want to make the story more compelling, add more details here about the contrast between the hero and antagonist or the damage caused by the antagonist. In the case of temperature anomalies, you can show data on the greenhouse effect or the role of CO_2 compared to other greenhouse gases. While in the reaction phase you presented data that delved into the hero's problem, here you present data that delve into the role of the antagonist. This phase indicates to the audience that the battle between the hero and antagonist isn't over yet.

At this point, the suspense has increased, and everyone in the audience will ask themselves: what will happen now? You'll find out in the third act, coming up in the next chapter.

Takeaways

- In storytelling, the antagonist is the character who contrasts the hero in reaching their object of desire.
- Five tips to build a complex antagonist include: 1) have a realistic and sympathetic backstory, 2) detail strong motivations, 3) exhibit power, 4) force the hero to make difficult decisions, and 5) cause the hero to grow.
- There are four antagonists: the villain, the conflict creator, the inanimate forces, and the hero. Depending on what type of antagonist you choose for your story, you will elicit different reactions from your audience.
- In data storytelling, the antagonist is the cause of the problem that the hero has. Explaining the causes of a problem requires skill and experience. Apply one of seven techniques to identify the antagonist in your story: five whys, brainstorming, chronological analysis, Ishikawa diagrams, Pareto analysis, Kepner–Tregoe, and fault tree analysis.

- Include a direct confrontation between the hero and antagonist in your story. If you have data relating to the antagonist, show it; otherwise, insert a comment or annotation that refers to the antagonist, making them present and visible in the story.

- The second act of the story is where you show the problem in action. Organize the second act into the following parts: reaction, first pinch point, second plot point, action, and second pinch point.

References

Bolton, J. and Scott III, B. 2016. *Problem Management: A Practical Guide.* Norwich: The Stationery Office.

Booker, C. 2020. *The Seven Basic Plots.* Dublin: Bloomsbury Publishing Plc.

K. Dasu, Y. H. Kuo and K. L. Ma. 2024. *Character-Oriented Design for Visual Data Storytelling in IEEE Transactions on Visualization and Computer Graphics* 30(1): 98–108. DOI: 10.1109/TVCG.2023.3326578

Jenkins, J. B. 2022. *How to Write a Complex Villain.* Retrieved on August 4, 2024, from `https://www.youtube.com/watch?v=6qMdRDwDzLE`

Lo Duca, A. 2014. *La Bambina e il Clown.* [Self-published.]

Masterclass. 2021. *The 4 Main Types of Antagonists.* Retrieved August 4, 2024, from `https://www.masterclass.com/articles/the-main-types-of-antagonists`

Miller, Donald. 2010. *Building a StoryBrand: Clarify Your Message so Customers Will Listen.* New York: HarperCollins Leadership.

Weiland, K. M. 2016. *Creating Character Arcs: The Masterful Author's Guide to Uniting Story Structure, Plot, and Character Development.* PenForASword Publishing.

Weiland, K. M. 2016. *The 5 Secrets of Story Structure: How to Write a Novel That Stands Out.* PenForASword Publishing. `https://www.kmweiland.com/wp-content/uploads/5soss.pdf`

Third Act: Setting the Climax and Next Steps

The third act is the moment of reckoning. Everything you opened in the previous parts of the story must now be ended. All the questions you asked the audience with your story before must now be answered. In this phase, the audience's hunger is finally satisfied. It is here that it's revealed whether the hero finally solves their problem and reaches the object of desire or whether the antagonist wins. The third act is the moment that the audience has been waiting for since the beginning of the story; it's the reason why you built the story and told it. It's the phase in which you finally reveal to the audience the controlling idea that you had planned from the very beginning. According to K.M. Weiland, an award-winning author and writing mentor, "The third act is the moment we've all been waiting for—readers, writers, and characters alike. This last section of the story is the point. It's what we've been building up to all this time" (Weiland, 2012a).

At the end of the third act, you will have nothing left to say, and the audience will be satisfied by your story so well that they will talk about your story in the future. If you've built and told your story well, the audience will be so excited that they'll be ready to put the message you've conveyed into practice. Weiland also states, "By the time the third act is finished, all the salient questions must be answered, the conflict resolved one way or another, and the reader left with a feeling of satisfaction" (Weiland, 2012a). To be clear, your story has a deep meaning, which will finally become evident only after the third act. I like to think that with the third act your story doesn't end. Instead, it finds its fulfillment, its full realization, its manifestation. And if, as a good storyteller, you have done an excellent job, your audience will become the new storyteller of your story, because they will tell it to other audiences, even in other contexts. You will have accomplished your mission only if you hear others talk about your story in the future, because the audience will have digested it so much that they, themselves, will become ambassadors of your story. But you will see this later in the book.

Within the third act, there is a particular moment, called the *climax*, in which the resolution of the problem that you conducted in the first two acts of the story takes place. The climax is a special moment in the story—it's the moment you give your thirsty audience water to finally quench their thirst. However, before this moment of final resolution, the hero usually goes through a dark moment—a crisis—that highlights all the drama of the problem and brings its effects to their extreme consequences. This moment is given various names in cinema and novels, including crisis, third plot point, and so on. I call it the *Dark Night* for reasons I'll explain later. For now, I'll just tell you that I encountered the term *Dark Night* many years ago in other contexts, and it is still very dear to me today. I use it here to indicate this moment, in which the problem's effects, which stop the hero from reaching their goal, reach their peak.

The climax determines the story's conclusion. In cinema and novels, you can have two types of story fulfillment. In the first case, the hero reaches the object of desire (here, we're talking about *comedy*, or, in a business scenario, *success*); or the hero doesn't reach it, and this happens in the *tragedy* (or, in a business scenario, you call it *failure*). In the case of comedy, the hero solves their problem because they have become mature in the sense that they have developed the virtue to solve the problem. In the case of tragedy, however, the hero has understood how to solve the problem but is not mature enough to solve it (Booker, 2004). However, even in the case of tragedy, the hero must experience some change at the end of the story, in the sense that the story cannot end as it began. What the hero matures is the awareness of how to solve the problem, even if they don't have the skills or virtues to solve it and, therefore, reach the object of desire.

In data storytelling, the situation changes slightly. In addition to having the comedy and tragedy styles, there is a third type: the one in which the hero reaches the object of desire, *with* the audience helping them solve the problem. In this case, the audience is brought into the story and can influence the ending because they play an active role within the story. Think, for example, about temperature anomalies. Only the virtuous attitude of an audience of decision-makers can lead to the problem's solution. In data storytelling, therefore, the audience is called to intervene to change the negative course of the story through a series of next steps. Only if the audience puts the proposed suggestions into practice will the hero finally be able to solve their problem and reach the object of desire.

If the audience doesn't intervene in the story, however, the hero will be separated forever from their object of desire, and the story will end as a tragedy.

The structure of the third act, therefore, includes three subsequent steps:

- The Dark Night
- Climax
- Next steps

In the rest of this chapter, I analyze these three parts individually and then in the structure of the third act. Let's begin with the first part: the Dark Night.

The Dark Night

Many years ago, I enrolled in a two-year spiritual study to better understand everything that concerns the spirit and its relationship with matter. It involved taking about 10 courses a year, organized into biweekly lessons on Tuesday and Thursday afternoons. The courses took place in a large classroom, where we sat on a chair with a protruding and inclined armrest (very uncomfortable), on which we could take notes. At the time, I was still taking notes by hand and filling sheet after sheet with blue ink. One course was about John of the Cross, a sixteenth-century Spanish mystic and poet known for his profound spirituality and cofounding the Order of Discalced Carmelites with Teresa of Ávila. One of John of the Cross's writings is titled "The Dark Night" (John of the Cross, 2003), and it was from that moment that the desire to delve deeper into this topic was born in me.

> **NOTE** For John of the Cross, the "Dark Night" is a spiritual experience of profound purification, during which the soul goes through a period of aridity and inner suffering to get closer to God. This painful process is seen as a necessary path toward a mystical union with God, where the soul is freed from all imperfections.

From that moment, for me, the term *Dark Night* became particularly important, and this is why, when I had to choose the name to give to the hero's moment of crisis in the third act, I had no doubt: *it will be called Dark Night*, I thought, without hesitation.

Before deepening the dive into the Dark Night moment of the story, let's recap the story structure. Each story comprises three acts. In the first act, you present the hero and their context. The first act ends with the first plot point, where you introduce the problem. The second act describes the problem, by presenting the antagonist in the first pinch point and how they cause the problem the hero has. In the middle of the second act, there is the second plot point, where you show the contrast between the hero and the antagonist explicitly. The second act ends with the second pinch point, which reinforces the contrast between the hero and the antagonist. Figure 8.1 illustrates what you have learned so far.

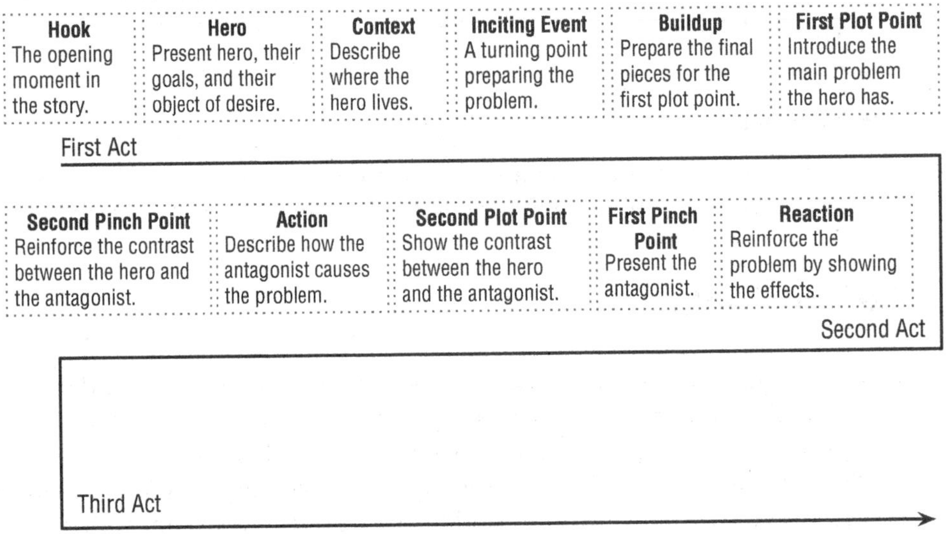

Hook	**Hero**	**Context**	**Inciting Event**	**Buildup**	**First Plot Point**
The opening moment in the story.	Present hero, their goals, and their object of desire.	Describe where the hero lives.	A turning point preparing the problem.	Prepare the final pieces for the first plot point.	Introduce the main problem the hero has.

First Act

Second Pinch Point	**Action**	**Second Plot Point**	**First Pinch Point**	**Reaction**
Reinforce the contrast between the hero and the antagonist.	Describe how the antagonist causes the problem.	Show the contrast between the hero and the antagonist.	Present the antagonist.	Reinforce the problem by showing the effects.

Second Act

Third Act

Figure 8.1: The story structure up to the second act

If you remember correctly, in the second act, you revealed to the audience the problem that the hero has and how the antagonist is the cause of it. In her book *Chart Spark*, Alli Torban, a senior data literacy advocate at Data Literacy LLC, says that a story must be *timely* in the sense that it must be current for the audience (Torban, 2023). Now is the time to take the problem to its extreme consequences. It is the hero's Dark Night. In this phase, your role is to convince the audience of the urgency of solving the problem, and they must act now; otherwise it will be too late.

So, how do you make the Dark Night so compelling? The answer depends on the type of data you have and the type of analysis you've conducted. In a bit, I suggest five possible ways to make the Dark Night in your story irresistible to the audience. These devices derive from a reworking of the seven story types identified by Adegboyega Ojo and Bahareh Heravi in their article "Patterns in Award Winning Data Storytelling: Story Types, Enabling Tools and Competences" (Ojo and Heravi, 2018). If you're curious, the seven story types identified by Ojo and Heravi follow:

- Refute claims
- Reveal unintended consequences
- Reveal anomalies/deficiencies
- Track changes in systems

- Reveal information of interest
- Enable deeper understanding
- Reveal information of increasing detail

For now, I won't explain the meaning of each story type. Figure 8.2 shows how I mapped these stories into the five types of Dark Night in data storytelling. Of course, these types aren't exhaustive; you can also think of other gimmicks. In all the cases, however, you should plan which type of Dark Night you want to include in your story, based on the objective you want to achieve with your story.

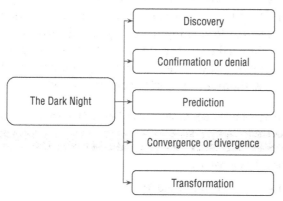

Figure 8.2: The five types of Dark Nights

The *Dark Night of Discovery* reveals new information, correlations, or trends that weren't previously known or considered. For example, you can reveal unexpected correlations of variables, significant data anomalies, an unexpected change that alters expectations, or an underestimated or unknown historical trend. Consider the example of temperature anomalies. The Dark Night of Discovery could be the revelation of a scientist's study, explaining, for example, that a glacier is melting much faster than expected due to rising global temperatures. This unexpected correlation suggests that current projections underestimate the speed of climate change, requiring urgent interventions.

The *Dark Night of Confirmation or Denial* consists of confirming hypotheses or denying expectations, based on the data analyzed. In the example of temperature anomalies, you could add new data confirming that heat waves and prolonged drought dramatically reduce crop yields in some agricultural areas.

The *Dark Night of Prediction* shows future trends, often with significant or urgent implications. For example, you can show a catastrophic projection, which predicts an imminent negative future if no actions are taken. Or you can describe the prediction of an imminent change. You can also show the prediction of a positive future or an opportunity that isn't previously evident. In the case of temperature anomalies, you could show forecasts of temperature increases in 20 years if no action is taken.

Another kind, the *Dark Night of Convergence or Divergence*, is based on the convergence or divergence of trends or datasets that lead to important conclusions. For example, in the case of temperature anomalies, you could show the difference between countries taking measures to reduce CO_2 emissions and those that are not.

The last type, the *Dark Night of Transformation*, highlights radical changes or transformations that are about to happen, often unexpectedly. For example, you can show an unexpected transformation or the discovery of new opportunities. In the example of temperature anomalies, you could show the effects of unexpected changes in ocean currents caused by rising temperatures.

In addition to the types of Dark Nights just described, you can imagine others based on what emerges from your data. Returning to the Ojo and Heravi story types mentioned earlier, Table 8.1 shows their mapping to the Dark Night types. I don't think this is particularly relevant to you; however, as a researcher, I ask you to be patient and let me review them in relation to scientific articles.

Table 8.1:   Mapping the Five Dark Night Types to the Seven Story Types Defined by Ojo and Heravi

TYPES OF DARK NIGHTS	STORY TYPES DEFINED BY OJO AND HERAVI
Discovery	Reveal information.
	Enable deeper understanding.
	Reveal information in increasing detail.
Confirmation or denial	Refute claims.
Prediction	Reveal unintended consequences.
Convergence or divergence	Reveal anomalies/deficiencies.
Transformation	Track changes in systems.

These types are a starting point for understanding what crises your hero can experience. In reality, each type of Dark Night produces different effects on the audience. Depending on the type of Dark Night used, you will probably get a different reaction from the audience.

In the case of the Dark Night of Discovery, for example, the revelation of new information might surprise the audience and create a sense of urgency and concern. The idea that hidden or underestimated factors accelerate the problem could lead to increased awareness and the need to act quickly. When you use a Confirmation or Denial Dark Night, the audience may experience frustration or a feeling of helplessness. The Dark Night of Prediction could cause the audience to worry about the impending consequences. This type of Dark Night can mobilize action or, conversely, induce a sense of uncertainty about the future, stimulating discussions about how to avoid or deal with predictions. The Dark Night of Convergence or Divergence might initially confuse, as the audience tries to understand how various seemingly unrelated factors influence the situation. However, once understood, this revelation leads to a greater awareness of complex dynamics, stimulating more critical thinking. Finally, in the Dark Night of Transformation, the revelation of radical changes or impending transformations might shock the audience, often leaving a sense of urgency to adapt to a new reality. Table 8.2 summarizes the audience effects just described.

Table 8.2: Mapping the Five Types of Dark Nights and Possible Reactions in the Audience

DARK NIGHT TYPE	DESCRIPTION	AUDIENCE REACTION	EXAMPLE
Discovery	The revelation of new, unknown, or underestimated information, correlations, or trends that change the understanding of the current situation.	Surprise and alarm	Describe a scientist's study, explaining that a glacier is melting much faster than expected due to rising global temperatures.
Confirmation or Denial	Confirmation of hypotheses or denial of previous expectations, based on analyzed data, which requires a revision of strategies or hypotheses.	Frustration or resignation	Show new data confirming that heat waves and prolonged drought dramatically reduce crop yields in some agricultural areas.
Prediction	Projection of future trends, often with significant or urgent implications, which outline possible positive or negative future scenarios.	Anxiety and worry	Show forecasts of temperature increases in 20 years if no action is taken.
Convergence or Divergence	Highlight the convergence or divergence of trends or datasets, leading to new conclusions or revealing unexpected contrasts.	Confusion or growing awareness	Show the difference between countries taking measures to reduce CO_2 emissions and those that are not.
Transformation	Highlight radical, often unexpected changes or transformations that foreshadow a new reality or require immediate adaptation.	Shock and need for adaptation	Show the effects of unexpected changes in ocean currents caused by rising temperatures.

The Dark Night isn't the ending point of the story. Its role is to pave the way toward the final battle between the hero and the antagonist. After encountering the Dark Night, the audience, regardless of the reactions they may have felt, will ask themselves the following:

- What will happen now?
- What will become of the hero?
- Who will come out on top?

It's your job to reveal this to them in the climax. "When you reach the point of maximum tension, jump ahead to the climax" (Hamand, 2014).

The Climax

The climax is the hero's last action. "No tomorrow. No second chance," says Robert McKee in his famous book *Story* (McKee, 1997). During the climax, "the audience experiences a sense of pleasure and relief, causing them to love the story" (Miller, 2010). After the climax, there will be no further story-significant actions on the part of the hero. Only actions to close the story remain, but those do not add any details. There will only be the "happily ever after" part if the story is a success story or a scene of a desolate environment in the case of a failure story. The climax is the moment of maximum intensity and suspense in the story and is often surprising (Masterclass, 2021).

The term *climax* derives from Ancient Greek, κλῖμαξ (klîmax), meaning staircase, ladder. Metaphorically speaking, the climax is the highest step on the ladder that the hero and the audience have climbed during the story. After the climax, the story is concluded, and everything that follows is a set of ancillary elements. To be clear, post-climax, the audience descends the ladder, satisfied with what they were able to experience at the top of the ladder.

According to Maggie Hamand, author of the book *Creative Writing Exercises for Dummies*, the climax of a story must resolve the central narrative question posed in the first act. In a detective story, this is the revelation of the murderer's identity; in a romance, it's when the characters choose to commit to each other. In a quest, the climax occurs when the hero attains their goal, while in a tragedy, it marks the hero's downfall (Hamand, 2014).

Let's try to take stock of what has been said so far with a simple example. Lately, my youngest son, Antonio, has been trying to learn to ride a bike without training wheels. You can imagine his challenge as a story in which the hero is Antonio, the object of desire is riding a bike without training wheels, and the problem is that he hasn't learned yet. This story can be summarized in four main moments, as shown in Figure 8.3.

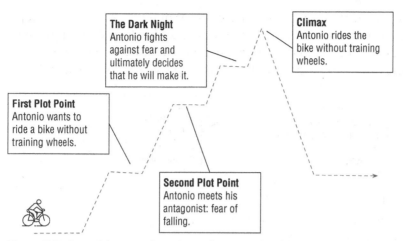

Figure 8.3: Antonio's story of wanting to learn to ride a bike without training wheels

With the first plot point, Antonio encounters the problem for the first time: riding a bike without training wheels. This is the point of no return. To go back would mean reassembling the wheels on the bike again and being considered a small child. This is not acceptable for Antonio, so he is pushed into the story. After some initial attempts, Antonio encounters his true enemy: the fear of falling. And this happens in the second plot point. As you can see from Figure 8.3, the story progresses, and Antonio climbs a ladder. As Antonio's attempts continue, the situation becomes more complex because he cannot succeed. This battle continues with ups and downs. At a certain point, Antonio thinks he won't make it because the fear of falling is too high. Thus, he enters the Dark Night (also known as the third plot point). As long as everyone encourages him, he eventually decides to succeed. At the top of the ladder (i.e., climax), Antonio succeeds in his aim of riding a bike without training wheels. The story can now end. At the time I'm writing this chapter, Antonio has just reached the climax after having fought for a long time, and he celebrated happily.

If the definition of climax is easy to understand in a novel, film, or Antonio's story, perhaps it isn't immediately clear what it is in data storytelling. What exactly is the climax in data storytelling? Let's explain it through an example. Consider the sales of a product over time. Suppose you have historical data that shows that, at some point, sales have dropped due to a reduction in product quality. Then, once the quality of the product is restored, product sales begin to rise again. Figure 8.4 summarizes the various story phases, with a focus on the climax, which is the moment of the problem's resolution.

After the initial phase in which you describe the product (i.e., first act), which I'm not detailing here, there is the first plot point, which shows the decline in product sales. In the second plot point, the product hero encounters the cause of its problem, that is, its antagonist: a low product quality. Then the plot enters the Dark Night, in which the extreme consequences of the problem are shown if action isn't taken immediately. Finally, in the climax, the story shows how the problem was solved, thanks to the reintroduction of quality into the product. You might summarize this story simply with a graph, as shown in Figure 8.5.

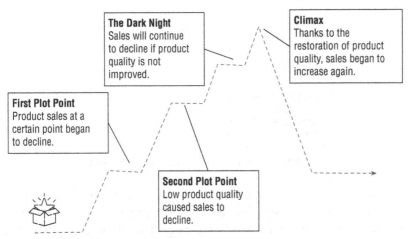

Figure 8.4: The sales history of the product

Figure 8.5: Product sales story represented in a single scene, with a single graph

However, the simple graph shows the entire story in a single scene, where you don't give the audience the opportunity to rejoice with the hero at the climax, after having suffered with them throughout the previous story. Therefore,

I suggest using a separate scene for the climax to avoid anticipating the answer to all the questions already when the questions are asked. It's the suspense that binds the audience to the story. If you reveal the climax ahead of time, you will lose the audience later.

What I have told you so far is fine if you already know the solution to the problem. What if you don't know it, however? Consider the example of temperature anomalies, where the hero is temperature, and the antagonist is CO_2 emissions. What could be the climax in this case? To find the answer, ask yourself this question: who wins the battle, temperature or CO_2 emissions? The answer to this question isn't simple. We'll soon see how to structure a climax in which you don't have a precise answer simply because you aren't aware of it. A quick answer could be asking experts to provide a solution, but what if even the experts didn't have an answer? We'll see it shortly.

Until the climax, the hero and the audience wait as suffering patients wait for a cure (McKee, 1997). The climax, therefore, is the outcome of the final fight between the hero and antagonist. The climax's revelation can also be brief, a single moment, necessary for the audience to understand not only what happened but also why it happened. During the climax's revelation, "You should show the criteria and values you discovered and used to find the solution" (Gonçalves, 2022).

The outcome of the whole story depends on how you build the climax. A well-constructed story with a hasty climax disappoints the expectations of the audience, who will be disappointed by the entire story. The climax must be dramatic, believable, and carry an emotional punch (Hamand, 2014). Indeed, if you have very little time or space to tell your story, you can summarize it in just the climactic scene. This scene is the moment of truth of the entire story, and you don't need tons of pages to tell it. The simpler and clearer this scene, the greater the audience's level of understanding of the entire story. A successful climax depends on how much you know your audience. You'll see how to adapt the climax based on the audience in the next chapters. For now, let me explain what the climax is and you can insert it in your story.

There are two climax types, as shown in Figure 8.6: confrontation and revelation (Hamand, 2014).

The climax of *confrontation* shows precisely who wins the battle between the hero and antagonist. Usually, only one of the characters wins. Obviously, if the hero wins, they reach the object of desire. Otherwise, they lose it. Even if the hero loses the battle, it must be clear that they have developed a new awareness, which has made them better than at the beginning of the story. Nobody wants to hear a story where nothing changes after the hero encounters a problem.

The second climax type is the *revelation*, which adds information that explains everything that's happened before or is the answer to the hero's problem.

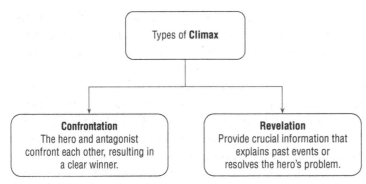

Figure 8.6: The two climax types

To understand the difference between the two types of climaxes, consider the examples shown in Table 8.3. The table takes some examples from the previous chapter and adds two columns relating to the two types.

Table 8.3: Examples of Stories Extracted from the Data, Enriched with the Two Types of Climaxes: Confrontation and Revelation

DATASET	PLOT	CONFRONTATION CLIMAX	REVELATION CLIMAX
Air pollution levels in different cities	The air quality (hero) wants to remain clean (object of desire), but high levels of pollution (problem) due to polluting industries (antagonist) prevent it from doing so.	After adopting new environmental regulations, polluting industries are forced to comply.	An additional hidden cause, such as an undetected industrial gas leak, exacerbated the emissions.
Blood sugar levels of diabetic patients	The health of a patient (hero) can be guaranteed if he maintains normal sugar levels (object of desire), but spikes in blood sugar (problem) caused by a diet rich in sugar (antagonist) put him at risk.	Thanks to the introduction of psychological support, patients can reduce sugars from their diet.	External causes, such as the side effects of a drug, aggravate high-sugar levels.

DATASET	PLOT	CONFRONTATION CLIMAX	REVELATION CLIMAX
Number of road accidents in a city	Road safety (hero) is guaranteed if the number of accidents is reduced (object of desire), but an increase in road accidents (problem) caused by distracted and imprudent driving (antagonist) doesn't enable this objective to be achieved.	An extensive prevention campaign leads to a significant drop in accidents.	A new data analysis reveals that a previously ignored intersection was the hub of the crashes.
The trend in university enrollments in recent years	The university (hero) wants to increase the number of enrollments (object of desire), but a decrease in enrollments (problem) caused by an increase in fees (antagonist) doesn't enable the objective to be achieved.	Thanks to an extensive advertising campaign, university enrollments increased.	It turns out that the cause of the drop in enrollment was the lack of a certain in-demand degree program.
Energy consumption of a city	Energy sustainability (hero) can be guaranteed if energy consumption is reduced (object of desire), but the increase in energy consumption (problem) caused by an inefficient use of resources (antagonist) doesn't enable the objective to be achieved.	The city implements an intelligent energy management system, drastically reducing consumption.	Much of the power consumption was due to undetected network leaks, which have now been resolved.

As you can see from the table, these types of climaxes are suitable if you already know the solution to the problem and want to tell it as a story. This happens, for example, in the case of historical data, where both the problem and the solution appeared in the past. But what if you still don't know the solution? How do you set up the climax in this case? Check out the next section.

Next Steps

The next steps represent the last story phase. In cinema and novels, the next steps are typically called *resolution* and represent the closing scene of the story, which adds nothing to the climax, but only serves to avoid closing the story directly with the climax. It is the wedding scene between the hero and his girlfriend in love stories, the scene of what happens after arresting the culprit in a detective story, and so on. In her book, *Stories That Stick*, Kindra Hall states that the third and final phase is the new normal. It is the moment when you share with the audience what the situation is like after the explosion, when you tell them what you know, why you are wiser and stronger, and what you have improved (or are still trying to improve) as a result. It can be a moral, a customer's happily ever after using your product, an invitation to act (Hall, 2019).

In data storytelling, you can use the next steps in the final story phase to invite the audience to do something (Lo Duca, 2024). The next steps, therefore, become a real call to action for the audience. You can insert the next steps at two different points in your story: during the climax and after the climax, as shown in Figure 8.7.

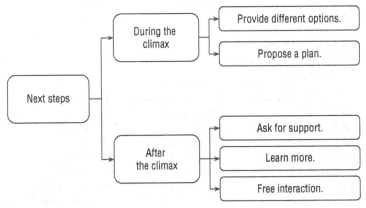

Figure 8.7: Possible placements of the next steps in the story

Insert the next steps during the climax to make the audience become a new character in the story—the critical character who helps the hero solve the problem. Use this type of next step if you don't yet know the solution to your problem. The message to be conveyed is this: the hero will achieve their object of desire if the audience acts in a certain way. In this way, the story becomes interactive, which is typical of the world of video games, where the player determines the story's actions. In his book *Fundamentals of Game Design*, Ernest Adams says that an interactive story is a story where the player actively participates by making choices or contributing actions to shape the narrative (Adams, 2013). This precisely happens with the next steps inserted during the climax: the audience's actions contribute to the problem's solution. There are basically two ways to insert the next steps during the climax. The first way is to provide the audience with several *options* from which to choose. Each option, if applied, will lead to the total or partial solution of the hero in the story. In the case of the story relating to the temperature increase, the options could include various virtuous attitudes to be put into practice to reduce CO_2 emissions, such as the personal use of green means of transport, respect for the environment, and so on.

The second type of next step to be included during the climax is the proposal of an *action plan* to solve the hero's problem, that is, a series of subsequent steps that the audience can put into practice. In the case of a temperature increase, the next steps could be the following: starting from reducing the use of the car and then moving on to the use of the bicycle. Obviously, these next steps are highly dependent upon the audience, so during the story planning phase, define generic next steps. Then, you will detail them during the delivery phase. You will see this starting in the next chapter. For now, focus on the generic concept of the next steps.

In case the climax already offers the solution to the hero's problem, there is no need to insert the next steps during the climax. Instead, add the next steps in the final part of the story, right after the climax. This way, you will give the audience the *mission* to continue the story after encountering it. And I say mission because we talk about mission. Telling the stories extracted from the data is the mission of those who want to give voice to the people that data represents. The audience's job isn't only to listen to the stories you will tell but also to be part of that mission to tell the story again to other audiences. The audience, therefore, has the mission of keeping the story alive.

There are three types of next steps to insert after the climax. The first next step is to *ask for audience support*, such as sharing the story in their networks. The second type is *learn more*, which consists of asking the audience to delve deeper into the topic covered in the story; for example, by proposing to read additional material. The last type is *free interaction* with the story, in the case of an interactive story to be enjoyed offline, or *discussion*, in the case of a story told in real time in front of the audience. The choice of one or another next steps type depends on the story objective. If you remember, in the previous chapters, I said that a story can have one of the following three objectives: to inform, entertain, or persuade. Based on this, you can use a specific next steps type, as shown in the decision tree of Figure 8.8.

The tree starts with the question "What is the goal of the story?" and branches into the three main objectives: inform, entertain, and persuade. If the goal is to inform or entertain, insert the next steps after the climax. Instead, for persuasive stories, the tree directly suggests inserting the next steps during the climax. Don't worry if you don't understand everything now. In the next chapter, I'll deep-dive into the audience objective, and I hope everything will be clearer.

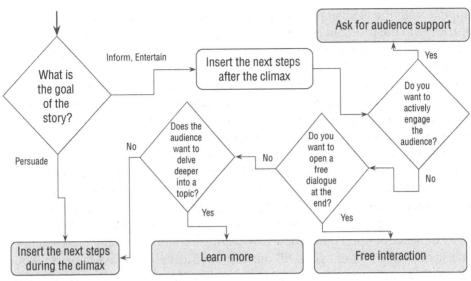

Figure 8.8: The decision tree for the next steps choice

You might think that after the next steps, the story is over. Instead, it's precisely now that the story begins. If you've done a good job, your story will start to have an impact right after you tell it. It is, therefore, essential to propose the next steps within the reach of your audience. You cannot propose to an audience of decision-makers to implement the code to improve the monitoring of a product, nor propose to an audience of technicians to decide on the next strategies to follow. I'd like to conclude this part with an ancient axiom of scholastic philosophy that I think summarizes the task of adapting the story to an audience. The axiom is: "Quidquid recipitur ad modum recipientis recipitur" (what is received in a subject is received according to the capacity of the recipient's nature). This means you should propose as the next steps something that the audience can realize. You can't propose to solve the problem of global temperature increase to an audience of professionals, because they don't have the means to implement this action. Instead, you can propose to them to implement a system that monitors the global temperature increase because they have the skills to do this. We will see in the next chapter how to adapt the story and the next steps for the audience. First, let's put the pieces of the third act together and see how to structure it.

Structuring the Third Act

Imagine that you haven't eaten in a long time and feel hungry. At a certain point, while walking on a street, you see a pastry shop and decide to buy a tasty slice of cake. Just as you are about to enter, however, a clerk comes out of the pastry shop and tells you that the shop is closing. Your sense of frustration is very high, while your hunger rises. You talk to the clerk and explain to them that you can't wait until tomorrow and that you would be immensely grateful if they could sell you that slice of cake. The clerk is initially perplexed, but after your persuasive conversation, they understand your needs and make an exception. They sell you that piece of cake. All happy, you can finally enjoy it sitting on a park bench.

You can divide that simple story into three acts. The first act describes the scene where you haven't eaten for a long time, you're hungry, and you see a pastry shop. In the second act, you encounter the antagonist, the clerk, who is closing the pastry shop. In the third act, you fight to convince the clerk to delay the shop closure and finally eat your piece of cake. As you can see from this simple little story, the third act is where things get complicated, and the story becomes more compelling.

The *third act* is the last part of the story and should last about a quarter of the entire story. It consists of three main moments: the Dark Night, the climax, and the next steps or resolution. I formalize the structure of the third act, starting from its sequential structure in the novels, as highlighted in *5 Secrets of Story Structure: How to Write a Novel That Stands Out* (Weiland, 2016). Figure 8.9 shows the timeline of the third act in novels.

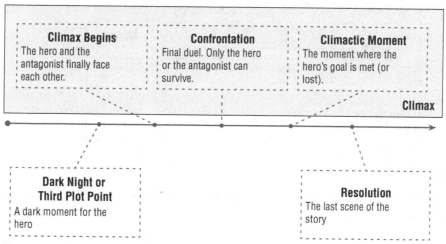

Figure 8.9: The structure of the third act in cinema and novels

The third act starts with the Dark Night or third plot point, representing a dark moment in the hero's life. Next is the climax, which is divided into three phases. The first phase is the beginning of the climax, in which the hero and the antagonist meet. In the previous example of the pastry shop, the beginning of the climax corresponds with you explicitly asking the clerk to keep the shop open. The second phase is the confrontation, during which there is the final battle, in which only one of the two can survive. During confrontation, the clerk tries to convince you that they must close the shop because they must go home. You also try to convince the clerk to keep the shop open because you are hungry. The confrontation, in this case, is a verbal discussion, but you could also imagine a different type of battle. The climax ends with the climactic moment, in which the hero's goal is definitively achieved or lost. In the pastry example, the climactic moment is when you eventually convince the clerk to keep the shop open. The last phase of the story is the resolution, which corresponds to the last scene and releases all the emotions of the audience or, as Weiland says, a little emotional mopping up (Weiland, 2012b). In the previous example, this last phase is when you eat your piece of cake.

In the case of data storytelling, the structure of the third act is similar to that of novels and cinema, with the only difference being that you can include the next steps directly in the climax or later, depending on whether the audience is essential to solving the problem. Figure 8.10 shows the structure of the third act if the climax also includes the next steps.

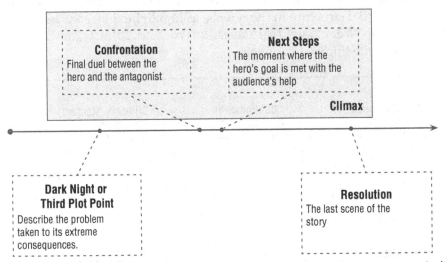

Figure 8.10: The structure of the third act in data storytelling when the next steps are included in the climax

The third act starts as usual with the Dark Night, in which you describe the problem taken to extreme consequences. Then you move on to the climax, in which you explain how the hero can defeat the antagonist and achieve the goal only through the intervention of the audience (in next steps). You can add a final scene (the resolution) describing the hero's life after the audience helps them achieve their goal.

In the second type of third act, the hero alone solves the problem without the audience's support (or loses the object of desire forever), as shown in Figure 8.11.

Losing the object of desire means that the story is a story of failure. Still, the audience can learn something from this type of story. However, in almost all stories the hero solves the problem.

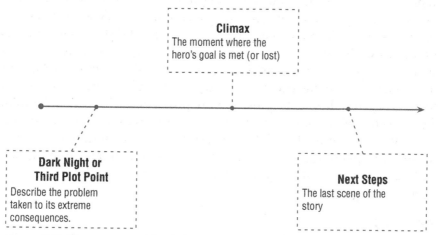

Figure 8.11: The structure of the third act in data storytelling when the next steps are inserted after the climax

This structure is simpler and more linear. Use it when you have historical data or when you already know who wins the game between the hero and antagonist.

Let's apply the structure of the third act to the example of temperature anomalies described in the previous chapters. Which of the two structures can you apply? Since, at the time of writing, the problem is still not solved, opt for the scheme in which you incorporate the next steps into the climax. In Chapter 3, "Making a Successful Data-Driven Story," you saw a preliminary outline of the third act (see Figure 8.12).

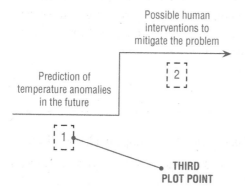

Figure 8.12: The third act of the story on global temperature anomalies from 1860 to today. We use two scenes, which begin with the exacerbation of the problem (i.e., third plot point) and then end with the possible solutions.

The structure described in Figure 8.10 inserts the next steps within the climax. To complete it, you can add a moment of resolution, in which you describe the positive effects of human intervention to reduce CO_2 emissions.

You have reached the end of this exciting story-building journey. Now that you have completed the third act, your story is complete, and you can open a bit of sparkling wine because you have completed the most difficult and arduous part of the story. I hope I've convinced you that telling a data-driven story is serious and requires some pre-planning. You can't just show a crude data graph and hope the audience understands exactly what it means. So, remember to divide the story into three acts: presentation, problem, and solution. Nothing simpler. Then follow the structure of each act that I have described so far, and you will have the common thread that you can present from time to time as you see fit. After this planning phase, you're finally ready to move on to the next step: telling your story to the world. So, what are you waiting for?

Takeaways

- The third act of the story consists of three parts: the Dark Night, the climax, and the next steps.
- The Dark Night, or the third plot point, is when the problem is brought to its extreme consequences. There are five types of Dark Nights: discovery, confirmation or denial, prediction, convergence or divergence, and transformation.
- The climax is where you reveal the problem's solution if you know it. If you do not, you invite the audience into the story to help the hero solve the problem.
- The next steps are what the audience is invited to do after encountering the story. You can insert the next steps during or after the climax. With these steps, your story ends, but if you have done a good job, the audience's action time begins after the next steps.

References

Adams, E. 2013. *Fundamentals of Game Design*. Indianapolis: New Riders.

Booker, C. 2004. *The Seven Basic Plots: Why We Tell Stories*. London: A&C Black.

Gonçalves, A. 2022. *Social Media Analytics Strategy: Using Data to Optimize Business Performance*. New York: Apress.

Hall, K. 2019. *Stories That Stick. How Storytelling Can Captivate Customers, Influence Audiences, and Transform Your Business.* Nashville: HarperCollins Leadership.

Hamand, M. 2014. *Creative Writing Exercises for Dummies.* Hoboken: Dummies.

John of the Cross. 2003. *Dark Night of the Soul.* Mineola: Dover Publications.

Lo Duca, A. 2024. *Data Storytelling with Altair and AI.* Shelter Island: Manning Publications.

Masterclass 2021. *Mastering Story Arc: How to Structure a Climax.* Retrieved on August 8, 2024 from `https://www.masterclass.com/articles/how-to-structure-a-climax`

McKee, R. 1997. *Story: Substance, Structure, Style and the Principles of Screenwriting.* Manhattan: Regan Books.

Miller, Donald. 2010. *Building a StoryBrand: Clarify Your Message so Customers Will Listen.* United States of America: HarperCollins Leadership.

Ojo, A., & Heravi, B. 2018. *Patterns in award winning data storytelling: Story types, enabling tools and competences. Digital Journalism* 6(6): 693–718.

Torban, A. 2023. *Chart Spark: Harness Your Creativity in Data Communication to Stand Out and Innovate.* Bellevue: Data Literacy Press.

Weiland, K. M. 2012a. *The Secrets of Story Structure, Pt. 9: The third act.* Retrieved on August 8, 2024 from `https://www.helpingwriters becomeauthors.com/secrets-of-story-structure-pt-9-third`

Weiland, K. M. 2012b. *The Secrets of Story Structure, Pt. 10: The Climax.* Retrieved on August 8, 2024 from `https://www.helpingwritersbecome authors.com/secrets-of-story-structure-pt-10-climax`

Weiland, K. M. 2016. *The 5 Secrets of Story Structure: How to Write a Novel That Stands Out. PenForASword Publishing.* `https://www.kmweiland.com/wp-content/uploads/5soss.pdf`

CHAPTER
9

From Making to Delivering
a Data-Driven Story

Some time ago, I got a life lesson from my then five-year-old son Antonio. We were in the waiting room of my son's music school, and to pass the time, he asked me to look at a recipe magazine. I accepted his request, picked him up, and began leafing through the magazine. At a certain point, we found a recipe that seemed quite tasty; it was a recipe for coffee creme caramel, accompanied by a beautiful photograph that made our mouths water. It was as if by instinct, I took my smartphone from my bag and took a photo of the recipe, in the hope of being able to make it later.

My son asked me the reason for that photo, and I told him that I was interested in the recipe and that we would prepare it too. He was happy to hear this answer, unaware of the reality. If you only knew how many photos I keep on my smartphone of events, situations, or things that have been forgotten over time! But this time it was different. The next day, Antonio came to me with his big eyes and asked me to prepare the creme caramel photographed the day before. To tell the truth, I had completely forgotten, just as I constantly forget to consult my notes or photos. But he did not. With his little voice, he called me to attention: "Mom," he told me, "You took the photo so we could prepare it later, so now we must cook it!" And so, we went to the kitchen and prepared the famous coffee creme caramel.

The dessert was enjoyable. However, to tell the truth, the result wasn't that great. The creme caramel wasn't as good as it appeared in the magazine photo.

The message that Antonio sent me was twofold. On the one hand, you must select only the things that are truly interesting to avoid a lot of noise, and on the other, you must find the time to create the chosen things.

Data storytelling is the same: You must select only the exciting things and leave aside those that make noise. If you have too many charts, don't try to fit them all into your story. Select only those that move the story forward. The rest is noise. And that's what you've done so far, by building a story from your data. You have explored and analyzed your data and extracted an essential discovery from your data.

Your discovery is independent of the people to which you want to communicate it. It exists because it emerged from the data and absolutely cannot depend on the people to which you want to communicate it. What you have done so far, by reading this book, is to transform your discovery from the data into a data-driven story: *data-driven* because you built it starting from data, and *story* because it has a plot and characters. You relied only on the data and sources linked to them, also including the opinion of experts. Your story is now powerful from a credibility point of view, because it is anchored in something certain (i.e., the data). So, your story is real: It's about your discovery. It is a data-driven story in the true sense of the word.

For now, though, your story is in your head, or at most on a rough sheet of paper (or on a PC text document). This is because you have completed the pre-production phase, which, in cinematic terms, corresponds to writing a screenplay. Your task now is to transform it into something concrete, visible, and usable. You must now move on to the production phase, with the implementation of the individual scenes of the story, and postproduction, with the editing of the scenes according to a well-defined criterion.

With editing, you conclude the story-making phase, in which you have implemented the rough draft of your story. It's time to communicate your data-driven story to the world. Let's clarify one concept: The story is always the same, but the audience can change. So, if the story's content is always the same, the form you present changes from time to time based on the audience. This is why I thought of dividing the making phase from the book's delivery phase. The making phase concerns the content, and the delivery phase concerns the form. Making a story means defining its message and structuring it with characters and a plot. Delivering a story means adapting it to a specific audience.

More precisely, in this chapter, you will see how to complete the making phase and move from making to delivery, with a particular focus on these topics:

- Completing the making phase

- Production

- Postproduction

- Starting the delivery phase

Let's start with the first step: completing the making phase.

Completing the Making Phase

In the first chapter, you saw how making a story comprises three main phases, as shown in Figure 9.1: preproduction, production, and postproduction.

Figure 9.1: The three phases of making a data-driven story include preproduction, production, and postproduction

In the preproduction phase, you define the story's script. Starting with the data, you extract the story's theme, subject, and scenes from the data supplied. During this phase, you also define your entire story with the three-act structure. In a nutshell, you can summarize the structure in three acts in presentation-problem-solution. As you have seen in the previous chapters, this summary is very reductive, but it still enables you to focus on how the story evolves. At this stage, it's crucial to consider what sparks the need for a data-driven story. What drives you to turn data into a narrative? Whether uncovering a critical insight, solving a pressing problem, or meeting stakeholder demands, identifying this trigger adds clarity and purpose to your process. This moment—the catalyst for data storytelling—grounds your narrative in real needs and ensures it serves a meaningful purpose.

In his book *Effective Data Storytelling*, Brent Dykes defines the storytelling arc with a structure very similar to the one proposed in this book: hook, rising action, climax, thinking, and next steps (Dykes, 2019).

During the preproduction phase, you don't worry about the channel you will use to tell your story, nor the audience you want to address your story to. Just focus on the story's structure and the message you want to convey.

In the production phase, write the text and the accompanying visual elements consistent with the story you have just written. In this phase, divide your story into sequences and then into scenes that more or less correspond to the pieces of your story, and choose the tool to implement them. For example, you can implement the first plot point using a sequence of three scenes with three different graphs or two graphs and a text element.

In the final postproduction phase, choose the order to narrate the scenes and eliminate some that aren't necessary for the narrative. In this phase, you also select the channel to deliver the story. For example, you can decide to present your story through a video, a presentation, or a journalistic article.

After the making phase, you start the delivering phase, in which you adapt your story to your type of audience. Whatever your audience will be, the general structure (i.e., plot and characters), the scenes you have implemented, and the channel you have chosen to tell your story remain the same.

In reality, even if the production and postproduction phases belong to the making phase, they also start the delivery phase. Starting from these two phases, you can already think about how you will present your story to the audience. So, if it is true that the implementation of individual story scenes may be independent of the audience, it is also true that the individual details you add to each scene will depend on the audience. I propose you implement complete scenes as much as possible (with numerical information, linked to the context, etc.), and then, during the delivery phase, you will decide which elements to cut based on the audience. However, if you don't have time to do all this work, already in the production phase, think about the audience and adapt your scenes and the means of communication, based on it.

Let's move on to how to implement the defined scenes, that is, the production phase.

Production: Data Story Shot

In the production phase, proceed with creating story sequences and scenes. A sequence is a collection of scenes. A sequence corresponds to a piece of the story (e.g., the hook, a plot point, the climax, etc.). In Chapter 3, "Making a Successful Data-Driven Story," you saw four main types of sequences:

- *Temporal sequences* focus on change over time.
- *Spatial sequences* highlight the comparison between two or more places.
- *Relational sequences* highlight relationships or differences.
- *Cause–effect sequences* show the factors at play in a story and describe their causes.

In his book, Dykes extends this list by also adding drill-down, zoom-out, cluster, and outline (Dykes, 2019). *Drill-down sequences* enable you to explore a topic at progressively deeper levels, *zoom-out sequences* give a broader perspective by connecting individual details to a larger context, *cluster sequences* group related scenes to highlight common themes, and *outline sequences* provide a high-level story overview, guiding the audience through a structured path.

A *sequence* comprises one or more scenes. Each scene can be seen as a story fragment represented through visual and textual elements that communicate a clear and coherent message (Clabough, 2014). To implement a scene, you must focus on just a single action that the hero or other characters perform. Each scene has a specific goal of moving the story forward. A scene must be clear and immediately understandable to the audience. It occurs in a specific place, in a defined period, and involves well-defined characters. You can think of a scene as a mini story within the larger narrative, with its own structure (Hamand, 2014). You can use different tools based on the content of the scene and the message to convey. In this book, I will not focus on existing tools but define the general concepts. Then, you can use the tool you like best to implement the various scenes. For example, if you are a programmer, you can think about implementing scenes in Python or R. If you use style sheets like Excel every day, you can implement scenes using Excel. If you are a fan of Power BI, use that. You can also use PowerPoint or other tools to make presentations. Whichever tool you use, you have eight scene types available in each, as shown in Figure 9.2.

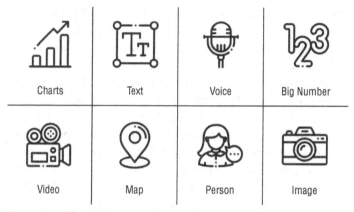

Figure 9.2: The eight types of scenes for the representation of a piece of the story

Charts are the primary tool for visualizing data and can take various forms, such as bar charts, timelines, scatter plots, or maps. The choice of graph type depends on the data's nature and the scene's objective. For example, a line graph can help show trends over time, while a scatter plot can highlight relationships between variables. As a good data analyst, you will surely know which graph shows your scene best. Just remember not to overload the chart with too much information. The graph must precisely represent only what you want to say in your scene, without adding other details.

Consider, for example, a scene that must present the second plot point, contrasting the hero's temperature and the antagonist's CO_2 emissions. In this case, a possible graph shows the trend lines of temperature and CO_2 emissions. It makes no sense to also include trend lines of precipitation or ocean-rise levels over time in this graph. Remember, the scene must be clear and have a single goal: moving the story forward. Remove all frills and implement only what is helpful in the economy of the story.

The second type of scene is the *text*. Use it to provide context, explain data, or introduce new concepts. In some cases, text may be the primary means of conveying a complex message that cannot be adequately represented with a graphic. The text must be concise and closely linked to the data it accompanies. An alternative to the text is the *voice*, if you present your story directly in the first person. In this case, you can write on a piece of paper the text corresponding to the scenes you have chosen to implement as scenes, and then you can read them or, better yet, repeat them in your own words during your presentation. A particular type of text is the *Big Number*, which is a single number or key metric that summarizes a critical aspect of the story. The Big Number is valid for drawing the audience's attention to an essential piece of data, avoiding overloading it with too much information. It is an effective technique for focusing on a solid and immediate message.

Another type of scene is *video*, such as animations that show the evolution of data over time or highlight gradual changes that would be difficult to capture with a static image. Videos are especially useful when you want to create a strong emotional impact, for example, by showing the visual effect of an environmental variable that changes over time.

Other scenes include *geographic maps* to represent geospatial data. Use them to show regional differences, geographic trends, or the distribution of a phenomenon. For example, you can use a thematic map to highlight the temperature value over different geographical areas. If you remember, in Chapter 3, we saw a map released by the National Oceanic and Atmospheric Administration (NOAA) of temperature anomalies in 1860 (see Figure 9.3). You can use this map as a scene in the buildup phase of your story, where you prepare the final pieces for the first plot point (i.e., where you describe the hero's problem—the fact that temperatures are rising).

Another type of scene you can use only in live presentations is a *real person* who acts as a sidekick. It can be an expert or the famous human case we saw in the previous chapters regarding the sidekick. In this case, you must have someone willing to come and act as a witness during your presentation.

A final type of scene is the *image*, which visually presents content. For example, you can show a photograph of a melting glacier or a desert to convey the idea of drought. Use images to capture your audience's attention or create an immediate emotional impact.

So far, I have presented you with different types of scenes as if they were watertight compartments. In reality, the most effective approach is often to use a combination of techniques. For example, you can start a scene with a graph to present the data, add text to explain the context, and then end with a Big Number to highlight the most relevant conclusion. It all depends on your skills and graphics choices.

When implementing a scene, in addition to considering scene types, consider adding *special effects*, which can significantly improve the audience experience, increase engagement, and make the narrative more memorable (Parikh, 2024).

Use these additional effects to emphasize key messages, create a specific atmosphere, and guide the audience through the story. The special effects that you can use involve the five senses, as shown in Figure 9.4.

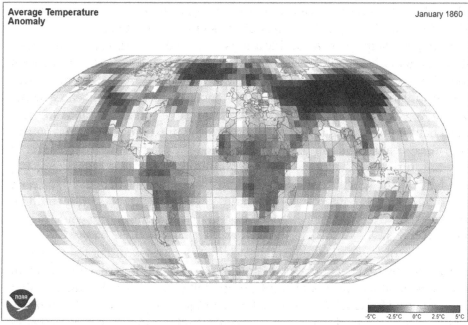

Average Temperature Anomaly

January 1860

-5°C   -2.5°C   0°C   2.5°C   5°C

Figure 9.3: A possible implementation of the buildup phase in the first act shows the plani-sphere with global temperature anomalies in 1860

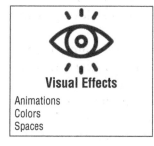

Visual Effects

Animations
Colors
Spaces

Sound Effects

Music
Ambient sound
Sonorification

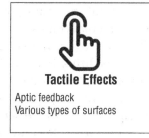

Tactile Effects

Aptic feedback
Various types of surfaces

Smell Effects

Perfumes

Taste Effects

Tastings of flavors

Figure 9.4: The possible special effects to include in a scene

Visual effects make data presentation more attractive. For example, you can use animations to show changes over time or to guide the audience through a graph. You can also play with colors, shadows, or lighting effects to highlight the most important data. This helps guide the audience's attention to the crucial points of the message. For example, you might change the color of a bar in a diagram to indicate a critical threshold or significant change.

Sound effects help create a specific atmosphere and underline particular narrative moments. You could add background music to influence the audience's mood and set the story's tone. Slow, thoughtful music can be used for stories with serious or emotional themes, while more dynamic music can accompany more energetic or optimistic stories. You can also add ambient sounds, which help immerse the audience in a specific context. For example, you can use nature sounds to accompany a story about the environment, while traffic noise can emphasize the theme of urban pollution. You can also consider using sound effects for specific data, for example, to accentuate changes in the data or to signal critical moments. For example, a "click" or "pop" sound could be used every time a given key appears, or a more dramatic sound could signal a crossed threshold.

In the case of *tactile effects*, use materials that change texture or temperature, such as surfaces that heat up or cool down, to represent different environmental conditions or situations. For example, if you tell your story using devices that support haptic feedback (like smartphones or tablets), you can add vibrations or haptic feedback to signal essential events. In the previous chapters, I suggested changing the environment's temperature to make the audience experience the discomfort caused by the increase in temperature anomalies. You can also include tactile experiences, such as touching smooth or textured surfaces, to represent increasing or decreasing humidity or temperature levels in an environmental context.

The *smell effects* help create a deep connection with the story, mainly if you use scents diffused at specific times to evoke particular settings. You can even think about the timed diffusion of fragrances. Using these effects helps make the story more engaging, but be careful not to overdo it, avoiding excess. The principle is always the same: use sensory elements if they carry the story forward and enable the audience to better understand the meaning of your story.

Finally, taste effects are mainly effective if the hero of your story is a food product.

Let's take a practical example to understand what I have said. Consider the story of the temperature anomaly, which we have used as a common thread throughout the book. Suppose you want to deliver your story as a live presentation in front of an audience. In this example, you implement the story's second piece of the first act: the hero's presentation. In Chapter 3, you saw how the temperature hero presentation answers the following questions:

- Who is the hero?
    - **Name:** Anomalies in average annual temperature
    - **Features:** Climate indicator, measured in degrees Fahrenheit/Celsius
- What is your hero's object of desire? To remain within a sustainable range to ensure climate stability
- What challenges does your hero face? Global warming and increasing emissions of greenhouse gases

You can implement this piece of the story using a sequence with three scenes, one for each question. Figure 9.5 shows a possible implementation of the first scene, which combines text and images (i.e., symbols).

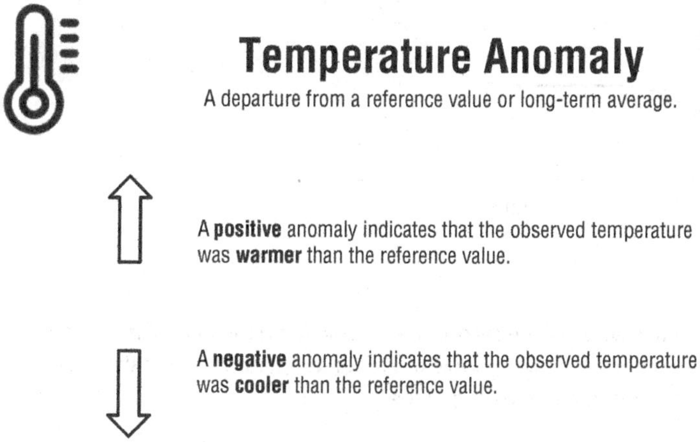

Temperature Anomaly

A departure from a reference value or long-term average.

A **positive** anomaly indicates that the observed temperature was **warmer** than the reference value.

A **negative** anomaly indicates that the observed temperature was **cooler** than the reference value.

Figure 9.5: A possible implementation of the first scene describing the hero. The scene is a slide that combines text and symbols. Use animations to reveal the contents of the scene progressively.

The first scene simply and clearly provides definitions. As special effects, you can use text animations, which progressively reveal the scene's content. *Challenge: Think about how you could implement this scene using graphics.*

This scene contains many details that explain its subject to various audiences. In the next chapters, you will see how to adapt the various scenes based on the specific audience to whom you want to speak. For now, keep it generic, trying to be as complete as possible.

The second scene shows the temperature hero's goal of staying within an acceptable range. You can show an explanatory graph, like the one in Figure 9.6.

The scene explains the various ranges of temperature anomalies, including normal values (<1.5°C or 34.7°F), values of a risk of moderate extreme weather events (>1.5°C or 34.7°F), and values of a risk of severe weather events (>2.0°C or 35.6 °F). The goal of this scene is to inform the audience on how to read the subsequent graphs. If you have an audience of climate experts in front of you, you can eliminate this scene and move directly to the next one. But we will see this later, starting from the next chapter. Also, for this scene, as special effects, you can use animations that gradually reveal the slide's content. For example, you can start by showing the normal values and then gradually show the other two levels.

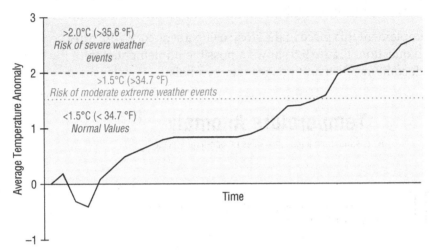

Figure 9.6: A possible implementation of the second scene describing the hero. The scene is a slide showing an explanatory graph of the acceptable ranges of temperature anomalies. Use animations to reveal the contents of the scene progressively.

The third scene answers the question, what challenges does your hero face? The answer we gave at the time was *Global warming and increasing emissions of greenhouse gases*. You could show a short video with the obstacles the temperature faces in staying within range. In the video, you could include the melting of glaciers, the increase in desertification, and so on. You can also use images or photos instead of video.

After you have implemented these three scenes, the hero description phase of your story is ready. You can proceed in the same way to implement the other phases of the story, with the division into three acts, which you have seen in the previous chapters. Many books and resources explain what charts to use based on the data type. An excellent book to start with is *Storytelling with Data* by Cole Nussbaumer Knaflic (2015), while an excellent web resource is *The Data Visualisation Catalogue* (n.d.).

Once you have implemented all the scenes, you are ready to move on to the editing phase of the story.

Postproduction: Data Story Editing

Think about the last film you saw at the cinema. Focus the story on the various characters and plot. Now, think about all the shots, such as when you felt like you were inside the film, when you looked at something with the same eyes as a character, or when you felt the same sensations as the character. Think of the thrill you felt when a character was about to fall into a ravine: in the previous scene, you saw the character dangling from a branch at the top of the ravine, and in the next scene, you saw the ravine through the character's eyes. Well, dear reader, this is called a *point of view*. A story combines different points of view to obtain something meaningful and emotional. This combination process is called *editing*. A great data storyteller sees these multiple points of view and realizes how to immerse the audience in the story through editing. Editing is the phase that brings the story alive, making it real. It involves crafting a story from the scenes you have implemented during the production phase (Boykin, 2018). In the cinematographic field, the success of a film depends on good editing. Think of your favorite movie, remove all the transitions, and turn it into an aseptic sequence of scenes. What's left? A very boring flat story. Now, project the aseptic sequence of scenes to your latest presentation. What is it after all? A very boring flat presentation. Editing brings the story to life, transforming it from a very boring sequence of scenes to an engaging and memorable story.

In the editing phase, you refine the story by ordering the scenes, eliminating superfluous ones, and selecting the best format for the final narration. This crucial step ensures the story is clear, cohesive, and engaging for the audience.

There are different editing techniques. I will describe only the main ones in this book, as shown in Figure 9.7.

Chronological Editing	**Flashback**	**Parallel Stories**
Present events in the order they occurred.	Jump back to an earlier event to provide context or background information.	Show two or more storylines that unfold simultaneously.

Figure 9.7: The editing techniques described in this book

Chronological editing consists of presenting the scenes in temporal order, following the natural sequence of events. This technique is used for stories that develop in a linear and progressive way. Basically, you edit the story exactly the same way you created it: the story begins with the first scene of the first act and ends with the last scene of the third act.

The *flashback* consists of starting the story at a different time from the chronological beginning to create narrative tension. In his book *The Art of Creative Nonfiction: Writing and Selling the Literature of Reality*, Lee Gutkind states that to find the point at which to begin the story, look in the story for the moment where the most important event occurs and begin the narration a little earlier (Gutkind, 2007). Usually, the opening scene directly precedes a plot point or climax. Immediately after this scene, the story flashes back to explain how you got to the opening scene. Use this technique to keep your audience's attention and prepare them for a key moment. In the example of temperature anomalies, you could start with the Dark Night (the moment that sets up the climax), in which you show an apocalyptic scenario where temperature anomalies are taken to extreme consequences (see Figure 9.8).

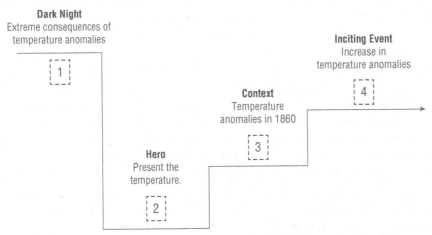

Figure 9.8: An example of a flashback that uses the Dark Night as a hook and then moves on to tell the story chronologically

In this case, the Dark Night fulfills the function of the hook, which is no longer necessary in your story. So, immediately after the Dark Night, move on to the hero's introduction.

Another type of editing is the *development of parallel stories*, which present multiple narratives that develop simultaneously with thematic or temporal connections. For example, you can use this technique to compare data from different geographic regions or to present the hero and the antagonist in a parallel way, as shown in Figure 9.9.

In this type of montage, however, at some point, the parallel stories must meet and resolve (as shown by the figure's black circle, the point from which the story normally proceeds in chronological order). In the example of temperature anomalies, you could present the story of the temperature hero and the CO_2 emissions antagonist in a parallel way, alternating traits of one and the other. In practice, you could overlap the first act's first part with the second act's middle part. This technique is advantageous when you want to show that the antagonist also has their reasons for existing. Another example of applying this technique could be the comparison between two products. You could alternate scenes relating to one product with scenes relating to the other.

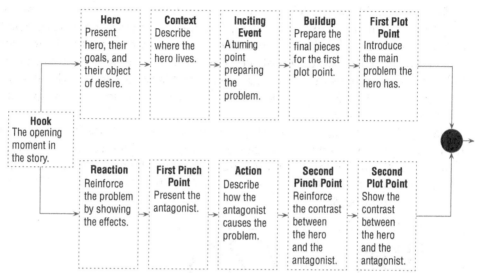

Figure 9.9: A possible editing of parallel stories, showing the story of the hero and the antagonist in parallel

Deciding which editing technique to use each time can be challenging. You can perform various editing tests and see which story works best for you. After some time, you will know you have acquired enough experience to understand which editing works best for your story.

Editing is not just deciding the order in which to present the scenes. Editing is also about selecting which scenes to show and which are unnecessary because they don't add value to the story or might distract from the main message. Choosing which scenes to keep should be based on how much each helps develop characters, build tension, or provide essential information to move the story forward. For example, if you have multiple graphs that always represent the same phenomenon but in a different way, without moving the story forward, keep only one graph and eliminate the others.

There is one last aspect to consider when editing a story, and that is how to connect the various scenes. Said in very banal terms, I am referring, for example, to the transition from one slide to another in a presentation. Often, in live presentations, the transition from one scene to another is completely neglected, so you move from one slide to another in a brutal way. Or, in other cases, more or less random effects are used, which seem to liven up the presentation but do nothing but make the narrative more bizarre. Personally, before delving deeper into the topic, I inserted more or less random transitions into several slides based on how much I liked the visual effect. In reality, the transition from one scene to another is also a scene in the story, and therefore you should elevate it to that dignity. Any slide creation tool, be it PowerPoint or another tool, provides animations, including transitions between the various slides.

To understand how to use transitions, I take inspiration from the cinemato-graphic field, which par excellence bases the story's success not only on the plot but also on editing. In technical terms, the transition from one scene to another is called a *cut*. There are different types of cuts, but in this book, I will focus only on the main ones that can help you enter this wonderful world of story editing. If you are interested in learning more, you can read books or look up resources in that sector.

Figure 9.10 summarizes the main types of cuts you can use to define a transition from one scene to another in live presentations (i.e., video or slide presenta-tions). To fully understand what we are discussing, I suggest you watch the *Ultimate Guide to Scene Transitions—Every Editing Transition Explained [The Shot List, Ep 9]* (StudioBinder, 2021).

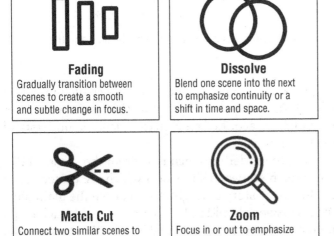

Fading
Gradually transition between scenes to create a smooth and subtle change in focus.

Dissolve
Blend one scene into the next to emphasize continuity or a shift in time and space.

Match Cut
Connect two similar scenes to draw a visual parallel between them.

Zoom
Focus in or out to emphasize specific details or to change perspective on the narrative.

Figure 9.10: Some of the most popular types of editing, which you can also use in data storytelling

A *fade* is when a shot dissolves to or from a solid color, usually black or white. A *fading from black* is a way to open a story, while a *fading to black* gives the audi-ence a moment of pause. Fading to black corresponds to the end of a chapter in the case of a book. In data storytelling, use fading to black, for example, to separate the end of one act from the beginning of the next or when you want to push the audience to reflect on something important. In the case of the temperature anomaly story, you could use a fading to black after presenting the problem (i.e., the temperature increase). This gives the audience a pause that enables them to reflect on the severity of the problem.

A *fading to white* is used at the end of the story or to represent a character dying or entering a dream. It also denotes ambiguity. In data storytelling, you can use fading to white to indicate an ambiguous situation. For example, if you don't know in the climax who wins the battle between the hero and the antagonist, you can end with a fading to white, leaving this sense of ambiguity open.

There are transitions very similar to fading: *iris*, which is circular with respect to fading; and *wipe*, in which scene A is gradually replaced by scene B, from bottom to up or right to left or diagonally, star, or clockwise (or counterclockwise). These two techniques are no longer used, as they seem a little old-fashioned. Use them only if you want your presentation to look vintage.

Another transition type is the *dissolve*, which utilizes a gradual transition to another scene. It is used to define the passage of time, or to signal a memory or a dream. In data storytelling, you can use this transition type when the two scenes connect to show data relating to the same topic but at different moments, such as the value of global temperatures in 1860 and 2024. Using the dissolve technique, you create the feeling that time has passed for the audience.

The *match cut* connects two visually similar scenes that represent different elements. The similarity between the two scenes enables the audience to perceive a logical or emotional connection between what is shown, even if they are in different temporal or spatial contexts. In data storytelling, you can use a match cut to relate two graphs or visualizations with a similar structure. For example, you could connect a map showing a city's pollution levels one year, with an updated map showing the same data years later.

> **TIP**   **Dissolve or Match Cut?** Use a dissolve to convey the idea of a gradual and inevitable change and if you want the audience to perceive a smoother transition between the data.
>
> Use a match cut to underline a clear and shocking change, where the contrast between before and after is the narrative's focal point.

A *zoom* focuses attention on specific details within a scene. Instead of moving from one shot to another, zoom involves moving closer or farther away from the element of interest, without changing shots. In data storytelling, you can use a zoom, for example, with maps: start from a map detail, and then extend the vision to a larger region, or vice versa. A zoom, compared to other types of cuts, is particularly effective at guiding the audience's attention without interrupting the fluidity of the narrative. Additionally, it can create a sense of immersion.

Other more complex techniques exist, which I do not discuss in this book, and include the match dissolve, the passing, the smash cut, the J cut, the L cut, and so on.

The techniques I have presented are fine if you have chosen slides or a video as a channel for telling the story. But what if you use a different channel, such as a journalistic article or a written document, where you cannot use these techniques? In such a case, you can use other tricks to simulate transitions between one scene and another, such as transition sentences, rhetorical questions, summary sentences, division into chapters, or white space. My suggestion is to be creative! There isn't a single correct way to always do this, so you shouldn't feel locked in or forced to do it a certain way. Experiment and learn what they are good at and what the audience responds to!

To recap what I said about editing, choose the order to edit the scenes. For example, you can use chronological order (i.e., the exact order in which events occur during the story) or flashback or parallel stories. Once you've established the order in which you want to edit the stories, add transitions from one scene to the next. Transitions or cuts are also scenes that contribute to involving the audience more. I talked about the audience. But who actually is the audience? You see it in the delivery phase, starting from the next section.

Starting the Delivery Phase

I recently told the same story to two different audiences. The story wasn't about the data but was still a story. Following Alli Torban's directions about using creativity (Torban, 2023), I used creativity to tell the message of my book *Data Storytelling with Altair and AI* (Lo Duca, 2024a). I combined my passion for origami with that for data storytelling. I built an origami pyramid, which summarized the story told in my book: how to integrate the Data-Information-Knowledge-Wisdom (DIKW) pyramid and artificial intelligence (AI) to create data-driven stories. To get an idea of the result of my construction, you can freely download the pyramid, print it, and build it (Lo Duca, 2024b). I printed 10 copies of this pyramid and distributed them during an event aimed at a general audience, where I presented the difference between AI and augmented intelligence. The pyramid sold like hotcakes, and no copies were left. Indeed, some public members complained that they could not get their own copy of the pyramid. Following this success, I thought of reproposing the same pyramid at another event, a scientific conference, with an audience of researchers. This time, I printed 20 copies of the pyramid. Well, very few people were interested in my pyramid during the event, and even if those interested were enthusiastic, the vast majority didn't even look at it. What didn't work this time? The pyramid was always the same in the two cases. The difference, however, was in the audience. The pyramid contained a message that was too generic, which was fine for a general audience but not for an audience of researchers. It is, therefore, necessary to adapt the story to the audience. This happens during the delivery phase.

The delivery phase is when you adapt your story to the audience. I will talk indepth about the audience in the following two chapters and why it is better to wait until the delivery phase before talking about the audience. For now, it's enough to know that the audience is a group of people or a single person who interacts with your story. You'll see a more complete definition of audiences in the next chapter, including various types of audiences. For now, I will only focus on some techniques to get to know the audience.

Several techniques exist for studying audiences (Chingi et al., 2023), including surveys, interviews, and preliminary research (see Figure 9.11).

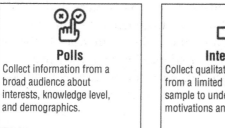

Polls
Collect information from a broad audience about interests, knowledge level, and demographics.

Interviews
Collect qualitative insights from a limited audience sample to understand motivations and expectations.

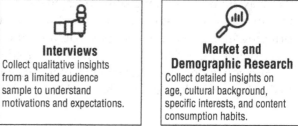

Market and Demographic Research
Collect detailed insights on age, cultural background, specific interests, and content consumption habits.

Figure 9.11: Some techniques to study the audience

Polls allow you to collect information from a broad audience. They can include questions about interests, level of knowledge of the topic covered, culture, demographics, and so on. *Interviews*, on the other hand, are a qualitative method to obtain more in-depth information on a limited audience sample. *Market and demographic research* can detail age, cultural background, specific interests, and ways of using content.

Once you have collected this information, segment your audience into subgroups with similar needs and expectations. For example, one expert group might want an in-depth detailed analysis, while another group might prefer a more straightforward visual explanation. Tailoring your narrative based on these segments enables you to engage each part of your audience more effectively. If your audience is very uneven, look for a balance between different levels of knowledge and interest. You can segment your audience into groups with similar characteristics and prepare suitable content for each group or use a mixed approach to present basic information for everyone but provide additional details for those who are more interested or experienced.

Use the techniques just described if you are able to contact your audience in advance. What can you do if you don't have access to the audience in advance?

In this case, analyze the context in which you will propose your story. Every story has its own context, precisely where and when it will be told. Study this context, and you will know who your audience is. For example, if you present your story at an event, collect information about the event: Who will attend? What types or categories of people will participate? Experts or the general public? If you present your story as a journalistic article, collect information on the audience of the magazine, blog, or newspaper that will publish your article.

Data storytelling often calls for a mix of skills: research, data analysis, design, and communication. You can tackle all these aspects on your own, but teaming up with experts—like researchers or data analysts—can make your storytelling stronger and more effective. A researcher could help you dig deeper into your audience's behavior and ensure your segmentation is rooted in real insights. Helped by these figures, you might uncover patterns or details you wouldn't have spotted alone, helping you create a sharper, more engaging narrative. Anyway, if you're working solo, focus on small, actionable steps and use tools that make the process easier. But don't hesitate to collaborate when you can. Bringing in experts lightens your load and often takes your story to the next level, delivering a richer, more impactful experience for your audience.

Once you understand who you're looking at, you can work to adapt your story to that type of audience. And that's what you'll learn about in the next chapter.

Takeaways

- The making phase of a story includes three main parts: preproduction, production, and postproduction.

- In the preproduction phase, you write the story, identifying the characters and the plot. As you have seen in previous chapters, organize your story into three acts: *the story's presentation, the problem, and the solution with next steps.*

- You implement individual story scenes in the production phase using your favorite tool. For each scene, use one of eight suggested scene types: chart, voice, text, big number, video, map, person, or image. You can also use special effects during the production phase to involve the audience more. Connect special effects to the five senses for more significant impact.

- In the postproduction phase, you edit the story, deciding the order in which to present the scenes and the transitions between them. You can use chronological editing to present the story in the same order in which the events happen. You can also use a flashback to introduce a later event in the story, and then go back to what happened previously. You can also use parallel stories to tell multiple stories simultaneously, such as the story of the hero and the villain.

- During the postproduction phase, you also decide how to move from one scene to another, implementing cuts, which are transitions between scenes. There are different types of cuts, such as fade, dissolve, match cut, and zoom.

- Before adapting your story to your audience, analyze the potential audience interacting with it. If you have access to the audience in advance, administer surveys or interviews, or analyze demographic or cultural data related to them. If you don't know the audience in advance, study the context (where and when) your story will be presented.

References

Boykin, B. (2018). *Final Cut Pro X 10.4—Apple Pro Training Series: Professional Post-Production*. San Francisco: Peachpit Press.

Cingi, C.C., Bayar Muluk, N., Cingi, C. (2023). Analysing your audience in advance. In: *Improving Online Presentations*. Springer, Cham. `https://doi.org/10.1007/978-3-031-28328-4_8` (accessed November 29, 2024).

Clabough, C. (2014). *Creative Writing*. United Kingdom: DK.

Dykes, B. (2019). *Effective Data Storytelling: How to Drive Change with Data, Narrative and Visuals*. New York: John Wiley & Sons.

Gutkind, L. (2007). *The Art of Creative Nonfiction: Writing and Selling the Literature of Reality*. New York: John Wiley & Sons.

Hamand, M. (2014). *Creative Writing Exercises for Dummies*. Hoboken: For Dummies.

Lo Duca, A. (2024a). *Data Storytelling with Altair and AI*. Shelter Island: Manning Publications.

Lo Duca, A. (2024b). *The DIKW Pyramid Origami*. `https://github.com/alod83/origami/blob/main/DIKW.pdf` (accessed October 15, 2024).

Nussbaumer Knaflic, C. (2015). Storytelling with data: A data visualization guide for business professionals. Hoboken, NJ: Wiley.

Parikh, S. (2024). *The Ultimate Guide to Storytelling in Business*. New York: John Wiley & Sons.

StudioBinder (2021). *Ultimate Guide to Scene Transitions—Every Editing Transition Explained* [The Shot List, Ep 9] by StudioBinder. `https://www.youtube.com/watch?v=TKXBAaQB03U` (accessed October 15, 2024).

The Data Visualisation Catalogue. (n.d.). Retrieved from `https://datavizcatalogue.com` (accessed November 29, 2024).

Torban, A. (2023). *Chart Spark: Harness Your Creativity in Data Communication to Stand Out and Innovate*. Data Literacy Press.

What the Audience Wants and Knows

The story-making phase is finally over. The plot of your story is structured in three acts, with the various characters well-defined. You have also implemented and edited the scenes. Now, it's a matter of adapting your story to the audience or, better yet, looking at it from the audience's perspective (Davis et al., 2021).

In Chapter 1, "Why You Need to Become a Data Storyteller," you learned that data storytelling comprises two phases: make and deliver. In the "make" phase, you define the story's objective, plot, and characters. You also implement and edit the story and while in the "deliver" phase, you adapt your story to your audience. In the previous chapter, you have seen a general overview of the audience and how to do some research on them to essentially know who they are. However, up until now, I presented the audience veiledly as something nebulous, asking you to be patient because I would talk about the audience later in the book. Starting with this chapter, you will see who the audience is in more detail, learn how to refine the story to engage them as much as possible, and ensure that your audience, in turn, becomes a new storyteller of your story.

However, I first would like to explain why you had to wait until now to hear about audiences. I've mentioned it previously, but now I must be more explicit in defining them. Every story can be told in a thousand ways and to a thousand different people, using a thousand different channels. You can talk about *repurposing*, that is, using the same element for different purposes and with different means. So, once you've struggled to construct your story, why not repurpose it in numerous ways and reuse it several times? For example, you could create a presentation for your boss, an infographic for the general audience, or a technical report for nearby departmental technicians. Your story is always the same though—what changes are the audience and the means with which you tell it.

The effort you made initially, in defining the story, might seem enormous, but now all your efforts are rewarded. You already have all the material ready! All you must do is adapt it to your audience, and you're finished. Think big! Don't just use your story a single time. Reuse it, repurpose it, and spread it to masses. Believe in your story—believe that it makes sense to tell it more than once.

I recently discovered that the best way to assimilate concepts is to study them multiple times. Do you know what the next book I'll read will be? What I'm reading now! I will repeatedly reread it, until I have assimilated it well. This is because I try to read only high-quality books. And, when I find a good book, I will reread it several times. The second time I reread a book, I discover things I didn't comprehend the first time. Someone said that life is too short to read low-quality books. In a world where everything occurs immediately and people have very short attention spans, all your effort you sink into preparing your story flies away in five minutes of a presentation or a quick post on social media. The same goes for stories: tell them many times and in a thousand ways. It's only in this way that your audience will remember them.

I hope I've convinced you of the importance of separating the "making" and "delivery" phases. If I haven't, you can always combine the two phases and apply what I'm about to tell you directly in the "making" phase. However, I firmly believe combining the two isn't advantageous because you put form and content together. The form is the audience you want to communicate the message to, and the content is your story. Keep form and content separate so you can adapt content to different forms.

So far, we have generically discussed audiences. But what exactly is an audience? Or rather, *who* is your audience? Let's talk about audience types and their needs and thoughts. In this chapter, you will see:

- Who the audience is
- What the audience wants
- What the audience knows

Let's start by defining who the audience is.

Defining the Audience

You don't have a single audience. Even if you have three or four people from your same workgroup in front of you, you should never speak in general.

No audience is a monolith—it is always made up of individual people. The *audience* is, therefore, the set of people who interact with your story (Longnecker, 2023).

So, remember that you aren't speaking in general, but to people, each of whom is a unique and unrepeatable reality, who lives their own experiences, and who has their own life. You can't expect to reach and engage everyone in the same exact way. Each audience member will respond to your story differently, based on their beliefs, culture, and attitudes. You will learn about the values and beliefs of the audience later in the book. For now, I focus on other aspects of the audience.

You will never be able to predict with absolute certainty how individuals in your audience will respond to your story. What you can do, however, is to apply the general principles that I will suggest shortly to convey your story's message in the best way. The audience is, therefore, not a shapeless mass, but a group that is always made up of people. Your goal is to speak to *each* of them in their uniqueness.

The good news is that people in the audience can be grouped based on their interests, attitudes, beliefs, culture, ethnicity, and so on. In technical jargon, it is said that the audience can be *segmented*. So, you can have homogeneous audiences if they are made up of people with similar characteristics and interests, or nonhomogeneous ones if the people in your audience have nothing in common. If you're dealing with a very homogeneous audience, you can adapt your story to that specific audience. If you are dealing with a heterogeneous audience, leave the story as you planned, without adapting it to any particular audience type. An alternative strategy for a nonhomogeneous audience could be to segment the audience and adjust the story to each segment. In this chapter, we focus on the homogeneous audience, or in any case, on a homogeneous audience segment, keeping in mind that the audience is not a shapeless mass but always made up of people for whom the concepts I describe are generally valid. Still, the last response to your story depends on the individual's freedom.

I believe that your mission, as a storyteller, is to act as a bridge between the data and the audience to ensure that the audience understands what your data tells. You can propose the next steps that the audience can follow, but then the audience's response to your message may vary. There will be those who will enthusiastically welcome your message, and those who will ignore it completely. There will also be those who think totally differently than you and will comprehend your message differently.

According to data storytelling expert Brent Dykes, after communicating a message, it is appropriate to analyze how much the audience (in his case, the decision-makers) have implemented the change. Still, unfortunately, this is not normally done (Dykes, 2024). In any case, you will have achieved your goal of clearly transmitting the message in your data.

Before undertaking any communication action toward the audience, you should study who you are in front of to understand with whom you are dealing. In technical terms, this is called *audience analysis* (Cingi et al., 2023). You have already seen this covered in the previous chapter.. In this chapter, I focus on an initial classification of the audience.

An audience can be classified in three different ways, as shown in Figure 10.1.

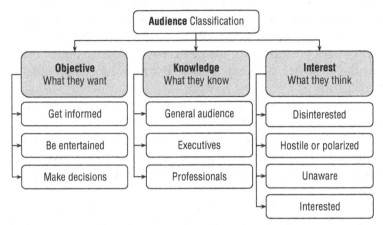

Figure 10.1: Classification of an audience based on the objective, topic knowledge, and interests

The first classification is based on the *objective*, or what the audience wants to achieve. Every time a person encounters a story (whether data-driven or not), they have a goal. The goal is precisely what the person expects from the story. Their goal may or may not coincide with what you defined when you built your story. If the person's goal coincides with your goal, then you are more likely guaranteed that the person will understand your story and act on what you propose as the next steps in the story. In the previous chapters, you learned that a story can have three objectives: to inform, entertain, and persuade. Well, the audience can also have one of these three objectives: to inform themselves, to be entertained, and to make decisions.

A second way of classifying people within the audience is based on their level of knowledge about the topic. Some will know the topic superficially or not at all (your general audience), some will know the topic in depth (your professionals), and some will know the topic but not in depth (your executives).

Finally, a third way of classifying the audience is based on their interest in the topic. There are those who have a great interest in the topic and have the same thoughts as you (your audience deficit), and then there are those who aren't interested at all in your topic. In the middle, you'll find that some are interested in the topic but think differently from you. Finally, you'll find that some have yet to learn the topic but might be interested *if* they can learn about it (your unaware or untapped audience).

These various audience types can be combined. For example, you may have an audience who knows and is interested in the topic and wants to make decisions.

The worst-case scenario of an audience is one who is disinterested in the topic, does not know it, and still has to make decisions on it.

Every audience type has different needs. Your task is to adapt the story based on these needs to engage them as much as possible. It's time to learn how to adapt your story to different audiences. Using the story of temperature anomalies developed in the previous chapters, let's see how to adapt it to various audiences, by focusing on what the audience wants and knows. In the next chapter, you will see what the audience thinks. Let's start with the different objectives: being informed, entertained, and making decisions.

What the Audience Wants

Why do people read stories? And why should an audience read your story? The main reason is that audiences hope to achieve a goal—to get something out of it. Every action taken has a motivation and an objective, so those who encounter your story will have an objective. In general, there are many and varied objectives, which can be grouped into three macro categories: to get informed, be entertained, and make decisions, as shown in Figure 10.2.

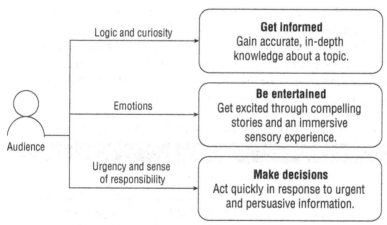

Figure 10.2: The three objectives that the audience wants to achieve when they encounter a story

"Getting informed" means gaining accurate, in-depth knowledge about a topic. "Being entertained" is about getting excited through listening to compelling stories and having an immersive sensory experience. Finally, "making decisions" is acting quickly in response to urgent and persuasive information. Depending on the audience's objective, you can use different motivational and cognitive factors in your data storytelling. If your goal is to inform, leverage the logic and curiosity of your audience. If you want to entertain them, exploit their emotional levels. Finally, if you want to push the audience to make decisions, then leverage urgency and a sense of responsibility. A practical example will be introduced later. For now, let's focus on the general concepts.

According to the elaboration likelihood model (ELM) of persuasion, there are two different ways to process stimuli: the central and peripheral routes (Petti and Cacioppo, 1986). Suppose a person considers a message they receive at the central route level. In that case, the effort required to process the information is very high, but the message's effect lasts over time. If, however, a person processes a message at the level of the peripheral route, then the processing effort is less. Still, the effect that the message has on the person's attitude is less long-lasting. Adapting a story to the audience's objectives means simplifying the level of information processing as much as possible to reduce the central route's effort.

To practically implement the different motivational and cognitive factors, you can play on some aspects that are transversal to the plot of the story but that have a significant impact on it. The four transversal aspects are language, tone, time and rhythm, and sensory elements. Language enables the storyteller to express thoughts, convey emotions, and share information through structured systems of words and grammar (Rathcke et al., 2015). Use the tone to convey emotions, intentions, and emphasis, with tonal shifts influencing the meaning of words (Rathcke et al., 2015). Rhythm organizes speech into patterns, helping the audience predict upcoming sounds and meaning (Auer et al., 1999). Sensory elements like sight, sound, touch, and smell enhance communication by engaging multiple senses, making messages more vivid, memorable, and emotionally impactful (Jones & LeBaron, 2002). Table 10.1 shows how to use these elements based on the audience's objective.

Table 10.1:   The Main Elements You Can Play with Based on the Audience's Objective

	GET INFORMED	BE ENTERTAINED	MAKE DECISIONS
Language	Clear and precise	Lively and descriptive	Direct and persuasive
Tone	Professional	Engaging and narrative	Urgent and motivating
Rhythm and timing	Calm and steady	Variegated	Quick and pressing
Sensory elements	Simple and clear	Vivid images and evocative sounds	Bright colors and alarming sounds

The purpose of informing is to educate and not persuade, focusing on the subject or matter under discussion. To help the audience become informed, use clear and precise language with a professional and objective tone. Present information, not opinions, and write with maximum objectivity, which helps convey information accurately and believably (Chaturvedi and Chaturvedi, 2012). Maintain a calm and steady pace, giving the audience time to absorb and understand the information presented. Use simple visual and auditory elements, such as graphs, charts, and clean audio, to support understanding of information.

If you want to entertain the audience, choose lively and descriptive language with an engaging and narrative tone, which keeps your attention and makes the story more exciting and memorable. Vary the pace, speeding up in moments of tension and slowing down in reflective ones, to create suspense and maintain attention. Integrate vivid images, evocative sounds, and intense colors to create a rich and engaging sensory experience that stimulates the audience's emotions (Eijkelenboom, 2024).

If you want to help your audience make decisions, use direct and persuasive language with an urgent and motivating tone. This will push the audience to act immediately, underlining the importance of decisions. Set a fast pace to convey urgency, pushing your audience to make decisions without delay. Use visual and audible cues that emphasize urgency, such as bright colors or alarming sounds, to highlight the need for immediate action. Don't focus on details because usually decision-makers don't have the time to listen to long presentations (Parnell et al., 2013).

Stop now for a moment and think about what might happen if you went to the circus with your children or friends and the clown used a professional tone. Imagine the clown telling jokes, using technical language with a flat rhythm. At best, you would think their tone was out of place. More realistically, you would think that you could have spent the ticket money differently. The same is true in data storytelling: adapt the language, tone, time, rhythm, and story elements based on who you have in front of you. Their level of engagement will change significantly.

In addition to the transversal elements just described, you can also work on the single parts of the story, to adapt it based on the audience's objective. In the previous chapters, you learned how to build the story's plot and how to structure it in three acts. Figure 10.3 outlines the parts of the story that you can work on to tailor it to the audience's goal.

Work mainly on three elements: the first plot point, the second plot point, and the next steps. Let's see how to adapt these three points, based on the audience's objective.

First Plot Point

As previously mentioned, the first plot point happens at the end of the first act and introduces the hero's main problem. Figure 10.4 shows how to adapt the first plot point, based on the audience's objective.

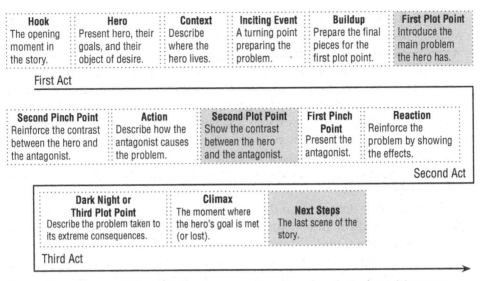

Hook	Hero	Context	Inciting Event	Buildup	First Plot Point
The opening moment in the story.	Present hero, their goals, and their object of desire.	Describe where the hero lives.	A turning point preparing the problem.	Prepare the final pieces for the first plot point.	Introduce the main problem the hero has.

First Act

Second Pinch Point	Action	Second Plot Point	First Pinch Point	Reaction
Reinforce the contrast between the hero and the antagonist.	Describe how the antagonist causes the problem.	Show the contrast between the hero and the antagonist.	Present the antagonist.	Reinforce the problem by showing the effects.

Second Act

Dark Night or Third Plot Point	Climax	Next Steps
Describe the problem taken to its extreme consequences.	The moment where the hero's goal is met (or lost).	The last scene of the story.

Third Act

Figure 10.3: The parts of the story that you can work on, based on the audience's interests

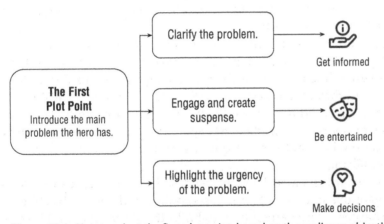

Figure 10.4: How to adapt the first plot point, based on the audience objective

To satisfy the hunger of an audience who wants to know more, paint a clear and detailed picture of the problem. Your job is to bring out the hard facts without embellishment, provide the essential data, and contextualize the information. For example, in the case of the increase in temperature over time, talk about how, in recent decades, global temperatures have risen, creating a tangible threat to ecosystems and infrastructure. This is the moment when the truth takes center stage.

For an audience who wants to be entertained by your story, present the problem in a more engaging and dramatic way. Create suspense or curiosity, turning the problem into an exciting challenge or mystery. With every word, keep the audience on the edge of their seats, eager to discover how this story will end. In the case of the temperature rise example, you can use text like this: "The temperature of the planet began to rise abnormally. But what was behind this sudden change?"

If an audience needs to make decisions, highlight the need for an immediate choice or action. Emphasize the practical and urgent implications. Bring your audience to the crossroads, where indecision is not an option. Paint an urgent, inescapable picture: "Global temperatures are rising above critical levels. The crisis is now, and the time to act is running out." In this scenario, your audience cannot remain passive; they must take a stand and do so now.

In the examples described, I have shown possible texts that you could use to structure the first plot point. Obviously, you can also act by involving the other senses on a sound or visual level.

You might find it strange to adapt the story to the audience after having already done the editing (the final moment of the making phase). In reality, the adaptations I propose are refinements of the scenes you have already implemented, which help make your story more fluid for a specific audience. The theoretical workflow should be this: first you define the scenes of your story, then you implement them, and finally, you adjust them based on your audience. If you don't have time to adapt your story to the audience after editing it, carry out the production, editing, and adaptation of the story to the audience in a single moment.

Second Plot Point

The second plot point occurs in the middle of the second act and indicates the contrast between the hero and antagonist. Figure 10.5 shows how to adapt the second plot point, based on the audience objective.

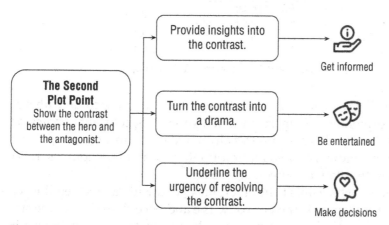

Figure 10.5: How to adapt the second plot point, based on the audience objective

To correctly inform the audience, paint a precise and detailed picture of the conflict between the hero and the antagonist, focusing on numbers, trends, and analyses. In the case of increasing temperatures, introduce graphs comparing temperature and CO_2 emissions. If you want to entertain the audience, turn the struggle between the hero and the antagonist into a gripping drama. Increase the tension and emotionally involve the audience as if they were spectators of an epic battle. For example, in addition to showing the graphic comparison between temperature and CO_2 emissions, use vivid narration, focusing on epic language. You can also add images related to the theme.

Finally, if your focus is pushing the audience to make decisions, underline the urgency of resolving the confrontation. For example, in the case of temperature, you could use text like this: "Faced with the inevitable rise in temperatures, there is no more time for hesitation. The choice is clear: reduce emissions now."

Next Steps

Next steps, discussed previously, are the last scene of the story and indicate what the audience is invited to do after interacting with the story. Figure 10.6 illustrates how to adapt the next steps, based on the audience's objective.

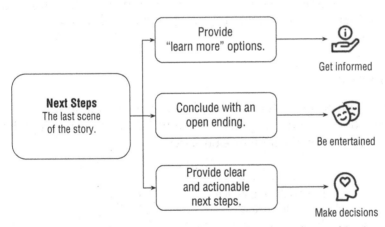

Figure 10.6: How to adapt the next steps, based on the audience objective

If you're dealing with an audience who wants to learn, conclude with a call to continuous exploration. Suggest authoritative sources, constant updates, and simple actions that can keep awareness alive. In the example of rising temperatures, invite the audience to obtain information from other sources, follow updates from authoritative sources, and so on.

For an audience who wants to be entertained, end with an open ending, creating a sense of anticipation and curiosity. The audience should leave the story wanting to know what will happen next, as if they are on the verge of discovering something new and essential. In the example of rising temperatures, you might conclude with an ending like "But the battle for the climate is far from over. Temperatures continue to rise; glaciers continue to melt. The question remains: Will we be able to reverse the broken temperature in time?" In this case, it is also essential to leave a message that goes beyond pure entertainment, such as the need to use respect for the environment.

For an audience that must make decisions, invite the reader to transform awareness into concrete action. Provide a clear picture of what the next steps might be. In the case of an increase in temperature, provide steps that can be implemented by the audience, such as the use of green vehicles and a responsible attitude toward the environment.

By adapting the next steps to the audience's objective, the part that defines what the audience wants is complete. Before moving on to the next step of defining what the audience knows, I would like to focus on one issue. As you know, the objectives must match both on the side of those who tell the story, and on the side of those who receive it. So, what happens if the objectives of the narrator and the audience do not coincide? Table 10.2 details what happens if the audience's objectives do not coincide with the storyteller's.

Table 10.2:   What Happens If The Audience's Objectives Do Not Coincide with Those of the Storyteller

	GET INFORMED	BE ENTERTAINED	MAKE DECISIONS
Information	OK	Boredom Distraction	Frustration
Entertain	Dissatisfaction	OK	Dissatisfaction
Persuade	Manipulation Pressure	Stress Oppression	OK

When the narrator wants to inform but the audience wants to be entertained, the result is that the audience may become bored, distracted, or even not pay attention to the story. The informational message is not received or is partially received, reducing the effectiveness of the communication. If the narrator wants to inform but the audience wants to make a decision, the result could be audience frustration because they expect to receive practical, decision-oriented information. The audience may be unable to use the information to make a concrete decision, leading to a lack of action or an uninformed decision.

When the narrator's goal is to entertain but the audience wants to be informed, the audience may find the narrative superficial or not relevant to their interests. If the audience is looking for helpful or educational information and are faced with a story constructed primarily for entertaining, they may feel dissatisfied, consider the narrative a waste of time, or not perceive the value of the content presented. When the narrator wants to entertain but the audience wants to make a decision, the audience may find the narration distracting or irrelevant.

If the narrator's goal is to facilitate a decision and the audience wants to be informed, the audience may feel that the narrative is manipulative or too oriented toward a specific outcome rather than informative. They may feel pressure to decide without feeling informed enough to make it, leading to distrust or resistance toward the message being conveyed. Finally, if the goal is to facilitate a decision and the audience wants to be entertained, they may find the narrative stressful or oppressive. The narrative may be perceived as too serious or overly action-oriented, thus reducing the audience's enjoyment and emotional involvement in the story.

Summing up what has been said here, when you adapt a story to your audience, always consider what they want to get from your story, that is, the objective, which, generally speaking, can be one of these three: to get informed, to be entertained, or to make decisions. At this point, you are ready to discover what the audience knows.

What the Audience Knows

Before writing this part of the chapter, I went with my father and family to my father's little countryside house to pick pears from his tree. To collect the fruit, my father used a stick with a hook at the top, which he uses to bend the highest tree branches to collect the highest fruits. The children picked the lower pears, while we adults picked the higher ones. However, thanks to the use of the hooked stick, even the children were able to pick the pears located high up. It is as if the stick had acted as a "facilitator," enabling children to access even the highest fruits they usually can't reach. It was a beautiful experience. In the end, we harvested only part of the tree's fruit, but we filled two boxes. This experience led me to reflect on how a story can be represented as a tree, whose fruits represent the information that enriches it, as shown in Figure 10.7.

The "fruits" found higher up are those that only the audience who knows the story's topic well can collect, while the "fruits" lower down are the ones that everyone can collect, even those who do not know the topic. At the lowest branches, there are "fruits" for the general audience; at the intermediate branches, those "fruits" are for executives; and at the highest branches, those "fruits" are for domain experts. Well, your role as a data storyteller is precisely that of the hooked stick that lowers the highest branches and makes them accessible even to those at the bottom.

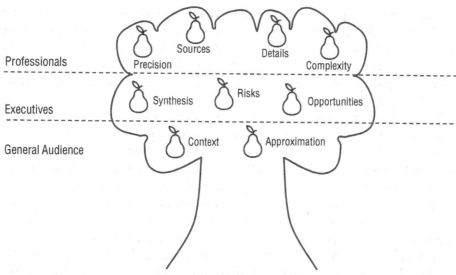

Figure 10.7: The audience tree with respect to what it knows

You will see in the chapter focusing on the data storyteller, how to exploit this role of facilitator. For now, let's focus on the three types of audiences: general audiences, executives, and professionals (Lo Duca, 2024). The general audience includes all people who do not know the topic or have general knowledge of it. For this type of audience, it's crucial that you present the story's context thoroughly in your story. *Context* is all the background surrounding the story, including the hero's description, their object of desire, the situation in which they live, the problem they have, their antagonist, and so on. (You will soon learn how to adapt all these elements based on the various types of audiences.) Furthermore, the general audience does not require precise numbers, so you can easily approximate them. For example, for this type of audience, it isn't necessary to say that the temperature is 37.23456 degrees. It is sufficient to say that the temperature is around 37 degrees. The number after the decimal point only adds noise (Heath and Starr, 2022).

Executives are the people who usually must make decisions. In addition to presenting context and approximating data, it is essential for them to grasp a summary of the topic, as well as the risks and opportunities related to the story. For this, you will need to focus on the hero's opportunities and the risks caused by the story's antagonist. In his book *Data Mining for Dummies*, Meta S. Brown says that the only numbers executives are interested in are those with dollar signs in front (Brown, 2014). This is to say, don't use detailed numbers when presenting the results of your analysis to executives! Also, try to build trust with executives, by being respectful, accountable, and prepared to address their concerns and questions (Carey and Jin, 2020).

Finally, professionals are technicians who know the topic very well (Mieg and Evetts, 2018). They want to know the data precisely (the 37.23456 degrees of the previous example), the sources and references from which the data were taken, the level of detail of the information, and the complexity of the relationships. For this type of audience, the context is not crucial, as it is assumed that they already know it.

At this point, you might wonder how to understand what the audience knows about the topic and, therefore, precisely classify the people in front of you. Two cases can occur: 1) you directly know the people to whom you will present your story, and 2) you don't know them. The first case occurs, for example, if you must present the results of your data analysis to your boss or colleagues or, if you are a data journalist, to the audience of the newspaper or magazine for which you write. In this case, you already know in advance what your audience knows. Suppose your boss is the company's CEO and you must present the results of your data analysis to them. In that case, they indeed belong to the executive category. If you work in a group of technicians and must present the results of your analyses to your colleagues, they will also be technicians, so you can use the strategies we are about to see relating to an audience of technicians. Finally, if you are a data journalist and work for a magazine that deals with generic topics but does not go into detail, then you will speak to a generic audience. This is the first case when you already know your audience. If you don't know who you will be in front of when you must present your story, you can do a preliminary analysis of the audience. We will see this better later in the book.

Now, let's see which elements are transversal to the story that you can use to adapt the story based on what the audience knows. There are three elements: language, level of detail, and precision. Language refers to the choice of words, tone, and complexity of terminology used to convey your story. It varies from simple, everyday words to complex, technical jargon depending on the audience (Shulman et al., 2020). Details refer to the level of information provided to the audience. It ranges from broad overviews to specific, technical explanations (Nature Education, 2014). Precision refers to the accuracy and specificity of the information presented. It includes the use of exact data, graphs, or approximations, depending on the audience's need for detail (Alley, 2018). Table 10.3 describes how to adapt these three elements based on the audience's knowledge.

Table 10.3: The Main Elements You Can Play On, Based on the Audience's Knowledge

	GENERAL PUBLIC	EXECUTIVES	PROFESSIONALS
Language	Simple, without jargon	Formal and business-oriented	Industry-specific technical terminology

	GENERAL PUBLIC	EXECUTIVES	PROFESSIONALS
Details	Simple and clear information, explained with concrete examples	Relevant data for strategic decisions to show risks/ opportunities	Technical and specific details, using studies and models
Precision	Approximation, with simple graphs	Aggregation, with comparative graphs	High precision, with raw data and analytical models

When addressing a general audience, use simple language without specific terminology or technical jargon. This information must be simple and clear, accompanied by concrete examples that help explain the concepts. The goal is to make these messages easily digestible. In this case, opt for a rough level of precision, supported by simple graphs that illustrate the concepts in a visual and immediate way.

For an executive audience, use formal, business-oriented language. This type of language highlights the strategic importance of the information provided. Executives need relevant data to help them make strategic decisions. Therefore, provide information that highlights risks and opportunities, without getting bogged down in excessive technical detail. Aggregate data, presenting it with comparative graphs that enable them to quickly evaluate different options or scenarios.

When speaking to industry professionals, use specific technical terminology that aligns with their level of expertise. Doing so demonstrates a mastery of the topic and promotes effective communication between experts. Professionals require technical and specific details, which can be illustrated through industry studies, analytical models, or advanced research. Provide all the information necessary for an in-depth analysis. Use a high level of precision, which must include raw data and the use of complex analytical models, which allows for a thorough and accurate understanding of the information.

Now stop and think for a moment. Have you ever watched a presentation where you understood practically nothing? This has happened to me several times, especially at scientific conferences where very technical articles are presented. In some cases, the authors even go so far as to describe the formulas and even try to explain them with very technical jargon. Personally, I have always found it very difficult to understand the formulas presented, not because I don't understand mathematics, but because I don't know the context to interpret that formula. Therefore, it is very important to understand what the audience wants. As I've already told you, we will see techniques for analyzing the audience in advance, later in the book.

In addition to adapting cross-cutting aspects based on audience knowledge, you can also work on specific story pieces. Figure 10.8 outlines the parts of the story you can work on to adapt to the audience's knowledge.

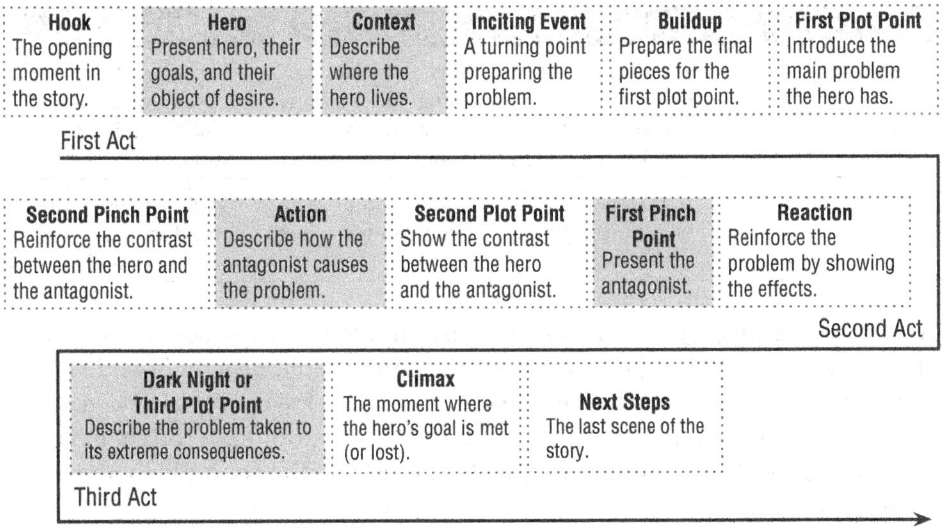

Hook
The opening moment in the story.
Hero
Present hero, their goals, and their object of desire.
Context
Describe where the hero lives.
Inciting Event
A turning point preparing the problem.
Buildup
Prepare the final pieces for the first plot point.
First Plot Point
Introduce the main problem the hero has.
First Act
Second Pinch Point
Reinforce the contrast between the hero and the antagonist.
Action
Describe how the antagonist causes the problem.
Second Plot Point
Show the contrast between the hero and the antagonist.
First Pinch Point
Present the antagonist.
Reaction
Reinforce the problem by showing the effects.
Second Act
Dark Night or Third Plot Point
Describe the problem taken to its extreme consequences.
Climax
The moment where the hero's goal is met (or lost).
Next Steps
The last scene of the story.
Third Act

Figure 10.8: The parts of the story you can work on, based on the audience's knowledge

You can work mainly on five elements: the hero's description, the context, the first pinch point, the action, and the Dark Night. Let's see how you can adapt these three points, based on the audience's knowledge.

Hero

In this part of the story, you introduce the hero, their goals, and their object of desire. Figure 10.9 shows how to adapt the presentation of the hero, based on what the audience knows.

Hero
Present hero, their goals, and their object of desire.
Simple and relatable description
General Audience
Description of the strategic importance of the hero
Executives
Analytical and technical description
Professionals

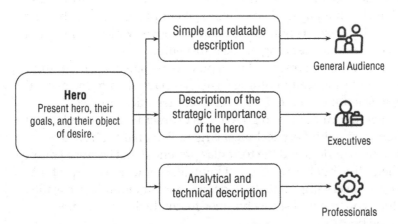

Figure 10.9: How to adapt the hero's presentation, based on the audience's knowledge

In the case of the general audience, present the hero in a simple, relatable, and accessible way. Avoid technical jargon and use clear, concise language. For example, use the following text to describe the temperature hero: "Global temperature helps us maintain climate balance. It is very important that it does not undergo too many variations over the years to guarantee the survival of all animal and plant species."

If you're dealing with executives, present the hero in a strategic and results-oriented way. Emphasize how the hero is crucial to the long-term success or sustainability of the company or organization. For example, you can use the following text to describe temperature: "Global temperature stability is critical to the sustainability of our operations and managing future risks. Protecting this balance is a strategic priority for our business."

For professionals, present the hero by providing technical details and using an analytical approach, leveraging the audience's skills and specific knowledge. For example, describe temperature by explaining the analytical models that govern it.

Context

The context describes where the hero lives and their cultural environment. Context helps the hero to become familiar to the audience. Kindra Hall, a well-known storyteller, for example, suggests adding details that are familiar to the audience. For example, if you're telling a story to people born in the 1980s, you might add the boombox into context. This detail helps not only to outline the context but also to engage the audience more, especially from an emotional point of view (Hall, 2019).

Figure 10.10 shows how to adapt the context based on what the audience knows.

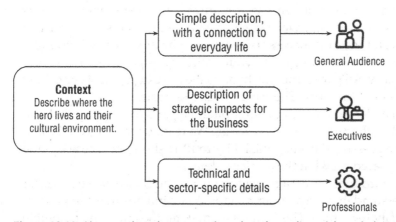

Figure 10.10: How to adapt the context, based on the audience's knowledge

In the case of general audiences, describe the context in a simple way, using familiar images and everyday references. The focus should be on how the context directly affects people's lives. For example, you might describe the temperature context as follows: "Our cities are getting hotter, and climate change is affecting everything from the seasons to agricultural crops."

For executives, present the context in terms of economic and strategic impacts, linking it to business challenges and opportunities. To describe the temperature context, use the following text: "We live in a global context of increasing climate instability, which is reshaping business risks, impacting supply chains, and creating new regulatory pressures."

For professionals, describe the context with technical and industry-specific details, highlighting relevant data, research, and trends. For example, for temperature, you could focus on climate change, which indicates an increase in average global temperatures beyond safe limits established by international agreements.

First Pinch Point

So far, you have seen how to adapt the various parts of the story, based on the objective or knowledge level of the audience. Obviously, you can also make other types of adaptations based on your needs and tastes. What I want to show you is that each part of the story is relevant and has a particular purpose. In every story, there are not and must not be useless parts, but everything contributes to carrying the story forward. I recently attended the online presentation of Cole Nussbaumer Knaflic's children's book *Daphne Draws Data: A Storytelling with Data Adventure* (Knaflic, 2024). During the presentation, Cole explained that the most significant difficulty when writing a children's book is the word and page limit. The book must be exactly 32 pages and have fewer than 1,000 words, while in an adult book the number of pages is around 250 and the number of words is 80,000. This means that every word you write in the children's book must be calibrated. You can't insert unnecessary words or phrases because you must use the little space you have to convey your entire message. The same is true when you tell a story. All parts, from the hook to the next steps, must contribute to the development of the story. There are no useless parts.

Having said that, let's refer back to describing the parts of the story that you can adapt, based on the audience's knowledge. We're going to focus on the *first pinch point*, which presents the antagonist. Figure 10.11 shows how to adapt the first pinch point, based on what the audience knows.

If you want to introduce the antagonist to a general audience, do so in a clear and easily understandable way, using metaphors or images that the general audience can easily recognize. The focus is on making the antagonist tangible and close to everyday reality. In the case of the rising temperature case study, you might say, "The real enemy is CO_2 pollution, an invisible gas that is emitted by cars and factories, contributing to global warming."

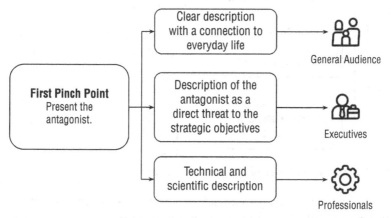

Figure 10.11: How to adapt the antagonist based on the audience's knowledge

For an executive audience, present the antagonist as a direct threat to the business or strategic objectives. Emphasize how the antagonist could hinder growth or increase operating costs. In the temperature example, use a sentence like this: "The growing impact of CO_2 emissions is not only an environmental problem but a direct threat to the long-term economic sustainability of our operations."

For professionals, describe the antagonist in technical detail, focusing on scientific data and analysis that explains its functioning and impact. The focus is on accuracy and industry-specific relevance. In the temperature case study, you could describe CO_2 emissions through predictive models that indicate exceeding climate safety thresholds.

Action

In the story's flow, the action is the moment that follows the second plot point, in which the antagonist is introduced. The action describes how the antagonist causes the problem. Figure 10.12 shows how to adapt the action, based on what the audience knows.

When speaking to a general audience, explain how the antagonist causes the problem using practical, concrete examples that the audience can easily understand. The focus is on making the problem tangible and close to their daily experience. For example, in the case of rising temperatures, use text like "CO_2 emissions from cars and industry are accumulating in the atmosphere, trapping heat and causing global temperatures to rise."

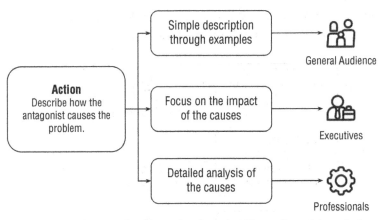

Figure 10.12: How to adapt the action, based on the audience's knowledge

For executives, describe the antagonist's actions in terms of impacts on a global or corporate scale, highlighting how they represent a threat. For example, "Increasing CO_2 emissions are destabilizing the climate, leading to extreme weather that threatens supply chains and increases operational risks."

If you are speaking to a professional audience, provide a detailed and technical explanation of the antagonist's action, using scientific data and analysis to demonstrate the mechanism through which the problem develops. The focus is on the precision and depth of the analysis. For example, "The accumulation of CO_2 in the atmosphere alters Earth's radiative balance, increasing the greenhouse effect and causing global warming measurable in terms of annual thermal anomalies."

Dark Night

The Dark Night introduces the third act and describes the problem taken to its extreme consequences. Figure 10.13 shows how to adapt the Dark Night, based on what the audience knows.

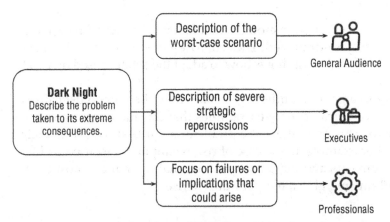

Figure 10.13: How to adapt the Dark Night, based on audience knowledge

When speaking to a general audience, illustrate the worst-case scenario in a way that emphasizes the tangible impact on daily life, like widespread disruptions or loss of resources. For example, "Earth becomes a hostile place: Cities are submerged, forests burn, and life as we know it begins to disappear."

In the case of executives, present the extreme consequences as a crisis that threatens the survival of the business, with long-term economic, legal, or reputational implications. The focus must be on the urgency of intervening to avoid a disaster. For example, "Climate change spirals out of control, leading to global economic crises, infrastructure collapses, and devastating regulations for businesses."

For professionals, describe extreme consequences with scientific precision, using the results of predictive models. For example, "Climate simulations indicate a rise in global temperatures of 4°C (39.2 F) in the not-too-distant future, with catastrophic effects on ecosystems, rising sea levels, and irreversible collapse of glaciers."

You have reached the end of this introductory chapter to the audience. There is no single audience, but there are many facets. You have seen how you can classify the audience, based on objectives and knowledge. In the next chapter, you will see how to classify it based on interests. Before concluding this chapter, I would like to point out that I have not focused on the cognitive and emotional aspects of the audience but only on a general classification. In the following chapter, you will also see this, and in particular, you will learn about a new theory to engage the audience: the stomach-heart-brain theory.

Takeaways

- The audience is a set of people who interact with your story. You don't speak to the audience in general but to people, each of whom is a unique and unrepeatable reality with values and attitudes.

- When a person encounters a story, they may have one of three goals: to get informed, be entertained, or make decisions.

- Adapt the following cross-cutting aspects of the story, based on the audience's goals: language, tone, time and rhythm, and sensory elements. Also, work on the first plot point, the second plot point, and the next steps.

- The audience can also be classified based on what they know: general audience, executives, and professionals.

- Adapt the following cross-cutting aspects of the story based on what the audience knows: language, details, and accuracy. You can also work mainly on five story elements: the description of the hero, the context, the first pinch point, the action, and the Dark Night.

References

Alley, M. (2018). *Balancing Precision with Clarity*. In *The Craft of Scientific Writing*. Springer, New York. https://doi.org/10.1007/978-1-4419-8288-9_2

Auer, P., Couper-Kuhlen, E., and Müller, F. 1999. *Language in Time: The Rhythm and Tempo of Spoken Interaction*. New York: Oxford Academic.

Brown, M. S. 2014. *Data Mining for Dummies*. Indianapolis, IN: Wiley.

Carey, M. J. and Jin, J. 2020. *Tribe of Hackers Security Leaders*. United States of America: New York: John Wiley and Sons.

Chaturvedi, P. D. and Chaturvedi, M. 2012. *Fundamentals of Business Communication*. Dorling Kindersley: Pearson Education India.

Cingi, C. C., Bayar Muluk, N., and Cingi, C. 2023. Analysing your audience in advance. In *Improving Online Presentations: A Guide for Healthcare Professionals* (pp. 93–103). Cham: Springer International Publishing.

Davis, C. H., Gaudiano, B. A., McHugh, L., and Levin, M. E. 2021. Integrating storytelling into the theory and practice of contextual behavioral science. *Journal of Contextual Behavioral Science*, 20, 155–162.

Dykes, B. 2024. Demystifying the data-driven mindset to power better decision-making. *Forbes*. Retrieved on September 4th, 2024. https://www.forbes.com/sites/brentdykes/2024/08/15/demystifying-the-data-driven-mindset-to-power-better-decision-making

Eijkelenboom, G. 2024. *Data Storytelling—From Insight to Impact: Turning Complex Data into Compelling Narratives*. Birmingham: Packt Publishing.

Jones, S. E. and LeBaron, C. D. 2002. Research on the relationship between verbal and nonverbal communication: Emerging integrations. *Journal of Communication*, 52(3), 499–521. https://doi.org/10.1111/j.1460-2466.2002.tb02560.x

Hall, K. 2019. *Stories That Stick. How Storytelling Can Captivate Customers, Influence Audiences, and Transform Your Business*. Nashville: Harpercollins Leadership.

Heath, C. and Starr, K. 2022. *Making Numbers Count: The Art and Science of Communicating Numbers*. New York: Simon and Schuster.

Longnecker, N. 2023. Good science communication considers the audience. In *Teaching Science Students to Communicate: A Practical Guide* (pp. 21–30). Cham: Springer International Publishing.

Lo Duca, A. 2024. *Data Storytelling with Altair and AI*. Shelter Island: Manning Publications.

Mieg, H. A. and Evetts, J. 2018. Professionalism, science, and expert roles: A social perspective. In K. A. Ericsson, R. R. Hoffman, A. Kozbelt, and A. M. Williams (Eds.), *The Cambridge Handbook of Expertise and Expert Performance* (pp. 127–148). Cambridge: Cambridge University Press.

Nature Education. 2014. *Addressing specific audiences. Nature Education.* (Retrieved on October 4th, 2024). https://www.nature.com/scitable/topicpage/addressing-specific-audiences-13952917

Parnell, G. S., Bresnick, T., Tani, S. N., and Johnson, E. R. 2013. *Handbook of Decision Analysis*. New York: John Wiley and Sons.

Petty, Richard E. Cacioppo, John T. (1986). *Communication and persuasion: Central and peripheral routes to attitude change*. Berlin: Springer-Verlag.

Rathcke, T. V., and Smith, R. H. 2015. Speech timing and linguistic rhythm: On the acoustic bases of rhythm typologies. *Journal of the Acoustical Society of America*, 137(5), 2834–2845. https://doi.org/10.1121/1.4919322

Shulman, H. C., Dixon, G. N., Bullock, O. M., and Colón Amill, D. 2020. The effects of jargon on processing fluency, self-perceptions, and scientific engagement. *Journal of Language and Social Psychology*, 39(5–6), 579-597. https://doi.org/10.1177/0261927X20902177

What the Audience Thinks

Some time ago, I traveled to London as my intermediate stop on the way to a conference in Cyprus. I had purposely booked the flight ticket to Cyprus for the next day to have some time to visit London, even though I had already visited it several times. I decided to go up in the London Eye, a Ferris wheel located on the south bank of the Thames. It's a 135-meter-high Ferris wheel that was built in 1998. By going up in a cabin of the wheel, you can admire the whole London landscape, and if you go up in the evening, as I did, you can see all the lights of London and, I assure you, it is a beautiful experience.

Now, imagine going up this Ferris wheel and keeping your eyes fixed on your smartphone for the entire duration of this spectacular panoramic ride, while your friends, who went up with you, admire the beautiful landscape. Once you step off the wheel, what are you left with? Practically nothing, because your interest was elsewhere. This is precisely what happens to a disinterested audience in your story. You can tell the most intriguing story in the world, but if the audience isn't interested in your topic, your story will not affect them whatsoever.

Now, imagine that, instead of standing on the Ferris wheel and admiring the scenery, you fix your gaze on the wheel's mechanics, critiquing and highlighting all the possible safety issues related to the wheel. Gazing at the detail of this or that screw mounted more or less safely, you begin to criticize the wheel's entire construction. The result at the end of your panoramic tour is always the same:

you haven't seen anything of the London panorama. Similar to the attitude just described is that of a hostile audience, who are against your story, regardless of whether you talk about exciting things. Again, your story won't have much of an impact if your audience is hostile.

Now imagine returning from London and telling your best friend, who has never been on the London Eye, about the wonders you can see when the wheel reaches its highest point. Your friend, who was completely unaware of the existence of this Ferris wheel in London, represents an example of an unaware audience, that is, a group of people who don't know the topic of your story but, if they did, they might be interested.

Finally, imagine that you are still under the Ferris wheel, have just paid for your ticket, and are eager to get on the wheel to admire the view. Before you even board the wheel though, in your head you've already imagined the beautiful lights of London and see the London Bridge and Big Ben. When you finally do board, your eyes remain wide open throughout the tour, as you try to take in every corner of the view. This is an example of an interested audience who enjoys the topic of your story before even reading it. This audience type also has high expectations, so your goal is to satisfy them.

Through this simple example, I wanted to highlight the different types of audiences, classified based on their thoughts: disinterested, hostile or polarized, unaware, or interested. In this chapter, you will see which story elements you can work on to engage various types of audiences. In summary, this chapter covers the following:

- What the audience thinks
- Details on the stomach-heart-brain theory
- How to adapt your story to what the audience thinks

Let's start right away with what the audience thinks.

Introducing the Audience's Thoughts

In the previous chapter, you learned that you can classify your audience, based on three different criteria: what they want, which corresponds to the audience's objective; what they already know about the story; and what they think about the story. You have also learned that the audience can have three different goals when they encounter a story: to be informed, to be entertained, or to make decisions. To ensure that your audience achieves their objective, the story's objective should coincide with that of the audience. You can work on the First and Second Plot Points and the Next Steps at the story structure level. In practice, you can adapt these main points of the story, based on the objective to be achieved. These points are the moments in which something new happens in the story: In the First Plot Point, you presented the problem; in the Second Plot Point, you described the contrast between the hero and antagonist. Finally, with the Next Steps, you described what happens when the problem is solved (if the Next Steps are after the Climax), or what must happen to solve the problem (if the Next Steps are during the Climax).

Regarding what the audience knows about the topic covered in the story, you can have three types of audience: the general audience, which does not know or knows little about the topic of the story; the professionals, who know the topic very well; and the executives, who are between the general audience and professionals: they know the topic, but not at a level of detail as the professionals. Based on what the audience knows, you can work on the hero's description, the context, the First Pinch Point, the Action, and the Dark Night. All these elements of the story correspond to their descriptive parts of the story, which enable you to enrich your audience's knowledge regarding the story's topic. For example, for a general audience, you will need to provide them with a lot of detail about the hero, the context, the antagonist (who is introduced in the First Pinch Point), how the antagonist causes the problem (i.e., the Action), and the extreme consequences of the problem (i.e., the Dark Night).

The last type of audience classification is based on their thoughts. Obviously, a person can think of anything when encountering a story. However, as shown in Figure 11.1, there are generally four types of attitudes (Longnecker, 2023).

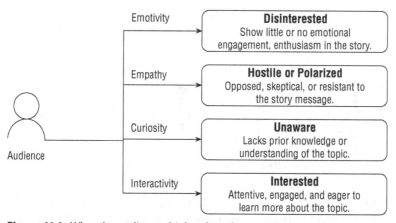

Figure 11.1: What the audience thinks when they encounter a story

Disinterested audiences show zero interest in the topic or message of your story. They are the ones who look at their smartphone, instead of admiring the landscape of the Ferris wheel. To engage such an audience, introduce your story with something important to them or with a problem they face daily. You can play on their emotional level (Green and Brock, 2000). I remember that some time ago, I had to present a project on the benefits of data storytelling at an event attended by several people with a technical background. I knew they had a technical background because they worked at the same institution where I work, and my institution works in the field of computer science. In this case, I didn't do any formal audience analysis because I already knew the shape of the audience. Precisely because they had a technical background, almost everyone sat in their chairs with their computer sitting in front of them. Even before speaking, I could hear keys clicking on the various computer keyboards. A terrible scenario was in front of me: Nobody would listen to me. Nobody looked at me. They were all hunched over, typing away on their computers. I was faced with less than 30 people who were completely uninterested in my presentation. Instead of starting to present my project, I showed them a slide with the graph shown in Figure 11.2.

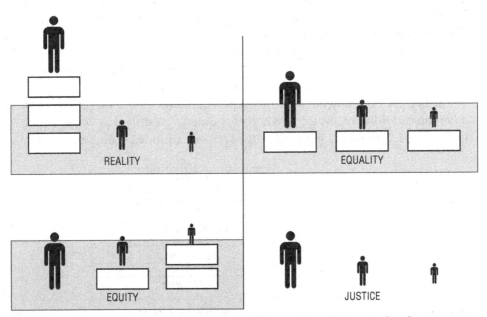

Figure 11.2: An example of a spaghetti graph used to provoke a disinterested audience

I began my presentation by saying, "Who among you has never had to deal with a graph of this type?" It was a terrible graphic design, without focus, telling practically nothing and presenting a tangle of threads. It was what, in technical jargon, is called a *spaghetti graph*, because it shows many tangled lines, appearing just like spaghetti does in a good pasta dish. Everyone (or almost everyone) looked up from their computers and smiled. I had hit the mark. The tangle of lines was also their problem. They were technicians who analyzed data every day and represented said data through graphs. The first graph that (almost) every technician implements is the spaghetti graph. So, my problem was precisely their problem. I continued my presentation with two more terrible graphs (see Figure 11.3): a terrible, illegible pie chart and a bar chart, slightly more readable but still equally as terrible.

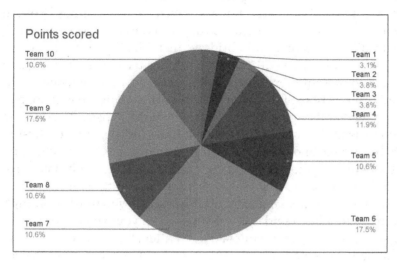

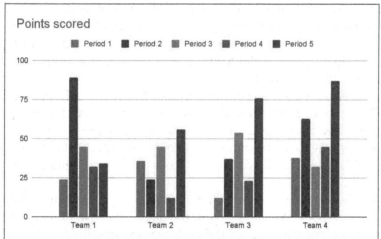

Figure 11.3: Two examples of difficult-to-read graphics used to provoke a disinterested audience

These graphics built a bridge between the presentation and the audience because they were precisely their problem. I had played on the emotional levels of my audience, which, therefore, woke up. I had hit the mark because I had played on two main aspects: my audience's emotional involvement and personal relevance. After the presentation, a colleague from the audience said precisely these words to me: "You woke up the audience!" To awaken a disinterested audience, it is, therefore, essential to play on the hook, as we will discuss shortly.

Challenge: Think about the last time you presented your data to someone. What kind of hook did you use to pique their interest?

The second type of audience is the polarized or hostile audience. This audience type already has well-defined opinions, which are often opposite of the message of your story. Their opinions are strongly tied to their own ideas and may even contradict your story. Build bridges, then identify any commonalities. The best way to dialogue with someone isn't to try to convince anyone of your ideas but to present them respectfully, accepting that someone might think differently. In this type of dialogue, even a hostile audience will not feel fingers being pointed at them and might be more willing to listen to you. One of the least "publicized" but most effective techniques for speaking to a hostile audience is to be humble and present yourself as someone who has the same problems as the audience, and not as someone who has all the ready solutions. We will see this later, however, when I talk about the role of the storyteller. For now, just know that when speaking to a hostile audience, you must show high empathy toward them. What I said is fine if you present your story live and can speak directly to your audience. If your story is written, however, you have no way of controlling the reactions of a hostile audience. However, you can control the tone and language you use in your story. For example, if you have a strong position on a topic, try not to denigrate those who think differently from you, but always be respectful and aware that the world is beautiful because it is varied, and you do not possess the truth. At most, you are its servant while seeking it. But the truth is not yours.

The unaware audience is one that could potentially be interested in your story but is not familiar with the topic being discussed. For this audience type, use a straightforward approach that makes the topic discussion simple to understand. In this case, the only way to make your story known is to spread it as much as possible to reach this type of audience. How? Through different communication channels or social media.

The last type of audience to discuss is the interested one—one who already knows the topic and is open to receiving your message. There isn't much to say about this type of audience: It's simply the best-case scenario that can happen to you in storytelling. This audience type might already know you because they have read other stories of yours, or they know the topic and think like you. In this case, there is no need to convince anyone. They are already convinced. However, this audience has high expectations, so your job is to tell them great data-driven stories.

So far, we have seen four types of audiences based on their thoughts. Obviously, your audience will not be compartmentalized but will be a mix of all types of audiences. This is because you cannot know in advance what your audience thinks. In the case of your objectives and knowledge, you can, more or less, know which category the audience belongs to (if you have done some preliminary analysis). But in the case of what the audience thinks, in most cases, you will not know them in advance, unless you've interviewed them first. So, what can you do? You can still focus on one type of audience, hoping to make inroads with at least that type. You can try to talk to everyone a bit, but the risk is not speaking to anyone specifically here. If you are a beginner, I advise you to focus on the type of audience that is interested or unaware, and to at least talk to them. You can try speaking to a disinterested audience if you have more experience and have already written several stories. Finally, I advise you to write stories for hostile audiences because I assure you, in that case, you'll need a lot of authority, humility, and patience.

Once you know what the audience might think of your story, let's see what aspects you can work on, based on what they think. Let's look at what I call the Stomach-Heart-Brain theory.

The Stomach-Heart-Brain Theory

The Stomach-Heart-Brain theory is a nice way to represent the three dimensions of processing a story or, more generally, information. I thought of this model because it is easier to remember than the big words that hide behind it—the instinctive, affective, and behavioral levels (Lane, 2023). Figure 11.4 shows the three levels of the Stomach-Heart-Brain theory.

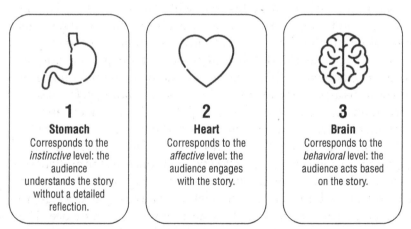

1
Stomach
Corresponds to the *instinctive* level: the audience understands the story without a detailed reflection.

2
Heart
Corresponds to the *affective* level: the audience engages with the story.

3
Brain
Corresponds to the *behavioral* level: the audience acts based on the story.

Figure 11.4: The Stomach-Heart-Brain theory

According to this theory, there are three levels at which a person receives a message. The first level is the stomach. If you haven't eaten for a while and you're starving, it doesn't matter what you eat. The important thing is to eat. However, after you have eaten and are full, you will have no interest in understanding what ingredients were used to prepare the food you just ate, nor will the flavor of the food you just enjoyed matter. This is the first level of reception of the story—the instinctive level. At this level, the audience understands the story, but once they have understood it, they are not interested in going further. There is no continuation. The story does not penetrate deeply into the audience, so it ends there.

The second level is in the heart—the affective level. If you are already quite full and still need to eat more, you are looking for refined, tasty food on the palate. It's not enough to eat anything, but you want something good. While eating it, you savor every detail—an aftertaste that engages your palate deeply. The second level of reception of the story is the emotional level. At this level, the audience is looking for great emotions. It's not enough for them to just understand the story; they need to feel something when they interact with the story. However, even at this level, feeling emotions doesn't mean that the audience changes their behavior, in the sense that the story could have a lasting impact over time.

The last level is the brain, or behavioral level. Suppose you have already eaten and enjoyed every flavor of your meal and are full. Imagine being so excited about what you ate that you go to the chef and ask for the meal's recipe, so you can cook it again at home and eat it again the next day. This is the third level of your story—the behavioral level—in which the audience's experience of your story becomes part of their life. Only at this level will your story have a lasting effect on the audience and bring about change. After all, anything that remains at the level of the stomach and heart does not turn into a real-life change.

Formalizing what I have just said, the audience can understand a story at three levels: instinctive (stomach), affective (heart), and behavioral (brain). The *instinctive* level concerns aspects related to intuitive understanding. It focuses on conveying information, facts, data, and logic to help the audience understand the message. The instinctive level also depends on the audience's prior knowledge of the topic and the way they come to know, meaning that each person has their cultural baggage and learning curve. The *affective* level concerns the audience's emotional aspects and sentimental involvement. It leverages emotions, such as surprise, curiosity, fear, hope, or the personal relevance of the message, to capture attention and create an emotional connection with the audience. The *behavioral* level focuses on aspects that stimulate the audience's active response and practical involvement. It pushes the audience to participate, interact, or take concrete action in response to the message.

You can play on these three levels (i.e., instinctive, affective, behavioral levels) to engage your audience based on what they think, as shown in Table 11.1.

Table 11.1: Main Elements You Can Play On, Based on What the Audience Thinks

AUDIENCE	INSTINCTIVE	AFFECTIVE	BEHAVIORAL
Disinterested	Simple and direct information Clarity and basic concepts	Strong emotional involvement Personal relevance	Simple calls to action Curiosity triggered through questions
Polarized	Facts and rigorous logic Objective and verifiable data	Show empathy Avoid emotional conflict	Discuss respectfully Avoid direct provocations
Unaware	Basic education and explanations Gradual introduction to new concepts, also through metaphors	Arouse curiosity Make topic personal and relevant	Encourage small-learning actions Stimulate questions
Interested	In-depth analysis and solid arguments	Strengthen beliefs and values	Active interaction Stimulate participation with debates

To hit the mark on an instinctive level, convey simple and direct concepts to a disinterested audience, while for a polarized audience, you can use objective facts to support your position. The unaware audience requires a progressive introduction of new information, while an interested one is looking for in-depth content and detailed analysis. For example, if you want to introduce the antagonist CO_2 emissions into the story of how temperature anomalies increase to a disinterested audience, use phrases like "CO_2 is like a blanket that heats Earth too much." For a polarized audience, leverage scientific studies that prove the responsibility of CO_2 in the increase in temperature. To an unaware audience, introduce CO_2 emissions with a metaphor like this: "CO_2 traps heat in our atmosphere, a bit like leaving the car in the sun with the windows closed." Then, gradually introduce the story's antagonist in more depth. Present CO_2 emissions at a more detailed level to an interested audience, perhaps directly involving the audience by triggering a debate.

Once you reach the instinctive level, your audience is assumed to have understood your story. Now, it's simply a question of involving them more indepth. To affect a disinterested audience on an affective level, play on their emotions. For a polarized audience, play on their empathy instead. With the audience unaware, try to arouse curiosity and connect the topic to their daily lives. With an interested audience, however, it is necessary to maintain a solid emotional involvement linked to the audience's values and beliefs.

Consider again the example of the increase in temperature and the presentation of the antagonist, CO_2 emissions. To emotionally engage a disinterested audience, add concrete images to the story that show where CO_2 emissions originate, such as industries or car exhaust. For a hostile audience, for example, who does not believe that the temperature increase is due to CO_2 emissions, focus on empathy. Instead of attacking their position, show common concern for air quality and the well-being of future generations. To an unaware audience, describe how CO_2 emissions are part of their daily life, for example, if they use the car daily to go to work. Finally, for an interested audience, provide details about CO_2 emissions, such as the average amount of CO_2 a car produces during a year, or how specific industrial sectors and agricultural practices contribute more to global emissions.

Once the affective level is reached, the audience not only understands the story but is also emotionally charged. To ensure that the story generates a profound change in the audience, you must reach the level of the brain, that is, a behavioral level. To engage a disinterested audience at this level, propose simple and practical next steps. In the example of rising temperatures, propose turning off lights when they aren't needed or reducing plastic consumption. These are small contributions to help the hero Temperature maintain control.

Hostile audiences require non-provocative interactions. Avoid direct requests for immediate change. In the example of the increase in temperature, invite the audience to reflect or discuss the topic, through questions such as: "How can we guarantee a safer future for our children?"

With an unaware audience, you can stimulate learning by asking questions. For example, in the case of the increase in temperature, encourage the audience to carry out small awareness actions, such as personally researching the topic, participating in local projects to raise awareness on climate change, or following pages or groups on social media that concentrate on the environment.

Finally, actively engage the relevant audience with discussions and debates. In the case of rising temperatures, stimulate active participation by proposing petitions, group initiatives, volunteer activities, or the promotion of political advocacy actions. Invite the audience to be part of the change and influence those around them, becoming ambassadors of the hero Temperature.

Let's now see what effect the Stomach-Heart-Brain theory has throughout the story. As you well know, your story is organized in three acts, and the most representative moments of the story, those in which something significant happens for the hero, are the First Plot Point (in the first act), the Second Plot Point (in the second act), and the Dark Night (or Third Plot Point) and the Climax (in the third act). I remind you that in the First Plot Point, you present the problem; in the Second Plot Point, the antagonist; in the Dark Night, the extreme consequences of the problem caused by the antagonist; and in the Climax, the final battle between the hero and the antagonist. Every moment of the story has a specific effect on the audience. The first level is, as I said, the Stomach, which corresponds to the instinctive level. Audience engagement at an instinctive level follows the classic learning curve (Bills, 1934, p. 192), as shown in Figure 11.5. This means that the audience's understanding will be maximum at the end of the story.

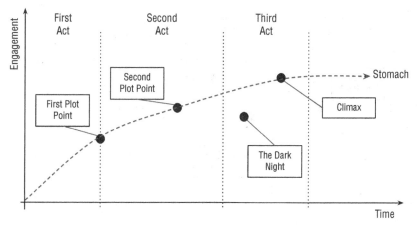

Figure 11.5: Engagement at the Stomach level of the audience during the three acts of the story

At an affective level, that is, at the heart level, the audience experiences a different involvement than the instinctive one. In fact, emotions follow up and down, with peaks corresponding to the First and Second Plot Points and the Climax. After the Climax, the emotional level drops a bit. Figure 11.6 summarizes the emotional level of audience engagement throughout the story.

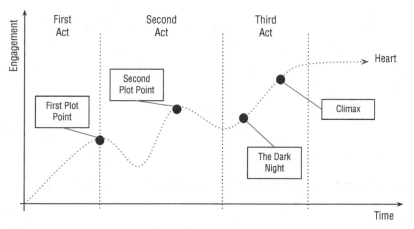

Figure 11.6: Engagement at the audience's heart level during the story's three acts

Finally, on a behavioral level, the audience experiences an involvement defined by the Kübler-Ross Change Curve (Kübler-Ross, 1969), as shown in Figure 11.7.

At this level, the audience experiences the same drama as the hero, who initially rejects the problem (the First Plot Point) with a negative peak and then decides to act during the Dark Night phase.

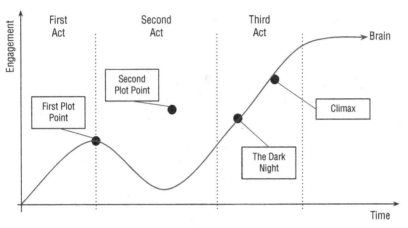

Figure 11.7: Engagement at the brain level of the audience during the three acts of the story

Therefore, the audience experiences different engagement at each level, which is maximum at the behavioral level, as shown in Figure 11.8, which simply groups together the three previous figures.

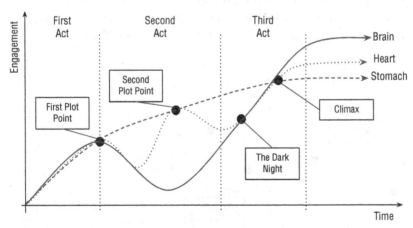

Figure 11.8: Engagement at the audience's stomach, heart, and brain level during the story's three acts

With this brief theoretical discussion, I wanted to show you which elements of the story you need to play to involve the audience at all levels. You might think you must play at the level of plot points and Climax, but that's not entirely true. The story elements to work on are those *immediately before* these points, so that the audience arrives at these critical points for total engagement. Let me explain better. Imagine you must shoot an arrow from a bow. The decisive moment is not when you release your hand from the bow but when you load the bow, which precedes the actual launch. The more you draw the bow, the longer your arrow will fly. The same goes with the story: The more you charge the moments before the crucial ones, the stronger the audience's reaction will be at the critical moment. So, let's see how to do it.

Adapting Your Story

So far, I have talked about four types of audiences based on what they think: disinterested, polarized, unaware, and interested. But how do you know in advance what kind of audience you have in front of you? How do you get into people's heads before you even meet them? As you saw in Chapter 9, "From Making to Delivering a Data-Driven Story," before adapting the story to your audience, you need to do a preliminary analysis and study of the audience to understand who you are in front of. Two cases can occur: Either you know the people you will have to speak to, or you don't know them. If you know them, you can imagine which category they belong to. For example, if you must present something innovative to your work team and you know that your team is hostile to change, you will undoubtedly have to speak to a hostile audience. If, however, you know that you must speak to colleagues who are fiddling with the computer while you speak, you will have to speak to an uninterested audience. If you must present your story to your family members, they are probably unaware of your work, so you will have to consider them as an unaware audience. If you publish your story in a trade magazine, you speak to an interested audience. And so on. With a little experience and common sense, you will be able to understand your audience.

If, however, you are speaking to an audience you don't know, the only thing that can help you is the preliminary analysis of the audience and the context in which you will present your story. Don't neglect the context, because it speaks much more than questionnaires and surveys. For example, the context tells you if your audience is technical or generic and in general also what they think. For example, if you talk about climate change in a context where there will be only industrialists, you will probably speak to a hostile audience. If you speak at an environmental event instead, your audience will be interested. Study the context and do an audience analysis to get a picture of who you are in front of. In the previous chapter, you saw how to adapt the various story pieces, based on what the audience wants or knows. You have seen how some pieces are better suited to deepening objectives and others for knowledge. Figure 11.9 shows the story pieces you can work on to adapt, based on what the audience wants or knows. Furthermore, the figure highlights which pieces must be adapted, based on the audience's thoughts. Obviously, the underlined story pieces are not watertight compartments, but you can adjust each piece even to what that part was not primarily designed for.

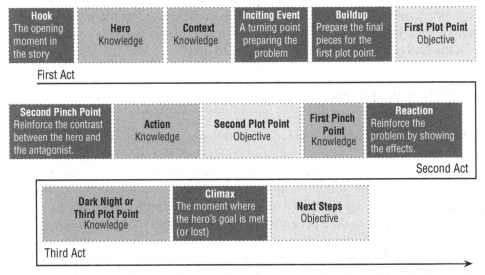

Figure 11.9: The parts of the story (in dark gray) that you can work on, based on what the audience thinks

As you can see from the figure, the story pieces on which you can work to adapt the story, based on what the audience thinks, are those that precede the turning points of the story (in the first two acts): the hook, inciting incident, buildup (before the First Plot Point), and reaction (before the Second Plot Point). Because the third act should be the maximum moment of audience involvement, I also suggest working directly on the Climax to have the maximum impact on the audience, using the previous example, when the bow is released from the arrow. Let's now see how to adapt these story pieces, based on the audience's thoughts, starting from the hook.

Hook

The hook is the opening moment of the story. Its main task is to attract and capture the audience's attention. It's your only opportunity to let an uninterested or unaware audience into your story. In addition to being intriguing, your hook must also demonstrate your credibility. In Chapter 5, "First Act: Defining the Sidekick," you learned that you could use five hooks: a personal anecdote, a provocative question, a surprising fact, a powerful quote, or a vivid display. Figure 11.10 adapts these hook types, based on what the audience thinks.

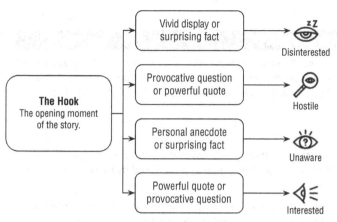

Figure 11.10: How to adapt the hook based on the audience's thoughts

The hook should be highly thought-provoking and surprising for a disinterested audience, immediately grabbing attention. Use a vivid display or an unexpected statement to make the audience think. To capture the attention of a polarized or hostile audience, the hook should avoid immediate conflict, aiming to create common ground, perhaps by raising an issue on which all parties can agree. For the unaware audience, introduce the topic with a familiar scenario or even an anecdote. Finally, if you are dealing with an interested audience, your goal is to establish mutual trust so that the audience trusts you. To establish this credibility, start with a powerful quote or provocative question.

To better understand how you can adapt the hook based on the audience in front of you, consider the example of increasing the temperature. Table 11.2 shows some examples of textual hooks by audience type.

Table 11.2: Text Hook Examples Based on What the Audience Thinks

AUDIENCE	TEXTUAL HOOK
Disinterested	**Vivid Display:** Imagine a summer where water is scarce, cities are sweltering in the heat, and air conditioning isn't enough to keep you cool. This is what could happen, as temperatures rise.
	Surprising Fact: Did you know global temperatures have increased by more than 1 degree Celsius since 1860? Even such a small change has resulted in extreme weather events worldwide.
Hostile	**Provocative Question:** What would happen if global temperatures continued to rise at the current rate? We cannot ignore the consequences, even if we think climate change is exaggerated.
	Powerful Quote: As climate scientist [X] said, "We are facing a planetary emergency." Temperatures are changing dramatically, and our time to act is running out.

Continues

Table 11.2 (*continued*)

AUDIENCE	TEXTUAL HOOK
Unaware	**Personal Anecdote:** I remember a summer in my childhood when the heat was so intense that it seemed unreal. Now I know that heat was not just an isolated event but part of a more significant climate change.
	Surprising Fact: Did you know that in the last century alone, the planet's average temperature has increased by more than 1 degree Celsius?
Interested	**Powerful Quote:** As the famous climatologist [X] said, "Rising global temperatures are the greatest danger our planet has ever faced."
	Provocative Question: What will happen if we don't act now to reduce rising temperatures?

Introduce your hero and the context once you have baited the audience with the hook. The next step is to maintain their attention. Let's see how to do it in the inciting event.

Inciting Event

The inciting event is a turning point in preparing the problem, such as the opinion of an expert gained from an interview, a particular event that will trigger the problem, and so on. Use the inciting event to keep the audience's attention high. More specifically, use the sidekick to present the inciting event. The sidekick is precisely the hero's sidekick and possibly a human case. In Chapter 5, you saw how to adapt the sidekick based on the story's objective, that is, what the audience wants. The persuasive sidekick supports and reinforces the hero's arguments, offering additional evidence, testimonies, or viewpoints to strengthen the main message. The informative sidekick is an internal narrator who explains complex concepts, provides historical context, or clarifies technical details. The entertainer sidekick adds humor, drama, or adventure to the story, enriching the audience's experience.

Now, let's see how to use the sidekick to structure the inciting event based on the audience's thoughts. Figure 11.11 shows what type of sidekick you can use based on your audience's thoughts.

For the disinterested audience, the sidekick could be the audience themselves experiencing something that could directly or indirectly impact their lives, even if they don't currently realize it. For example, in the story of rising temperatures, you might ask the audience if they have experienced power blackouts caused by excessive use of air conditioners.

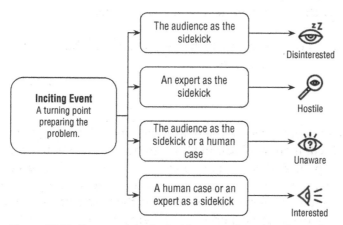

Figure 11.11: How to adapt the inciting event based on the audience's thoughts

For a polarized or hostile audience, use an authoritative sidekick, such as an expert who describes the inciting event as a concrete fact that challenges their beliefs. For example, if the audience does not believe or is hostile toward rising temperatures, you could involve an expert discussing factory closures and energy rationing in different world regions.

For an unaware audience, the sidekick could be the audience themselves or a human case, extracted directly from the data, who's experiencing the crisis, such as a patient if you have health data, a customer in the case of a product, and so on. In the rising temperature example, if you want to use the audience themselves as a sidekick, you can ask the audience if they experienced any problems watering their yard last summer. Finally, to an interested audience, the sidekick is still a human case or an expert who will provide details about the discovery.

You might think that the examples of inciting events I have just described are figments of imagination or unbridled creativity. In reality, they must result from an in-depth study of the topic involving domain experts. Start from the data and then read news, books, or other reliable material to learn more about the subject you are presenting. This way, the data from which you built the story is not isolated but has an overall context.

NOTE Data storytelling expert Brent Dykes, in one of his posts, discussed the difference between data stories and stories with data (Dykes, 2024). According to Dykes, data stories are the stories that are built from data. Stories with data, on the other hand, are stories that use data to confirm their theories. In this book, I talk exclusively about data stories, that is, stories built starting from data. All the material you add to the story (i.e., expert opinion, additional material, anecdotes) reinforces what the data says. Fidelity to the data is the first thing, as you learned in one of the book's first chapters where you extracted the hero from the data. In my opinion, stories with data could be manipulated, as they could use only part of the data to confirm their theories. So, remember to talk about data stories and not stories with data.

The buildup is the next story piece on which to work. Let's see how to structure it, based on what the audience thinks.

Buildup

The buildup piece is where you prepare the final parts for the First Plot Point; it's where the problem will manifest itself in all its grandeur. You should construct the buildup to keep the audience's attention high. In Chapter 5, you saw how you can use three strategies to construct the buildup: a specific event, an expert opinion, and recent news. A specific event splits the hero's life into two parts: before and after the event. An expert opinion helps the audience understand the gravity and legitimacy of the hero's experiences. Recent news creates a sense of urgency and relevance, showing that the hero's struggles are part of a more significant global issue. Based on your audience's thoughts, you can use one of the suggested buildups, as shown in Figure 11.12.

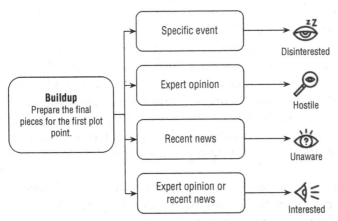

Figure 11.12: How to adapt the buildup based on what the audience thinks

For a disinterested audience, use a specific event, such as the temperature spike in 1977, to make the issue concrete and relatable. For the hostile audience, use an expert opinion to establish credibility and counteract their skepticism, citing respected scientists. For the unaware audience, use recent news to show the issue's relevance, linking the ongoing temperature rise to their daily life.

Finally, for the interested audience, use either expert opinion to deepen their understanding or recent news to stress the situation's urgency.

At this point, you can present the First Plot Point with the description of the problem. Once it is clear what problem the hero has, the next step is to describe the hero's reaction to the problem.

Reaction

The reaction is the story piece that opens the second act. At this stage, reinforce the problem by showing the problem's effects. Use additional data to strengthen your problem. You can present this data as graphs or simply in a conversational way, for example, incorporating qualitative data, such as interviews with populations like your audience. Choose this data to show based on audience type, as shown in Figure 11.13.

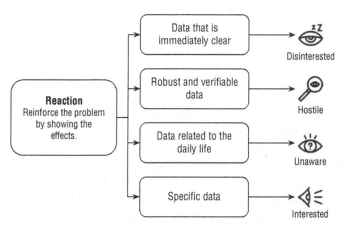

Figure 11.13: How to adapt the data presented during the reaction phase based on the audience's thoughts

For a disinterested audience, focus on immediately striking and easily understandable numbers, such as economic losses and visible damage globally, to try to grab attention. Use robust verifiable data from authoritative, independent sources with a hostile audience. This data makes it harder for this audience to deny the problem, and accuracy in data helps build credibility.

Data must be immediately relevant and connected to everyday life for the unaware audience. Provide more specific and complex data for an already interested audience. Such data provide depth on the problem and project it toward future scenarios. Table 11.3 shows some possible data to use in the case of the temperature increase story.

Table 11.3: Which Data to Use in the Reaction Phase Based on the Audience's Thoughts

DATA TYPES	DISINTERESTED	HOSTILE	UNAWARE	INTERESTED
Daily habits			x	
Climate change	x			
Economy	x	x		
Energy consumption			x	
Extreme weather events	x	x		x
Local weather events			x	
Impact on ecosystems		x		x
Sea level rise		x		x
Impact on health	x		x	
Long-term studies		x		x

If you don't have data available, use the sidekick to reinforce the concepts in the same way that you used them in the inciting event, obviously adding new details and not simply repeating the old ones.

After the reaction phase, the story continues with the presentation of the antagonist until you reach the Second Pinch Point, which reinforces the contrast between the hero and antagonist. Remember that in the Second Pinch Point, you describe the effects of the problem caused by the antagonist.

Second Pinch Point

If you remember correctly, in Chapter 8, "Third Act: Setting the Climax and Next Steps," I told you the story of Antonio, who wanted to learn to ride a bike without training wheels. On that occasion, I only presented you with the story's main pieces, such as the plot points and the climax: Antonio was the hero of the story, and his antagonist was the fear of falling. Now, stop for a moment and try to add the Second Pinch Point to the story, that is, the moment in which you add details on the contrast between the hero and the antagonist, or even the effects of the antagonist's action, even on elements not directly linked to the hero. In Antonio's story, in the Second Pinch Point, you could describe how this fear of falling is not new, because in other contexts Antonio fell. For example, once he fell off the bed and cried. Or you could describe how other children fell while riding their bikes. Your goal is to describe that Antonio's fear is not unfounded. The same thing is true in data storytelling. In the Second Pinch Point, you should strengthen the contrast between the hero and the antagonist by adding further details, once again using ancillary data or the sidekick. Use the data types suggested for Reaction, as shown in Figure 11.12, being careful to highlight details from the perspective of the antagonist and not the hero. In the example of rising temperatures, the antagonist is CO_2 emissions, so you could show data on the greenhouse effect, or the role of CO_2 compared to other greenhouse gases.

You have reached the last piece of the story that you can work on to adapt to the audience: the Climax.

Climax

The Climax is the moment where the hero's goal is met (or lost). If you've built the previous pieces of the story well, this should be an irresistible moment—one that all types of audiences have been waiting for since the beginning of the story. In addition, you can leverage various aspects, which you also considered in developing previous pieces of the story, as shown in Figure 11.14.

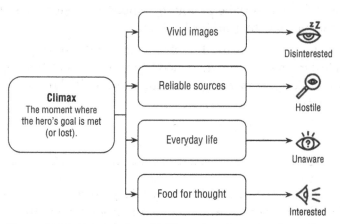

Figure 11.14: How to adapt the Climax based on what the audience thinks

To a disinterested audience, present the Climax as the moment when decisions really matter. Use vivid images that remain imprinted in the memory. If you want to speak to a hostile audience, use reliable sources to explain the end of the story. In some cases, you might even opt not to show an overall winner but open a debate or discussion. To an unaware audience, clearly explain the solution to the problem, using images and examples from everyday life. Finally, offer food for thought to an interested audience, offering in-depth information on possible future developments.

We have reached the end of this chapter, which has seen us reflect on how to adapt some pieces of the story based on what the audience thinks. Obviously, you don't have just one type of audience, and your task is to use the sugges-tions I gave you in this chapter and the previous one, based on the situations you will have from time to time. In the next chapter, you will see when and how you and your audience retell your story.

Takeaways

- Based on their thoughts, there are four types of audiences: disinterested, hostile, unaware, and interested.
- Disinterested audiences show little or no emotional engagement or enthu-siasm in the story.
- Hostile or polarized audiences are opposed, skeptical, or resistant to the story's message.
- Unaware audiences lack prior knowledge or understanding of the topic.
- Interested audiences are attentive, engaged, and eager to learn more about the topic.
- The Stomach-Heart-Brain theory helps you remember that a story acts at three levels: instinctive, affective, and behavioral.
- To adapt the story to the audience's thoughts, work on the story pieces preceding the critical moments of the story: hook, inciting incident, buildup (before the First Plot Point), Reaction (before the Second Plot Point), and the Climax (third act).

References

Bills, A. G. (1934). *General Experimental Psychology*. New York: Longmans, Green and Co. https://archive.org/details/generalexperimen00 bill/page/192/mode/2up (accessed September 29, 2024).

Dykes, B. (2024). Data story vs. story with data: What's the difference? https://www.linkedin.com/posts/brentdykes_datastorytelling-activity-7244384920117133312-ManU (accessed September 29, 2024).

Green, M. C. and Brock, T. C. (2000). The role of transportation in the per-suasiveness of public narratives. *Journal of Personality and Social Psychology*, 79(5), 701.

Kübler-Ross, E. (1969). *On Death and Dying*. New York: Macmillan Publishing Co.

Lane, Anne. (2023). Towards a theory of organizational storytelling for public relations: An engagement perspective. *Public Relations Review*, 49.1: 102297.

Longnecker, N. (2023). Good science communication considers the audience. In Susan Rowland and Louise Kuchel (eds.), *Teaching Science Students to Communicate: A Practical Guide* (pp. 21–30). Cham: Springer International Publishing.

12

Retelling the Story

Finally, after much work, you have told your data-driven story to an audience. The impact now has been significant. You have received your feedback, and many have been interested in your story. It was a great success. But then you notice that no one talks about your story after a week. Like water that flows into the river and then never returns, your story has passed, giving way to other stories and events. After all, in this world based on haste, even months and months of preparation are burned instantly. For example, think about when an important person dies. Everyone talks about them for a few days: magazines, newspapers, television, the Internet, and ordinary people. Then, after a few days, no one talks about their death anymore.

Why all this? The answer lies in the way our brain works, what Ebbinghaus called the *forgetting curve* (Ebbinghaus, 1913). According to Ebbinghaus, after a week, we tend to forget about 90 percent of what we have listened to, unless we have listened to something with significant impact. Ebbinghaus' theory is not something outdated, anchored in the late 1800s. In 2015, it was replicated in an experiment conducted by Murre and Dros (2015). This means even if you tell a great story, your story will most likely fall by the wayside after a week. Or at least, after a week, those who listened to you will remember only 10 percent of your story.

What can you do to prevent your story from being forgotten? You can tell it again. That's why, at the beginning of the book, I told you to keep the making and delivery phases separate and to think about the audience after designing your story. Having a clear story from the beginning enables you to quickly reformulate it through different channels and audiences without altering the theme, plot, and characters.

Retelling a story helps you keep it alive and remember it over time. A well-known influencer on LinkedIn, Lara Acosta, has repeatedly stated in her posts that to have a strong presence on social media, you must not always say new things, but repeating the same things in different ways is sufficient. The same goes for data storytelling. Tell your stories several times if you want them to be not forgotten and survive over time. Retelling a story means ensuring your data stays fresh in the minds of people who have already seen it and that it reaches new people. Plus, retelling enables you to adapt to changes in time and situations.

Retelling a story also enables you to reinforce your story's message. Any substantial change takes time and deserves deep reflection. No one makes an important decision if they haven't considered it deeply. The same goes for data-driven stories. If you want to help decision-makers with your data-driven stories, repeat them several times in several different ways like posters, email blasts, and flyers. Each medium is an advertisement for your story. Think for a moment about all the times that you've repeatedly seen the same ad on television or the Internet. Wouldn't it be enough just to watch it once? *Repetita iuvant* (repeating helps), as the Latins stated, in the sense that repeating things helps to memorize them better.

There are two ways to retell a data-driven story. The first way is for you to tell your story several times. The second way is that the audience advocates for your story and tells it again themselves. The two perspectives have different scopes. If you retell the story yourself, then the circle of your audience will always be more or less the same. If, however, you can get the audience to tell your story, then you could get a cascade effect in which more and more people will talk about your story. This is what happens with viral posts. They are told by someone and then spread everywhere, through the sharing of others. Even after some time, you'll see them circulating online again. So how might you best set up your story to become the next viral sensation your audience encounters? Let's proceed in order. In this chapter, you will see the following:

- An introduction to retelling
- You, as the new narrator of the story
- The audience, as the new narrator of the story

Let's start from the introduction to retelling.

Introduction to Retelling

Retelling is an essential component of human communication, a technique that cultures have used to transmit values, traditions, and knowledge. Retelling a story, or repeating something several times, is a technique students use to learn a concept. The more times you repeat it, the better you remember it. I remember with pleasure that, when I was about 13 or 14 years old, I studied almost all the capitals of the world's countries as a hobby. Periodically, I took an atlas and repeated them. I remembered them all perfectly. Then, I abandoned this practice, and now, many years later, I remember very few of them. Practice helps you remember. Even children ask us to listen to the same stories. They do it because it gives them security and enables them to learn more story details.

Retelling a story not only refreshes the concepts already acquired but also helps the audience grasp new aspects that they had not grasped before. This applies to the story's contents and the profound message that the story carries. Whenever the audience listens to a story again, they explore richer meanings.

Imagine graphing the level of story internalization versus the number of times the audience listens to it, as shown in Figure 12.1.

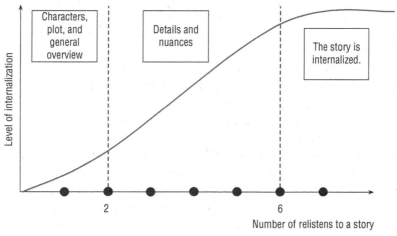

Figure 12.1: Level of internalization of a story compared to the number of times it is listened to

Figure 12.1 represents the typical *learning curve*, which initially undergoes a rapid acceleration and then flattens out over time (Yelle, 1979). There is no unanimous consensus in the scientific literature that establishes a precise number of listens required, such as 6 or 10, to internalize a story. However, heuristically, we can say that, more or less, after six relistens, the story is internalized.

When you encounter a story for the first time, the plot, main characters, and key moments are what strike you most. The overall impression is a general overview of the story without too many details.

On the second listen, being already familiar with the plot, your attention shifts to more specific and detailed elements, such as the details of the narrative, descriptions, emotions, and atmospheres. You can also grasp why the characters behave in a certain way or even their relationships. You can also notice the use of words, the pace of the story, the changes in tone, and the language used.

By the third time, with the story familiar, you focus on hidden symbols and themes. The story also begins to connect to your life and eventually pushes you to reflect on aspects of your life or universal themes.

After the fourth listen, you begin to internalize the story. Every emotion, detail, or phrase has sedimented. You even capture subtle aspects you would never have caught in the first listens. The story, by being listened to, begins to mix with your experiences, memories, and values. Somehow, it starts "talking" about you. You might give entirely personal meanings to some passages or recognize part of yourself in the characters and situations. You no longer just listen to it; you live it with an involvement beyond simply listening.

At the fifth time, the experience of listening to the story is further transformed. It becomes a ritual or internal rereading. The story takes on a ritual dimension, and an even more personal process of introspection and discovery can develop. You are no longer a spectator of the story; the story becomes a mirror for yourself because it invites you to reflect on yourself. The desire to share the story or rework it might also arise at this point. You might want to tell it yourself, transform it, or give it your own personal touch. The fifth listen, therefore, represents a fusion between the story and your life experience. It is no longer just a story but a bridge between you and something broader and more universal, which enriches your inner world.

After the sixth time you listen to the story, the experience becomes even more complex and subtle, almost as if it were now an integral part of your emotional memory and your inner world. Some phrases or scenes become almost mnemotechnics, ready to resurface when needed in other moments of life. The story begins to blend with your reality, and some of its details may become recurring references in your daily reflections or thoughts. You feel connected to certain characters as if they were real people, or you find that certain episodes mirror situations in your life. At this point, the story may have changed its meaning for you. Your experience and emotions have evolved since you first listened, and this personal change is reflected in how you interpret the story. Something that initially seemed light now seems profound, or a marginal aspect turns out to be a fundamental issue for you. The story has achieved the status of *emotional memory*. You don't just remember the plot or the characters; you remember how you felt when you listened. It becomes a place of return, almost a refuge, where you can reflect on yourself emotionally, seek answers, or even find a part of yourself. Figure 12.2 summarizes what you take away whenever you listen to a story again.

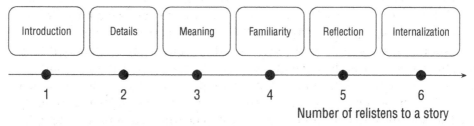

Figure 12.2: Level of understanding of the story based on the number of relistenings

The story can truly become one's own after a variable number of listens, depending on the person and the story itself, but in general, this process happens gradually and culminates between the sixth and tenth time. When a story becomes ours, it means that we not only understand it deeply but also integrate it into our identity and our daily reflections (Rao, 2016). An internalized story has a personal resonance and involves internal growth. This implies that the story influences our inner world, stimulating deep reflections and personal growth. Here, the story mirrors our innermost values, emotions, and aspirations, offering metaphors and archetypes that help us better understand ourselves. An internalized story is also integrated into our daily life in that it manifests itself in our way of thinking and speaking, reemerging spontaneously as an unconscious reference that guides us in everyday choices. Furthermore, it unites us with those who love it like us, creating a sense of belonging and sharing (Braman, 2023).

Finally, an internalized story is also a source of creative and thoughtful inspiration. It is no longer just a fixed story: It becomes a springboard for new ideas, inspires us to imagine variations or developments, and pushes us to reflect. The story becomes so rooted in us that it transforms into a personal memory, an internal space we can draw on to express and nourish our creativity. Figure 12.3 summarizes what it means for a story to have been internalized.

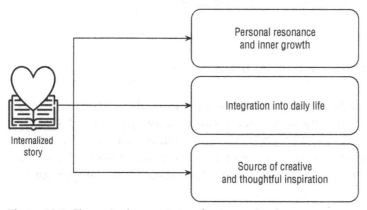

Figure 12.3: The main characteristics of an internalized story

Certainly, from the data storyteller's point of view (i.e., from your point of view), it is important to retell a story so the audience can assimilate it better. But from the audience's point of view, why should they listen to your story repeatedly? With all the rush around, the audience may not even have time to listen to your story again. Additionally, the audience may feel that they already understand the story and don't see the need for repetition, especially if they think the message was clear the first time. Some may also experience fatigue from hearing the same information repeatedly, particularly if it's not presented in a fresh or engaging way. In other cases, if the story lacks relevance or emotional appeal, the audience may lose interest in hearing it again. Although the audience may not be willing to relisten to your story, it is essential for you to retell it, using fresh and new means, to ensure that the message that the story carries is truly internalized. A story told only once rarely has a lasting effect. It is your job, therefore, to always look for new ways to talk about your story again. So, it's your job to tell it again, without the audience necessarily explicitly asking for it.

At this point, you have certainly understood the importance of telling the story several times. But how is it done? Let's see it in the next section.

You as the New Narrator of the Story

If you remember correctly, in the third chapter, I told you that every data-based story begins by developing a theme, precisely the story's main topic. The theme comprises three main elements: the controlling idea, the message, and the value, as shown in Figure 12.4.

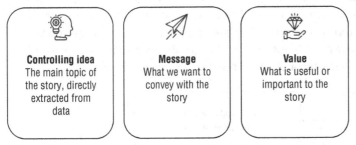

Controlling idea
The main topic of the story, directly extracted from data

Message
What we want to convey with the story

Value
What is useful or important to the story

Figure 12.4: The three main elements defining the theme of a story

The controlling idea is the insight extracted from the data. The message is what you want to convey with your story. It's the takeaway you want to leave with your audience after the story ends. Value is what is useful or essential to the story. It is a dichotomy between a positive and a negative element, such as preservation or destruction, in the case of the story about rising temperatures.

When you retell a story, you should not change the theme. You can describe different facets of the story, focusing on one character over another, or even vary the plot slightly, but the theme must remain constant. This is because your goal is to convey the theme to the audience: controlling idea, message, and value.

While keeping the theme constant, you can modify the following elements when retelling a story: channel, time, and context.

The Channel

The channel is how you tell your story, such as a slide presentation or email. Regardless of the channel you choose, when you retell a story, always consider the audience to whom you are retelling it. Suppose you retell the story to a different audience than the one who first heard it. In that case, you can use the same channel as the first time (for example, slides or an article), carefully adapting the story to different audiences. In the previous chapters, you have seen extensively how to refine a story already defined in its characters and plot for a specific audience. Simply personalize them based on what your audience knows, wants, and thinks.

If you retell the story to the same audience, it is a good idea to change the channel to maintain interest and avoid boring them (Bogue, 2023). Figure 12.5 shows a possible pattern of using different channels each time you retell the story to the same audience. It's not the only template you can use, but you can use it as a guideline to help your audience assimilate different aspects of the story with each listen.

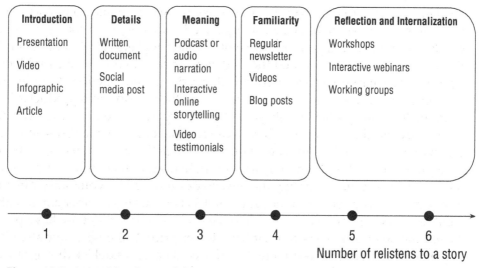

Figure 12.5: A possible scheme of channels used at each retelling of the story

The first telling of the story introduces the audience to the story. Use a slide presentation or article with a clear and concise story overview. You can also use a video or infographic.

On the second listen, the audience is focused on the details, so you might opt for a written document, such as a report, case study, or brochure, that provides the details the audience is seeking. For example, if the first version of your story was a data journalism article addressed to a well-defined community, you could opt for a series of posts on the community's social group. Each post might cover a different aspect of the story.

On the third listen, the audience elaborates on the story's meaning. You could retell the story through an audio narration or podcast, conversationally exploring the story's theme. You could also create a small website that enables interactive navigation of the story or collect video testimonials.

By the fourth time, the audience is already inside the story, so you could retell it using a regular newsletter, a series of videos, or regular blog posts to keep the audience interested, adding details and updates. At this point, the audience is entirely inside the story, so the fifth and sixth times you tell the story, you can go further, for example, by offering interactive webinars, workshops, working groups, and so on.

Everything I've told you might seem very theoretical. Let's take a practical example to understand. Imagine you work at a company that sells televisions, and at some point, sales of a particular model have dropped. Your boss has asked you to analyze the data to understand what is causing this drop in sales. You discovered that the decline is due to the increase in sales of a new television launched by the competitor at a lower price. You build your story from the data and tell it to your boss and the decision-makers. To tell your story, you use a slide presentation. Because you organized your story with characters and the plot into three acts, your audience of decision-makers clearly understood the message. You also proposed the next steps to take to resolve the problem. Everything seems perfect except for one thing: the forgetting curve. Caught up in other emergencies, the decision-makers delay the decision, and product sales continue to decline. After a week, your story is forgotten, and no one has acted. To ensure everything is recovered, you can send an email to your boss and the group of decision-makers in which you summarize the story, attaching a short in-depth document (not too long, as your boss doesn't have time). If you see that no one is yet implementing the next steps proposed by your story, after a few days, send your boss and the group of decision-makers another email with a link to video testimonials from customers who confirm that they have purchased the other product because it has a lower price. You might have already implemented these video testimonials and used them as a sidekick during story construction. Now, you can use them to strengthen your story. You can remind your boss about your story from time to time using different channels until the change is implemented.

At this point, you have understood which channels to use to retell your story. But how long do you have to wait before telling the story again? Let's see it in the next section, where I introduce the concept of spaced repetition.

Time

To understand how often to retell the story to the same audience, we use the technique of *spaced repetition*, which is used to learn new concepts, especially new languages, facts, or any information to be remembered in the long term (Ebbinghaus, 1913). The spaced repetition method suggests reviewing the information to be learned at gradually increasing intervals. This method is based on lengthening the forgetting curve, which I mentioned at the beginning of the chapter when I told you that after about a week, we forget about 90 percent of what we have heard. Figure 12.6 shows how spaced repetition works.

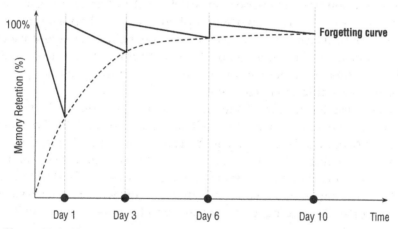

Figure 12.6: Memory retention using spaced repetition

Imagine telling your story for the first time at time zero. When you finish telling your story, the *forgetting curve* timer goes off. After a day, retell the story to reinforce the theme of the story. After you retell the story a second time, the forgetting curve timer goes off again, but this time the curve is less steep, so you can wait 48 hours before retelling the story a third time. On the third day, retell the story. The forgetting curve timer starts again, becoming even less steep because the audience is processing the story. Then, refresh the story on the sixth day to consolidate the story in your memory. At this point, the story is in the audience's memory, and you can extend the time for the next retelling to the tenth day.

So far, you have seen how to retell your story to the same audience, adapting the channel and the time. Let's now see how to retell the story to different audiences by redefining the context.

The Context

Redefining the context means adapting the story to the audience, based on their culture, interests, and so on, and the surrounding situation. In the previous chapters, you have seen how to adapt the story to the audience, so I will only go into some detail here. When you adjust the story to the audience, you can also incorporate elements of their culture, such as adding customs, habits, and traditions, to make the story closer to the audience.

In addition to the type of audience, adapting the story to the context also means considering the spatiotemporal circumstances in which you retell the story. These circumstances include where the story is retold (i.e., type of event, type of magazine or journal, in the case of an article, etc.) and time. For example, suppose you tell the story while a particular phenomenon is happening (e.g., COVID-19 or a political election). In that case, you can include it in the story to make it relevant now for the audience. In short, adapting the story to context means making it come alive here and now. Tomorrow, and in another place, your story will have a different declination.

So far, you have seen the benefits of retelling a story for the audience. However, retelling a story also benefits you, the storyteller. Every time you tell a story, not only is the audience enriched but so are you. You gain a deeper understanding of the topic through repetition, discovering nuances and connections that weren't obvious at first. This practice enables you to develop a richer understanding of the data and its meaning, bringing you to a higher level of awareness. Each story becomes an opportunity to refine your message and become a more sensitive and capable storyteller.

To recap what has been said so far, you can retell a story using three main elements: channel, time, and context. If the audience you are retelling the story to is the same, switch the channel to maintain interest. You can use presentations, emails, videos, social posts, and webinars. To decide when to repeat the story, use spaced repetition, a technique that lengthens the forgetting curve, reinforcing the memory at increasing intervals to consolidate the message.

As previously said, it's your job to retell the story to the same audience, despite their lack of interest or intention to relisten to it. Consider, for example, the case of a presentation to your boss. After the presentation, your boss is not motivated to relisten to your story multiple times probably because they don't have time. However, it's your job to retell them the story, perhaps when you meet them in the hallway or by email. Remember that a retold story is better retained.

If you are retelling the story to a new audience, adapt it to the audience's values, interests, and culture for greater relevance and connection. This also uses present time and space to make the story come alive here and now. Repeating the story enriches the audience and the teller, enabling them to deepen and strengthen their understanding of the data and its meaning.

So far, you've seen what happens when you retell the story. In the next section, we see the audience's role as the story's new narrator.

The Audience as the New Narrator of the Story

In my experience teaching at a university, I have noticed three types of students. The first are those who actively participate in the lesson (few and always the same), asking questions, coming to the office hours, and so on. When these students take the exam, they typically get relatively high grades. Then, some are entirely disinterested and perform on the exam based on how much they participated in the lessons (i.e., little). Finally, some don't ask any questions during the lessons and never come during office hours, but when they take the exam, they are brilliant, receiving top marks. This interaction–examination attitude can be mapped to the audience of a data-driven story. The lesson corresponds to the moment you tell the story and the retelling during the exam (see Figure 12.7).

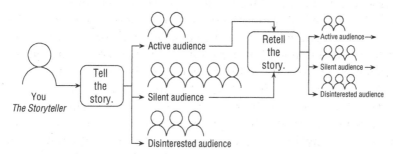

Figure 12.7: Who can potentially retell the story to the audience

The audience actively participating as you tell the story is similar to students asking questions (i.e., an active audience). Usually, in a group of many people, this audience is tiny. Still, they are precious because they could potentially retell your story in other contexts (for better or worse, as we will see shortly). A completely disinterested audience is unlikely to retell your story. With the techniques of adapting a story to the disinterested audience that I have illustrated in the previous chapters, you can still attract the attention of this type of audience, making them at least involved.

The silent but interested audience is precisely the one that could surprise you the most, retelling the story in other contexts.

We have seen who could potentially retell your story. Let's now see when and why they will retell it.

When the Audience Retells the Story

Potentially, the new retellers of your story could be those who actively participate with questions or reporting feedback, and those who are silent but attentive. Under what circumstances does the audience retell your story? There are two possibilities, as shown in Figure 12.8.

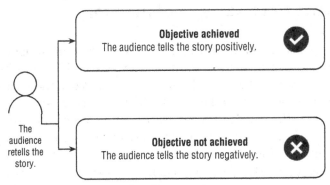

Figure 12.8: Two ways of retelling a story

In the first case, the audience achieved the objective. Think, for example, of a joke. You only tell it again if it makes you laugh. Nobody retells jokes that don't arouse any emotion in them. The same goes for data storytelling. If your goal is to entertain yourself, retell the story if it entertained you. To encourage the audience to retell the story, try to hit the objective the audience is looking for when you tell your story, as I described in the previous chapters.

In the second case, the audience did not achieve the objective. They achieved precisely the opposite of their objective. As a result, the audience will tell your story but in a negative way. In this case, the story will still be retold, but with a different twist than the one for which you imagined it. This retelling could hurt your story, transmitting a negative message to the new audiences whom it will be told. However, even these unexpected outcomes are valuable: They represent a new opportunity to reflect on how the message is interpreted, and which aspects may need further clarity. To avoid this negative retelling, work on the objective and try to adapt it to the audience as much as possible. Audiences might highlight moments in the story where things went wrong or didn't meet expectations. This "inverted" story could highlight different aspects, showing its versatility and inviting deeper reflection.

Why the Audience Retells the Story

Even if the audience reaches their objective, you don't know if they will tell your story again. So, how do you get them to tell your story again? The audience tells the story to others if they discover the *value* of the story, that is, the ultimate story meaning. Value goes beyond the data and focuses on the people behind the data. Each time someone retells the story, they discover and disseminate aspects of the value that may not have been apparent initially. In this process, data comes to life, takes on more profound meaning, and becomes elements of a shared narrative. The audience, therefore, become bearers of value, spreading a message that goes beyond the simple number or fact.

When the story is told again, the audience takes the original message and reinterprets it, imbuing it with their perspective, sensibility, and meaning. In this process, the audience transforms and enriches the story, making it evolve, and adapting it to new contexts and perspectives.

Don't worry about big numbers. Rarely will the entire audience respond actively to your story, becoming a new reteller. Just a few people are enough to help you spread the story, generating a retelling chain. Even just one audience member is enough to start the retelling chain to make your story infinite.

Retelling is not just a communication tool. It's a source of collective wisdom. Each time the story is told and reinterpreted, it grows in value and meaning. Retelling creates a space of shared awareness, an opportunity for each individual to enrich the narrative with their own experience. Ultimately, the value of a data-driven story expands beyond the data, reaching a deeper level of understanding that inspires how to change the world for the better.

Final Thoughts

Our journey together has come to an end. Through this long journey, you have seen how to build a story from data, extract characters and a plot, and organize it into three acts. You have seen how cinematographic techniques can be used for data storytelling, and how the audience plays a fundamental role in the final preparation of the story.

Throughout the book, you also saw a simple case study for building data-driven stories: rising temperatures over time. I am aware that I have simplified the theme, but I did it deliberately, to make the narrative as simple as possible. I chose this theme because it is very close to my heart. The message I wanted to convey to you with this temperature story is to take care of our planet, which has hosted us for millions of years. Let us try to leave a welcoming planet to the generations that will come after us.

There is something I would like to tell you before giving way to another book that will become your new travel companion. Storytelling is something that goes beyond data. As I told you at the beginning of this book, every person is born with the desire and ability to tell stories. And this is what I did too with this book. I organized the whole book as a story in which you are the hero, your object of desire is to become a great data storyteller, and the problem is acquiring the skills to do so. As learned throughout this book, the story is organized in three acts: the first act lasts a third of the story, the second act a half, and the third act a third. And that's what I did with the book, as Table 12.1 shows.

Table 12.1: Organization of the Book as a Story

PLOT	CHAPTERS	TOPIC
First Act	1–3	Present the hero (you).
Second Act	4–9	Present the problem (learn how to organize a data-driven story).
Third Act	10–12	Present the solution.

Within each act, I then arranged the various plot points, just like in a real story. The First Plot Point is in Chapter 3, "Making a Successful Data-Driven Story," where I first presented the problem, and the Second Plot Point is in Chapter 9, "From Making to Delivering a Data-Driven Story," when you understand that it's not enough to organize the story, you also need to know how to present it. In a certain sense, I also introduced you to the antagonist: the audience. In the third act, I described the final battle between the hero (you) and the antagonist (the audience), culminating with the climax in this chapter. You will achieve your goal if the audience retells your story.

After reading this book, I hope your passion for data storytelling has increased and you will continue to read and delve deeper into the topic. One of the new challenges of data storytelling is its integration with artificial intelligence (AI), which will have a notable impact in the coming years. I have deliberately not talked about it in this book, but I think you should consider this aspect, too. Few studies exist on the subject, including a study by Haotian Li et al. (2024), who define the ways in which AI can be used in data storytelling: as an automatic *content creator*, as an *assistant*, as an automatic *optimizer* of the contents produced by the human, and as an *evaluator/reviewer* of the content produced by the human. Another study is the one I am personally dealing with: how to use AI to adapt storytelling contents based on the audience (Lo Duca, 2024).

At this point, the time has really come to leave you, hoping to meet again in the future. I leave you with this poem:

> Seek the truth that data hides,
> Unveil it pure. Let none divide.
>
> Craft a story with plot and soul,
> Awaken hunger, make them whole.
>
> Infuse each word with life anew,
> And victory shall come to you.

—Lo Duca

Takeaways

- Repeating a data-driven story means continually exploring and deepening its meaning. Each story and adaptation adds something new and creates a stronger and more meaningful narrative. Retelling enables you to keep the theme stable, while varying the details to capture the audience's interest and increase the impact of the message.

- There are two ways of retelling. In the first case, it is you who retells the story. In the second case, it is the audience who listened to your story who retells it.

- When you retell the story, you can retell it to the same audience or to different audiences. If you tell it again to the same audience, change the channel to avoid boring the audience, and use the spaced repetition technique to decide when to repeat the story each time. If you retell the story to a different audience, adapt it to the specific context you are in.

References

Bogue, R. (2023). Communicating Effectively Through Repetition and Channels. `https://www.td.org/content/atd-blog/communicating-effectively-through-repetition-and-channels` (accessed November 14, 2024).

Braman, L. (2023). Why We Retell Stories. `https://lindsaybraman.com/why-we-retell-stories` (accessed November 14, 2024).

Ebbinghaus, H. (1913). Memory (H. A. Ruger and C. E. Bussenius, Trans.). New York, NY: Teachers College, Columbia University. Original work published 1885.

Li, H., Wang, Y., and Qu, H. (2024, May). Where are we so far? Understanding data storytelling tools from the perspective of human–AI collaboration. In Proceedings of the CHI Conference on Human Factors in Computing Systems (pp. 1–19).

Lo Duca, A. (2024). Data Storytelling with Altair and AI. Shelter Island, New York, Manning Publications.

Murre, J. M., and Dros, J. (2015). Replication and analysis of Ebbinghaus' forgetting curve. *PLOS One*, 10(7), e0120644.

Rao, S. (2016). The hidden benefits of reading a book more than once. The Mission. Retrieved from `https://medium.com/the-mission/the-hidden-benefits-of-reading-a-book-more-than-once-b0f68d0662ce` (accessed November 14, 2024).

Yelle, L. E. (1979). The learning curve: Historical review and comprehensive survey. *Decision sciences*, 10(2), 302–328.

Index